W. F.

M. F

THE F

TECHNOLOGY AND

THE CHANGING FAMILY

Houghton Mifflin Company

𝕿𝖍𝖊 𝕽𝖎𝖛𝖊𝖗𝖘𝖎𝖉𝖊 𝕻𝖗𝖊𝖘𝖘 𝕮𝖆𝖒𝖇𝖗𝖎𝖉𝖌𝖊

Preface

The reasons for this book, *Technology and the Changing Family*, are two.

One purpose is to learn why the family in the United States has been changing. Books on the family have generally been concerned with descriptions, problems, purposes, values, morals, and implications. We think there is need for a book that deals succinctly with causes of family changes, and with nothing else. Such a book should be useful in illuminating the problems that arise from the revolutionary changes that have been transforming this basic institution. We are interested also in trying to see how certain causes will change the family in the future — a matter which greatly concerns our children and our grandchildren. If we know the causes of change, we can make better plans for the future.

It is necessary, of course, to examine all kinds of causes. We had a theory that many causes would be found in technological changes and scientific discoveries, such as the tractor, the autobus, the apartment house, the theory of evolution, and psychoanalysis. This theory has been substantiated. In fact, a surprisingly large number of changes in family living in the past century or two in the United States can be traced to three clusters of inventions and discoveries, those centering around steam and steel, contraceptives, and scientific discoveries affecting forms of religious beliefs. There are, however, ideological forces producing changes in the family that cannot be adequately traced to technological or scientific origins.

The first reason for this book is, then, to study the causes of recent family changes. The second, and lesser, reason is methodological. Since the expectation was that changes in technology and science would be found as causes of many, though not all, changes in the family, we were interested in studying this relationship between technology and a social institution in a manner different from that used in previous studies. This relationship has already been studied by choosing a single invention such as the radio, the automobile, or the airplane, and then tracing its effects upon the different social institutions such as the family, church, school, government, agriculture, and business. The pattern is like that of a wheel, with the mechanical invention or scientific discovery at the hub and the influences upon society emanating outward like the spokes.

In this book the reverse is attempted. A single institution, the family, has been chosen and upon it are recorded the influences coming from many different inventions and scientific discoveries. The pattern is still that of a wheel, but the family is at the hub; and the influences directed toward it are the spokes. This analysis has yielded several processes of social change not evident when study is confined to the effects of a single invention.

In order to utilize the methodological approach outlined above, it was found desirable to develop a system showing the relationship of different causes one to another. This system enabled us to trace the basic and important causes of family change. It was not possible to make a statistical study of each one. Many could be ascertained through description, a large number by analysis, and some were obvious. In other cases we could make only approximate estimates of importance. But in all this procedure, a clear knowledge of the system of causes of social change was quite necessary.

In closing we wish to acknowledge the financial assistance provided by the Carnegie Corporation and the encouragement in particular of the President, Charles Dollard.

W. F. Ogburn
M. F. Nimkoff

Contents

PART ONE · *Introduction*

   1. What Has Been Happening to the Family?   3

   2. How Causes Are Studied   18

PART TWO · *Recent Changes in the Family*

   3. From Economics to Romance   35

   4. Starting Earlier   58

   5. Toward A Smaller Family   95

   6. Shrinking Functions   123

   7. More Working Wives   144

   8. Away from Authority   167

   9. Accent on the Child   192

   10. More Disruption   214

   11. How and Why the Family has Changed   250

PART THREE · *What of the Future?*

   12. Technology and the Future of the Family   267

   13. Scientific Discoveries and the Future of the Family   291

   Index   323

PART ONE

Introduction

1

What Has Been Happening
to the Family?

We propose in this initial chapter to sketch briefly some of the more important changes that have occurred in the family in the United States in relatively recent times, that is, within the last century or two. This book, it should at once be noted, is mainly concerned with discussing the reasons why the family changes and the book is therefore principally a study in causation. But to study the causes, it is necessary first to identify the changes. To introduce and describe these changes as a basis for the analysis of causation is then the principal reason for this chapter. However, the chapter may be justified also on the grounds that a discussion of recent family changes is valuable for its own sake, if it provides us with a fuller understanding of what has been happening to the family. In this chapter the treatment will be broad and general, with details and documentation reserved for later chapters devoted to the fuller analysis of certain selected changes.

Although most of us know that the family in recent times has been changing, we may be less mindful of certain changes than of others. For instance, nearly everyone knows that divorce has been increasing; but few realize that divorced persons are remarrying in increasing numbers, and that partly for this reason and also partly because more single and widowed persons are marrying, a much larger per cent of the marriageable population of the United States is married (1950) than was true a half-century or so ago. There seems to be no loss of faith in marriage.

While we may be unmindful of some recent changes in the family, as to other changes we are often actually misinformed or mistaken. For instance, many persons believe that the age for

3

marriage is later now than it was, say, fifty years ago. But this is not true, as will be shown in a later chapter. In view of the foregoing, there would seem to be some value in a reliable account of what has been happening to the family in recent times.

The Search for a List of Family Changes

A danger facing the authors was that they might, even unwittingly, limit their list of changes to those that fitted their theories of social causation. To guard against such possible bias, it seemed desirable, in arriving at an objective list of family changes for the purposes of this study, to canvass some of our leading authorities on the subject. Accordingly, eighteen [1] prominent students of the family were invited by letter to submit a list of "ten outstanding changes in the family in recent times." Since it was suggested that they make up the list rather quickly, to keep the assignment from being burdensome, the responses are probably to be viewed as representing the family changes which were uppermost in the minds of these experts rather than a comprehensive or even representative list of such changes. For the authors of this book, who are primarily interested in causation, the criterion of comprehensiveness was a secondary consideration, the primary consideration being merely to obtain a list of changes from outside sources. A tabulation of the replies appears in Table 1. The experts are designated only by number, since they were asked for anonymous replies.

The responses are highly interesting, both as to the consensus regarding a few major changes and the great variety of items submitted by the panel of experts. Perhaps the most striking feature of the list is the lack of agreement among the experts, if the great variety of items reported may be so interpreted. Altogether, sixty-three changes appear on the combined lists of the eighteen authorities. Only one change, the increasing divorce rate, is reported unanimously; and only eight changes are mentioned by at least half the experts. A total of twenty-nine different items are mentioned by only a single expert apiece, and eleven additional items

[1] Ray Abrams, Robert Angell, Ray Baber, Jessie Bernard, Ernest Burgess, Ruth S. Cavan, John Cuber, Kingsley Davis, Evelyn Duvall, Joseph Folsom, Reuben Hill, Clifford Kirkpatrick, Mirra Komarovsky, Harvey Locke, Bernhard Stern, Lewis Terman, Ernest Mowrer, Carle Zimmerman. Letter of June 10, 1947.

TABLE 1

Significant Changes in the American Family as Listed by 18 Experts

Recent Changes in the Family	Total Number of Mentions*
Increasing divorce (changing attitudes toward divorce)	18
Decline in authority of husbands and fathers	12
Increase in wives in labor force	11
Increasing premarital and extramarital sex intercourse	11
Increasing individualism and freedom by family members	10
Decline in size	10
Transfer of protective functions	10
Transfer of education	8
Wider diffusion of birth control	7
Transfer of recreation	7
Transfer of productive functions	7
Unfavorable attitude by children toward supporting their elderly parents	5
Increased mobility (time spent away from home)	5
Transfer of religion	5
Growth of secular and decline of religious behavior in marriage	4
Mechanization of the home	4
Increasing emphasis on romance (love and happiness)	3
More families of oldsters	3
Growth of interest in family counseling	3
Growth of interest in sex	3
More education for marriage	3

* Each of the following items received two mentions: earlier age at first marriage, extension of child care and nursery school centers, increasing differentiation as to types, higher standard of living, decrease in differences in sex roles, increased tendency toward multiple marriages, greater confusion of roles for family members, more sex education for children, increase in childless marriages, emphasis on the child, larger per cent married.

Each of the following items was mentioned by one expert: frozen foods, more intermarriage, from large houses to small, declining mortality rates, more casual relations between family members, greater demarcation between generations and their roles, more spontaneous behavior in courtship, trend away from romance?, greater average distance between residences of family and kin, beginnings of a reduction in differential birth-rate, increased urbanization of the family pattern, more financial help to newlyweds, more doubling up, more spending rather than saving, more children by older women, decreasing self-consciousness about family problems, increased tensions, more leisure for parents, trend toward familism, wives more neurotic, more parent-child conflict, more family dispersion, leveling off of decline in births, more marriage counseling, more emphasis on marriage and parenthood by college girls, more companionship, fewer kinfolk in household, more emphasis on personality.

by only two experts. In other words, about two-thirds of all the
reported changes are mentioned by only one or two persons. A few
of the items are perhaps closely related and could be combined,
such as "the growth of secular behavior in marriage," mentioned
by four persons, and "the transfer of religion from the home,"
reported by five persons. Other changes, although in the same
field, seem to represent different aspects and therefore are not
duplications. Thus eleven experts mentioned "increasing sexual intercourse apart from marriage," and three reported "growth of
interest in sex." Even if these two items were interpreted to mean
the same thing, which is questionable, the total for the category
would be twelve, not fourteen, since two of the experts reported
both items. Two mentioned "increasing sex education for children" which represents some overlap with "growth of interest in
sex" but probably not with "increasing sexual intercourse apart
from marriage." Despite a little duplication, most of the items
which are mentioned only once are separate and distinct phenomena and if combined with other items of the same class, lose their
specificity.

The responses of the experts indicate that the changes in the
family in recent times have been very numerous. The sixty-three
changes reported in Table 1 are, of course, only a fraction of the
changes that have occurred, for the experts were asked to list only
the changes which in their opinion were outstanding. Had additional authorities been asked to submit changes, the number would
doubtless have been increased. That so many changes should be
reported is not surprising, because the family is a complex social
institution, with many interrelations with other institutions, all of
which are undergoing extensive changes in our time; and the total
number of changes is great, especially when viewed in detail.

Why the experts chose to report the changes listed in Table 1 is
an interesting question. Of the many hundreds of changes that
have occurred, one authority makes a certain selection and another
a somewhat different selection, perhaps because of differing interests resulting from specialization. A student of the family who is
primarily interested in the general, theoretical aspects of family
life may report as noteworthy the fact that there are fewer kinfolk
in the household than formerly and that "the average distance between residences of family and kin is greater," whereas a student

mainly concerned with the practical aspects of marriage preparation may see as significant the increased financial help by parents to newlyweds and the growth in courses in education for marriage. There is a certain amount of consensus, for eight changes are mentioned by at least half the experts. These are, with their frequencies:

— increasing divorce rate (18)
— wider diffusion of birth control and/or decline in family size (12)
— decline in authority of husbands and fathers (12)
— increase in sexual intercourse apart from marriage (11)
— increase in number of wives working for pay (11)
— increasing individualism and freedom of family members (10)
— increasing transfer of protective functions from family to state (10)
— decline of religious behavior in marriage and family (9)

These eight changes, according to the responses of the experts reporting, may be considered the most outstanding recent changes in the family.

The question as to why there is not more agreement among the experts as to "outstanding recent family changes" is difficult to answer. A plausible explanation is that each expert may have sought to make his list somewhat original and therefore introduced items not commonly recognized. The variety of items probably does not mean that there is not a consensus among the experts as to the basic recent changes, or that the experts are not familiar with one another's thinking. On the contrary, such familiarity might very well cause social scientists who are interested in being original to propose new and different ideas. An examination of the published works of these same experts would probably show that there is considerable agreement as to the major changes in the family in recent times.

We note that certain of the changes listed by the authorities are of a speculative nature. Such are the reports that there is now more spontaneous behavior in courtship than formerly and that a trend "away from romance" exists. The same observation probably applies to the report that the trend toward familism, and away from individualism, has set in, as noted by a single reporter.

In this book we choose for analysis only a few of the family changes submitted by the experts. We choose only some of the more important changes which can be substantiated by evidence.

These changes will be described and analyzed one at a time, in later chapters.

In Table 1 we have a list of outstanding recent changes in the family. This is a bare outline, and we have thought it appropriate to weave these items into a brief narrative that we call "What has been happening to the family?" This is to be regarded as a thumbnail sketch, an over-all view that may serve as a kind of map for the reader. Later on we shall devote a separate chapter to each of these changes, setting forth the change in more detail, as a basis for the analysis of its causes.

The Account of Family Changes

Divorce on the increase. The most conspicuous change in the family is the increasing rate of divorce, if the unanimous listing of this change by the eighteen experts may be so construed. No other change received unanimous mention. In fact, the next most frequently reported change is mentioned by only twelve of the respondents.

Where respondents do more than just list the rising divorce rate as a trend, they mention the changing ideology associated with the trend, namely, the greater expectation of happiness in marriage. Marriage is for the duration of happiness rather than "until death do us part." There is an acceptance by young people of the possibility of divorce if marriage does not bring happiness; and with the acceptance of this possibility, divorce loses some of its emotional qualities, such as the feeling of failure or guilt, which tends to restrain the individual.

Fifty years ago, happiness was not so greatly emphasized; and if it failed to materialize in marriage, the marriage was not so often doomed.

Companionship. In earlier times, a man seeking a wife looked for someone who was strong, healthy, a good cook and a good housekeeper, while a woman looked for a husband who was a good provider and a good manager. While these virtues are still recognized as desirable, they are not valued as highly as they were in the past. Today, with the accent on happiness, men and women seek mates who will be good companions and for whom they will feel affection. Companionship means having congenial tastes, but this is not always recognized by young people. Instead the emphasis is generally on love and romance. It is felt that happiness in marriage is impossible without love and that to marry without love is shameful. The meaning of love is not, however, always clearly understood; and it is often confused with sex attraction. So great indeed is the emphasis in our culture on love as a proper basis for marriage that love is assumed to exist in nearly every marriage; at least, few couples go to the altar not avowing their love for each other. But the records of the divorce courts suggest that either (a) "love" was not present in many cases or (b) love alone is not sufficient basis for marital happiness.

Whether the strength of the romantic complex continues unabated, or has been intensified or weakened in recent times is not clear; but the shift from practical to personal considerations in the choice of a mate continues in large areas of the world. In the shift from utilitarian grounds to sentimental ones, the emphasis has often fallen on superficial personal qualities or in some cases even on purely imaginary ones. But lately the more thoughtful groups in the population, aided by the growing movement of education for family living, are recognizing more and more that certain traits of personality are conducive to happiness, such as dependability, loyalty, optimism, the will to succeed, generosity, and emotional stability. The growth of the psychological and social sciences may be expected in the future to provide knowledge of this kind which may be a basis for more intelligent choices of companions.

Self-determination in the choice of a mate. Since personal qualities are emphasized in the choice of a mate, it is recognized as important that the individual be free to make his own choice. When utilitarian virtues were thought to be predominant in a mate, the choice of a mate could be more readily made by others, say by the parents of the couple, or by professional matchmakers. Even compatibility of tastes could be assured by the intermediaries in earlier times, for persons belonging to the same social and economic groups, and therefore likely to share the same values, would be mated. At the present time, the increased educational and occupational mobility of individuals makes it more difficult to appraise an individual's tastes by the family he belongs to or the neighborhood he lives in. Where life is so highly individualized, it is desirable to know the individual rather than his group, if he is fully to be known. So there is emphasis on self-determination in the choice of a mate.

In earlier times, the parents usually chose a mate for their son or daughter, sometimes without the latter's knowledge; but if the choice was not acceptable, the young people could often exercise a veto, which was usually not overruled. Today the young people make their own selection, sometimes without their parents' knowledge; and it is the parents who may be accorded the veto power. Even today, however, many parents indirectly influence the choice of a mate, especially for a daughter, through arranging her social activities. The invisible guiding hand of the parents may be there, in choosing a neighborhood in which to live or a school to attend, thereby influencing the choice of friends.

Males less dominant. It is interesting that next to divorce, the experts reported most frequently as a recent family change the decline in authority of the husband and father. This, incidentally, was not mentioned by two of the three respondents who are women. A decrease in patriarchal rule is inferred from other changes, such as the increased employment of married women outside the home, the increase in the legal, educational, and civic rights of women, and the growth of more permissive attitudes as to child training. The loss in masculine authority is mainly a relative one accompanying the improved status of women and children. The absolute loss of privilege by males is not great. They now share with women some of the rights they previously enjoyed exclusively; and so they have experienced a relative loss of status, which leads to a decline in authority.

The foregoing change is described by a number of our respondents as a shift from authoritarian to democratic patterns. The emphasis is on equality. This contrasts with the patriarchal pattern, which stresses obedience to the husband and father. The patriarch has the power to give orders; and if the orders are not obeyed, he has the power to punish. In the democratic pattern, decisions are arrived at by discussion and consensus, by compromise, and by majority vote. After wifely obedience ceased to be a virtue, the word "obey" was dropped from the marriage service of many churches. In some areas of experience, women have obtained rights equal to those of men; they may vote, sit on juries, and hold public office. In other areas their rights are still somewhat less than those of men, and it is in these areas that recent changes may be noted. While women have the right to work for pay, certain fields of endeavor are still closed to them; but the trend is to reduce the number. Only two or three occupational classifications listed by the Census Bureau now have no women employed. Also the pay of women is being increased more nearly to approximate that of men.

Within the domain of the family, women in the United States have obtained most of the rights enjoyed by men. They are now, as they once were not, co-guardians of their children; they have the right to petition for a divorce; they have exclusive ownership and control over separate property. But in regard to property acquired after marriage, other than by gift or inheritance, there is inequality. Even in the community property states, where income earned after marriage is equally the property of both husband and wife, control rests with the husband. The trend is to minimize or eliminate these remaining inequalities.

As the rights of married women increase, so do the duties of husbands, as in the sharing of responsibility for the care of the household and the care of the children. Husbands do not, however, assume their new duties as fully or as speedily as their wives relinquish them; and this is a source of complaint on the part of women, especially those who do not have servants. Still, the trend is for married women to acquire more responsibilities outside the home, and for married men to assume more responsibilities within the home, so that the two sexes share more activities. A noteworthy result of the increased similarity in the roles of men and women is the tendency for the two sexes to become more nearly alike in their behavior, and accordingly, in personality also.

Authority over children has diminished; and in this case, the loss has affected both parents, although principally the father. Obedience in children is not valued as highly as in times past; and from infancy onward, the training of children is less rigid than before, and permissive attitudes in parents are encouraged. The earlier right of parents to the labor of their children has been abridged by the development of child labor laws, as well as laws requiring attendance at school.

The decline in the authority of parents continues as they get older and is reflected in the lessening responsibility of children for the economic support and care of their aged parents. These responsibilities are being increasingly assumed by government and industry in the United States through the provision of old age pensions and other benefits. Earlier, relief was granted to the needy aged only when it was shown that their children were financially unable to support them; but now the trend is not to hold the children responsible for the economic support of their parents. There also appears to be an increasingly unfavorable attitude toward having elderly parents live with their children.

More wives in the labor force. Formerly women who worked before marriage gave up their jobs at marriage or not long thereafter. Married women therefore comprised a minority of the female working population. More recently, the number of gainfully employed married women has increased; and in 1949, for the first time, the number of married women at work exceeded the number of single women.

At one time, marriage was virtually the only career for women, for there were few opportunities for employment outside the home. As a consequence, even when the number of available jobs increased, it was felt by many that a choice had to be made between marriage and a job. The question that was posed and debated was: Marriage or career? Now increasingly, we assume that wives will work or have a career if they want to; and the conflict of home versus job has been lessened, at least ideologically. In keeping, it is not so often taken for granted that a man must be able to support his wife when he marries. Often it is a matter of the wife working or not marrying at all.

Because of need, married women of the lower income classes were the first to be employed, while employment of wives of the middle class was thought to reflect unfavorably on the husband. With the increased employment of married women of the middle class, this attitude has changed. Also the new trend tends to blur somewhat the earmarks that help to distinguish one social class from another.

The effects of the increased employment of wives on family life are manifold. With the alternative of economic security in a job, women have more freedom in the choice of a mate and in the decision as to whether to continue an unsatisfactory marriage. The role of marriage in the life of a woman is greatly modified. Formerly, as the poet expressed it, marriage was for woman "her whole existence; for man, a thing apart." While marriage is still more important for women than for men, it is not, with jobs and outside interests, so exclusively important as it used to be. The range of choice has been widened for women.

An effect on children of the increase in working wives is probably a reduction in the number of children born, although this effect has not been measured. Since mothers with pre-school children tend not to be in the labor force, it may perhaps be inferred, that children are acknowledged to be an obstacle to the mother's employment; and if work is greatly desired or needed, the effect would be to limit the number of offspring. It is not suggested that the only reason some married women limit the size of their families is the desire to be free to take a job but only that this is one factor. Perhaps both the job and the small family are often expressions of the same influence, namely, the desire for a higher standard of living. Where there are children, the effect of a job is to reduce the amount of time the mother spends with her children, although — with the five-day week — this is not great where the children are of school age.

More work outside the home means less time spent at home and therefore probably less housework, since, as was indicated above, husbands do not share equally in this responsibility. Here we have one reason why some wives quit work, for they find the double burden of job and housekeeping too heavy, especially where health is not robust. Others who continue with their jobs simply do less housework. Sometimes the greater prestige and excitement of outside employment causes wives to lose interest in housework, which is relatively dull and unrewarded, and this attitude toward housework persists after the job is relinquished.

With more time spent at work, at the movies, in automobiles, at school, in restaurants, et cetera, there is naturally less time spent at home. With so many satisfactions derived from activities outside the home, the satisfactions associated with the home are relatively fewer. Consequently we tend to feel less sentimental about the home than we used to.

Changes in the double standard. The increased independence of women is reflected also in the changes in their sex behavior. A number of recent studies indicate an increase in premarital and extramarital sexual intercourse on the part of the women in the last few decades. A significant point in the findings is the report that these increases have occurred among so-called "respectable" women. In the past, the distinction between good and bad women was more clearly drawn, the good women being those who guarded their chastity. Middle-class males tended to respect this distinction; and if they consorted illicitly with women, the women were prostitutes or girls of a lower economic class. This picture has been changing. The amount of association with prostitutes has decreased, and the relative number of illicit unions with girls of the same socio-economic standing has increased. This is reflected in the increase in premarital sexual intercourse on the part of engaged couples.

That the sex behavior of women has changed seems indubitable, but it is not so clear that the sex mores have also changed. The change in the moral code must be independently demonstrated and may not be inferred simply from the change in sex behavior. To cite an analogy, an increase in crime may occur without any change in the criminal code of the community. Likewise, there may be an increase in sexual behavior frowned upon by the group. As to public attitudes toward chastity for women there is some evidence derived from public opinion polls which indicates a greater tolerance of premarital sexual behavior on the part of women than existed a generation or two ago, although the predominant opinion is still sharply opposed to such behavior. There are also some specialized studies which disclose a more liberal attitude.

Smaller families. A conspicuous recent trend, noted by ten of our respondents, is the decline in the size of the family. There is, of course, a good deal of folklore and mythology regarding the large size of the family in the past, resulting from our traditional adoration of the large family type. We oftentimes speak of families of ten or twelve as if they were common or even the average during our colonial period; however, an examination of available data gives us a figure half as big or less; thus in 1790 the average number of persons per family in the United States was 5.8. But even so, the decline has been marked, for in 1950 the number was 3.5.

Households are getting smaller not only because of the birth of fewer children but also because fewer adults are included, such as relatives, lodgers, and servants. The trend is for young married couples to establish homes of their own, apart from relatives; and the decrease in the size of the home reduces the need for servants, while the increase in real wages probably lessens the need to accept roomers or boarders.

The decrease in the number of offspring means, of course, that the relationship between husband and wife is emphasized more, obviously so where there are no children. A reduction in the number of children means also that the rearing of children becomes a more intensive art, for with fewer children to rear, the parents can give more time and attention to each child. In the larger families of the past much of the responsibility of child care rested on the older children rather than on the parents.

In the preceding paragraphs some of the salient changes in the family have been set forth, although not with any special particularity. We may perhaps generalize these changes by saying that what has been happening during the last century or two is that we have lessened our dependence on the family for the satisfaction of our needs and wishes. Formerly the family was the principal locus of economic activity, and the source of many educational, recreational, religious, and protective services. At the present time, the economic activities are largely separated from the home and are carried on by industry, commerce, banking, transportation, and the like, while recreation is being increasingly commercialized also. Education and protection, and recreation as well, are more and more functions of the state and/or industry. In a word, we depend less on the family and more on industry and the state.

When the family was larger and performed more economic and correlated functions, the family was a powerful institution; and the cooperation of all the members of the group was required if the family was to function effectively. But now that the business of the world is largely carried on apart from the home and by individuals rather than by family groups, the accent has shifted to the individual, so that the family is relatively less influential, the individual more so. The control of the family over its members is less; children choose their own jobs, their own mates, a separate place to live, et cetera. The power of the family over its members is less than it used to be.

The loss of power by the family. Another change in the family is its decline in power among the various social institutions. An illustration of family influence is the Medici in Renaissance Italy. Today there are few such powerful families. Power resides elsewhere.

The affairs of the world are run by power. Leaders can lead only by virtue of power, even though it be the power of persuasion or personality. Power means influence and is had in various ways, by ideas, by votes, by physical force. A big gorilla or a state with a big military establishment has power over contemporaries. Another source of power is wealth. With power come prestige and status.

The power of the institution of the family is to be found, then, in its leading families, in families of wealth, rather than in the average family. Such families, in earlier times when the family had great prestige and influence, were distinguished by being called the nobility, the aristocracy. During feudalism, wealthy families had private armies and relied on physical force as a source of power. With such force the Plantagenet family maintained rule over all England, and the head of the royal family was called king. On a smaller scale in the villages of an agricultural region community affairs were run by a few leading families. The struggle for power sometimes resulted in family feuds, especially when violence was resorted to.

Now lords have lost their power, and rule is not inherited through the family. The power of a President rests not upon family; and the influence of the lobby on Congress is expressed through the American Federation of Labor, the National Association of Manufacturers, the American Medical Association.

On the other hand, it can be argued that the power of royalty in former times lay really in government and in land ownership (an economic institution), and not in the family; and that it was an individual who was duke and not the family. This is true. But sovereignty was in the family line; and the ownership of landed estates was relatively stable, except when a transfer was made by dowry or by military force. Marriage was not only between individuals but into families and meant status and wealth if the family was prominent.

It can also be argued that today we have our prominent families of Rockefellers, duPonts, and Fords. But it is doubtful that these families have relatively much power as families. The power lies rather in the oil, chemical, and automotive industries where power is frequently associated with management. There are highly influential families in the United States in the middle of the twentieth century; but, compared to a century or two ago, they are much more rare.

It is social, economic, and military power that has shifted from the family to government, business, and associations. The exercise of moral training and of individual influence has been transferred very little from the family. In these the intrinsic role of the family is as significant as formerly, in shaping character, in inculcating morals, and in providing happiness.

Why the family has changed so radically will be analyzed in later chapters. But first we must consider the methods to be pursued in finding out why the family changes. To this problem we next devote our attention.

2

How Causes are Studied

We have seen that the family in the United States in the past century has changed very greatly. It is natural to ask what caused these changes. Were they due to any weakening in the character of the people? to the pursuit of individual selfishness? to a greater desire for pleasure? Or are we to seek an understanding of these changes in the urban way of life, in the economic forces that provide occupations for men and for women away from home? Such are some of the possible causes that are readily suggested.

To find out the causes of the changes in the family is not easy. In order to do so there must be a method; and it is the purpose of this chapter to set forth the method to be followed.

How Family Changes are Caused

Basic ideas. In the first place, we are trying to ascertain the causes not of the family but only of the changes in the family. One of the causes of the family is the desire for a mate of the opposite sex, but such a desire is hardly an explanation of the increased number of married persons from 60 per cent to 69 per cent of the population over fourteen years old in the United States from 1940 to 1950. We know of no evidence that there has been any increased desire for mates during the decade. The desire for a mate is a factor in the family but not in the increase in the number of families.

Change cannot be explained by a constant. A variation must be explained by another variation. Thus the marriages at earlier ages during the 1940's in the United States cannot be accounted for by the inherited sex impulse, which is constant for a large population over a ten-year period. The cause of the recent increase in early marriages in the United States must be sought in a variable such as war conditions or unusually prosperous business.

18

When anything changes we call it a variable whether it be sudden and the creation of something new, such as an invention, or whether it be continuous, such as the change of the median age of marriage of women from 21.6 years to 20.8 years. We call these phenomena *variables,* since they vary and do not remain constant.

In general in talking about why the family is changing, we mean changing in the course of time. The family may vary in other ways than across the years. It may vary geographically. In the present Chinese family, the position of women is much more subordinate than it is in the contemporary family in the United States. It is the variation in time, the past hundred years or more, in which we are interested. Data are much better for this period than for earlier times; and they are also better for the Western world than for the Far East or for primitive societies.

From the foregoing discussion, the reader will already have noted that the institution of the family is not just one simple phenomenon. It is really a composite of several constituents such as marriage, children, separated mates, home, activities, et cetera. The various aspects of this institution are indicated by the chapter headings of this book that deal with different phases of family structure and function.

Finding causes. When a variation in one variable is caused by a variation in another variable, the two variations occur together or one occurs after a lag. Thus the decrease in employment in the 1930's was accompanied by a decrease in the sale of marriage licenses. The two movements were approximately simultaneous. These are called concomitant variations. But not all concomitant variations have a causal connection. For instance, during the 1930's there was a lowering of the death rate as well as a decrease in the marriage rate; but we do not attribute the decrease of the death rate to the decrease of the marriage rate. A decrease in the marriage rate might have the effect of decreasing the death rate, but only after a time lag and then only slightly. A connection must be established beyond the mere concomitance of the variation.

Establishing this connection is not done simply by a statistical table, showing the concomitance. Thus there are statistical tables showing that families with tall fathers have on the average tall sons and that families with short fathers have short sons. But such a table does not by itself tell us which variable is the cause. From the table alone we might infer that tall fathers are caused by tall sons with as much reason as that tall sons are caused by tall fathers. The table is only data framed so the concomitance can be seen and measured. The causal connection becomes established from our knowledge about heredity and that fathers have already reached full stature before sons are born. Similarly a table showing a correlation between a high birth rate and business prosperity does not show which causes which. We derive our knowledge of which is the cause and which the result from information coming from outside the table. Newborn babies could hardly bring prosperity, but prosperity could bring more marriages and more babies.

When two variables change repeatedly and simultaneously over a stretch of time, as in the case with the decrease in the marriage rate and the decrease in the death rate and no direct causal connection between the two can be seen from knowledge outside the table, there is a strong presumption that there is some indirect connection, a connection through some third variable. In the case of marriage rates and death rates, the connection is through the business depression, which is the third variable. Both marriage rates and death rates in the nineteenth and twentieth centuries decreased during business depressions. The connection between business depressions and marriage decreases seems easy enough to establish because of unemployment which comes with depressions. The connection between depressions and deaths is not so clear, though it is not difficult to see how some causes of death, especially deaths from accidents, should decrease when fewer machines are running and when there are fewer persons at work. So the concomitance of these two variables is caused by a third variable, the business cycle.

Sometimes a very plausible connection can be established on the basis of one instance, even though there is not a series of concomitant variations. Such is done, for instance, by detectives in solving a single murder. So also in the case of the exceptionally high postwar divorce rate in the United States in the middle 1940's, we can, on the basis of this one period, find a plausible explanation, at least in part, in the earlier hasty war marriages, which meant in many cases enforced separation. Hasty marriages did not lead to the formation of families; and marriages are more easily broken than families. From such a causal connection, shown to hold for one war and in one country, we are not able to generalize about many wars and several countries. It is conceivable that some wars might be followed by fewer divorces.

The single cause infrequent. We have been speaking as if a change is caused by only one other variable. References have been made to the concomitant variations between two variables, whereas the change in one variable may be caused by concomitant changes in not just one other variable but several other variables. Thus the high post-war divorce rate may be caused by (a) hasty marriages, (b) wartime separations, and (c) the absence of children, all three influences operating at the same time. We often speak of *the* cause whereas we should speak of *a* cause. For, back of new or changing social phenomena, there is generally more than one cause. There is more than one reason why women work outside the home. In our society nearly all parts are changing at once — business, technology, religion, education, moral standards, population, legislation, et cetera. Since these various parts are all interconnected as, for instance, education is connected with the family and with economic institutions, and the family and economic institutions are connected, it follows that a social change is likely to be effected by changes in more than one factor. The working of women in factories, stores, and offices is related to many things: the size of the family income, the absence of children, and the demand for labor, all of which are variables.

Sometimes a causal variable is not stated very succinctly. Thus, we say the city increases the divorce rate over what it is among the farming population, for the divorce rate is generally higher in cities than in the open country. But the word city is a very broad term and includes many variables such as jobs for women, low birth rates, attractions outside the home, et cetera. We need to know what particular factors of the many in a city cause the divorce rate to be higher than that in the country. In this illustration there is not just one factor to be isolated, but many. Thus the employment of women away from home in many different occupations is greater in the city than in the country, as is also the anonymity of city life, which leads to less social pressure by one's neighbors over one's daily conduct. So also there are fewer children per marriage in the city. Thus in searching for causes, it is well to keep in mind that there may be several factors producing a greater result than would be produced by any one factor alone.

The Reasons for the Changing Family are Far-Reaching

A chain of causes. The causes of family changes thus far considered have been direct causes. The creation of factories is a direct cause of the loss of production from the home. Women buy factory-made cloth at stores and no longer weave in the home. But if we inquire what led to the creation of factories and find the answer in the invention of the steam engine, then the steam engine may be considered a cause of the loss of production from the homestead. It is a cause once-removed from the direct, proximate cause, namely, the creation of factories.

But if there is a cause once-removed from the immediate or direct cause, there can be a cause of that once-removed cause, namely, a cause twice-removed. And if a twice-removed factor, then a thrice-removed factor and so on. Thus there is a chain of causes. The process of causation is sequential. Since the direct cause is the one commonly given and the removed ones are omitted, it is convenient to think of the causes in this chain-like sequence as of two kinds, the proximate and the remote.

This process may be illustrated by the causes for the weakened ties of kinship. These ties were strong in the rural areas of our forefathers. An aunt, nephew, or cousin was considered a part of the family. Indeed, whole societies were in ancient times and among primitive peoples organized on a kinship basis. There were societies of clans. Later towns and cities became organized on a citizenship or civil basis, hence the term *civilization*. In the great cities of today bonds are often closer between friends than between relatives, and the obligations toward kin are sometimes felt as a burden. Marriage is between individuals rather than into kinship groups.

Why has there been this weakening of the ties of kinship commonly noted in cities? One reason is the separation or scattering of kin. Some live in the country and some in the city. Some live in one city and some in another. And ties generally do not stretch well over great distances without weakening.

The separation of kin has also a cause. Separation is due to mobility. Kin move away. Thus a once-removed cause of these weakened ties is mobility.

But back of mobility lies transportation development, a twice-removed cause.

A recent development of transportation is due to the railroad.

And without the steam engine we should not have had the railroad. Hence the steam engine is a still more remote cause of weakened kinship.

If we ask why the steam engine was invented, we note that the causes of any new invention are demand, inventive ability, and the existence of other inventions that compose the new invention. In the case of the steam engine there seems to be no outstanding particular cause among these three classes of cause. So it is not profitable to pursue the sequence of causes beyond the invention of the steam engine. We, therefore, stop at this link.

Many searches for causes go no further than the first, proximate cause. But an adequate analysis of causes considers the remoter causes, too.

Motives as causes. If the proximate cause of a change over time is psychological, that is, expressed in motives, it is often desirable to search further in causes more removed until a cause not psychological is reached. As an illustration, the cause of an increase in adultery may be found in an increase in sexual desire for someone other than one's legal mate. Such covetousness has probably always existed in every people. One of the "ten commandments" of Biblical times warns against it. Yet it may not be a constant. It may be more common at one time than another. We understand readily that covetousness is a factor in adultery, but it is not readily seen why covetousness has increased. Since the inherited biological base for sex desire is constant from one generation of people to another, the cause of increased covetousness is not to be sought in our instincts. There is some curiosity therefore as to what has brought about this increase in effective covetousness. The mere statement of increased motivation is not enough. We want to know why the motivation has been unusually stimulated. So we look beyond the motive to the conditions that brought it about. These conditions may be a decline in religious sanctions due to the

impact of science on religious rules of conduct. Or the increase
in covetousness may be due to the growth of populous cities where
evasion and concealment are easier. So from this illustration it is
readily seen why motives are not an adequate explanation of a
change in social behavior over a period of time. It is desirable to
explain the change in motives in terms of some change in conditions such as a change in science or in technology, as in the foregoing illustration. Hence in a chain of causes we seldom stop at
a psychological cause.

In considering the phenomenon of sequence, we have dealt with
only a single cause at each successive step. But, as previously
observed, there is rarely just one cause. Hence we shall widen our
observations to consider several causes at each particular step in
the sequence.

Convergence. Often a change results not from one cause but from
several. These several causes are said to converge. Thus the
growth of suburbs of modern cities is caused by several inventions
which converge to produce this growth. There are the steam engine, the diesel, the electric railway, the autobus, the private automobile, the telephone, the radio, television. We do not say that
the desire for space, clean air, and quiet are causes, for they are
a constant desire of families.

That there are several causes converging to produce a change is
seen from the observation that a coefficient of correlation of 1.0
in social phenomena is seldom if ever seen. A coefficient of correlation measures the degree of concomitance between two variables.
If the coefficient is 1.0 and the variables are causally related, there
is only one cause. If the correlation is large, say 0.8, then the concomitance studied is an important one. If the correlation is small,
say 0.2, it is not very important. If the correlation between the
result and all the causes could be measured, it would be 1.0.

The many causes that operate to produce a change in a phenomenon may be thought of as a cluster. Thus a cluster of transportation and communication inventions causes the growth of
suburbs. Similarly the Industrial Revolution which sprinkled so
many cities over the land and did so much to reduce the family
as a social institution was a huge cluster of mechanical inventions

and scientific discoveries which converged on the family and also on the city. It is not correct then to speak of one invention as the cause when there are many causes. It is common practice to do so, though, when one invention appears to be more important than the others. Thus we say the steam engine created cities and transferred functions from the home, when it was not one invention alone but a cluster of them.

The phenomenon of convergence is related to the phenomenon of sequence, as will be noted in the following further consideration of the causes of weakened kinship ties.

We have in an earlier paragraph said that a cause of the weakening of kinship is separation of kin. But there are other causes. One is population density. Where there are many persons living close together as in a city, there are many associates other than relatives. A person is less dependent upon relatives alone for friendship and assistance. More separation is therefore only one of two causes.

Similarly, there is more than one cause of separation. Besides mobility, differences in occupations are a cause of separation of relatives, in contrast to the rural situation where most male kin were farmers working often in one locality. Dissimilarities do not generally bring people closer together. A third factor in producing separation of kin is differences in tastes, income, education, and habits that are found in a heterogeneous urban society. Mobility is therefore one of three causes of greater separation of kin and one of five causes of weakened kinship ties.

As to the increase in mobility, there are causes other than transportation. For instance, mobility is stimulated by opportunities for new jobs and for greater income. So also trade and the desire for greater markets encourage mobility. Transportation is therefore one of three causes of increased mobility, and hence one of eight causes of weakened kinship.

It follows that the more remote a cause is in a sequence of causes, the smaller is its relative influence among the causes producing the result. When a cause is very remote and one among very many, its contribution appears very trivial. Thus the desire to pump water out of mines in England is said to have led to the steam engine. But the desire to pump water out of mines in England seems a very trivial cause of the weakening of the ties of kinship. This thinning out of a causal influence is emphasized by the concurrence of convergence and sequence.

Dispersion. The picture of the interrelationship of causes is not complete without the phenomenon of dispersion, which is the opposite of convergence. As many inventions converge to increase suburbs, so a single invention like the automobile disperses many effects on industry, hotels, families, wars, et cetera. In convergence, causal influences flow into a result the way the spokes of a wheel go into the hub. In dispersion, the effects flow out from the cause the way the spokes go out from the hub of a wheel. Thus, the effects of the invention of the radio are numerous, moving in various directions, such as the effects upon education, music, oratory, political activities, crime, transportation, et cetera. Many effects "fan out" from a single cause. The employment of wives affects their relations with their husbands and children, their dress, their manners, and their education.

The process of causation. The process of causation is not represented adequately by the illustration of a chain, though the conception of a chain-like sequence is important, since many observers look no further for a cause than the proximate cause and look no further for a result than the direct result. The most important results may be several times removed, and an important cause may be antecedent to the proximate cause. The process of causation is better represented by the illustration of a net, where the conception of sequence is joined with the conceptions of convergence and of dispersion.

Causation in social phenomena is thus complex, but not necessarily confusing, for not all parts of the net are appreciably activated at the same time; and the activation of an important cause may be vastly greater than that of an unimportant cause. Generally we are seeking important causes.

How to find important causes. There are several ways to tell which causes are important and which are not. An important cause is one which accounts for a large portion of the result. Thus if the correlation between the fluctuations in the marriage rate and the business cycle is 0.8, then the business cycle accounts for 64 per cent of the variations in the marriage rate and is an important cause. But if the variations in the divorce rate are correlated with the fluctuations in marriage rate by a coefficient of only 0.1, then changes in divorce are only a minor cause of changes in the marriage rate. Such correlation coefficients are particularly good determinants of importance when other variables are held constant. In the absence of such good measures, we must make approximations.

Sometimes importance can be inferred. Thus the increase in insanity among husbands or wives is a small cause of the increase in divorce. This inference is based upon general knowledge without measurement. Similarly we can infer that the increasing use of contraceptives is an important cause of the diminution in large families; though we may wish to go further in the chain of causes to learn the reasons for this increased use.

Important causes are not likely to be found where a very large number of causes are known to exist. Such a large number implies that individual causes are probably small ones. Thus the use of the can opener is a minor cause in bringing about woman suffrage. Also we usually find a large number of causes if we pursue them very far in the chain of causes. The more remote cause is likely to be a less important one.

Important causes are not commonly found much outside the period of time of the changes being considered. For instance, if we are considering changes in the family over a century or two from the days of subsistence farming, then the factory can be an important cause, for there were no power driven factories before that time. However, if we are considering changes in the family over the past decade, we would hardly seek the causes in an invention that occurred a long time previously, unless its use changed markedly in that decade.

An invention, be it social or mechanical, may be an important cause because its variation is so great; that is to say, the variation is from non-existence to existence. Before 1920, for instance, there was no radio broadcasting. Afterward there was. The swing from non-existence to existence is an extreme variation. The greater the variation, the greater the change it causes, other things being equal. So the atom bomb for this reason may be an important cause of future social changes.

Important causes are more readily found in clusters than in single factors, because of the phenomenon of convergence. For instance, transportation and communication are more important as causes than are the bus and the telegraph. The cluster called the Industrial Revolution is a particularly important cause.

Because of the phenomenon of dispersion, a single cause may have many dispersed effects which later converge. Such is strikingly the case with the steam engine, the dispersed effects of which were felt widely on production, transportation, communication, cities, and population. Influences from all these later converged to reduce the functions of the family. Such inventions become extraordinarily important because of the combining of convergence and dispersion.

Mechanical Invention as a Cause

Where there are several causes of a change in the family, the causes are often of two kinds. One is a variation in a material factor, such as a mechanical invention or a discovery in physical science, while the other type is a change in some non-material factor such as religion or government. It has been found useful to divide causes into the material and non-material factors, and inventions into mechanical and non-mechanical ones.

That variations in material objects cause social changes may appear strange to some who view the agencies of social change as always human beings. To these observers, it does not seem possible, for instance, that the invention of the hoe or digging stick could have changed the status of women in the primitive family. For a hoe is an inert object and not capable of changing anything, even the soil, except as handled by a person. So when the creation of a material object or the modification of one is spoken of as a cause, what is meant is that its use by people is the cause of the change.

The use of the digging stick or hoe by human beings is the cause. But we do not say that human beings are the cause, though we do say that the invention of the hoe is the cause. The reason for this statement is the principle presented in a previous paragraph, namely, that a change cannot be explained by something that has not changed, but must be accounted for by a factor that has changed. What we are here trying to explain is the change in the procurement of food from hunting to agriculture. The invention of the hoe (plus the knowledge of planting seeds or shoots) made this change possible. The cause then is the change from, say, the bow and arrow to the hoe. The motives of human beings are not the cause, though they be active agents, for they have not changed. They are the desires to obtain assured food supplies. A variable cannot be explained by a constant. A constant may be a factor in a phenomenon but not a cause of the change in the phenomenon. So the desires of human beings are factors in obtaining food (in agriculture as well as in hunting) but not causes of the change from hunting to agriculture.

Before there was a digging stick, peoples were hunters and food gatherers and hence generally wanderers. With the hoe and planting came a more settled life and a type of food production that was less hazardous than hunting and hence less dependent upon chance and also more readily done by women than hunting. The ratio of men to women probably increased. Women could cultivate but were not good hunters. The status of wives in the family after a time generally rose. Women in the hoe culture have a higher status than in the hunting cultures. So the creation of material objects does cause social changes.

The Lag in a Causal Influence

In considering the causes for the decline in the authority of the male head of the family, it should be remarked that the effect does not always occur simultaneously with the cause. The full effect is manifest only after a delay. To cite a different example, immigrants speaking a foreign language may require only a day or a week to move to the United States. Yet it will take months or years for them to learn to speak the new language fluently. But there is a correlation between residence and language, which in this case is manifest after a considerable lag in time. Again, many husbands and fathers in cities of the twentieth century still try to boss their wives and children as did their parents or grandparents in the authoritarian farm family of the nineteenth century. This custom appropriate to an earlier condition persists in a changed era; whereas the appropriate custom for the changed era should be one of greater freedom for wives and children who are not engaged much in home production.

Such a lag is more in evidence when one of the causes of a change is relatively slight, as compared with the strong influence of some of the other factors in family change. This is often the case in divorce. Cities have higher divorce rates than do farming communities. But where the religious influence in the family is stronger than the urban influence, the separation of maladjusted mates may be delayed. Such may be the explanation of why England, longer urbanized than the United States, has a lower divorce rate; in England church and state are more closely related than in the United States. Sometimes a causal relationship cannot be demonstrated until the passage of time has removed the lag. Indeed, if the influence of one causal factor is very strong, the influence of a lesser factor may not be visible at all. The city operates to reduce the birth rate; but if the religious opposition to birth control is very strong, the birth rate of communicants in cities may not be greatly reduced. In appraising causes, the phenomenon of lag should not be neglected.

The Pattern of Causes of the Changes in the Family

The map. We need a map to find our way about in the complex network of causes of the changes in the family. Such a map is based on three components.

1. Causes occur in a *sequence* like the links on a chain. These may be classified as the proximate and the remote. Thus the weakening of the ties of kinship is caused by the proximate factor, the separation of kin; and the remote causes are the instruments of transportation, which in turn were caused by the invention of the steam engine and the internal combustion engine.

2. A change is usually the result of several causes which may be said to *converge* to produce the result. Thus several transportation and communication inventions converge to increase the growth of the suburbs of cities. These converging causes are also called a cluster.

3. The effects of a single cause may be numerous and may *disperse* outward into many different fields. Thus the transfer of work from the home had many different effects upon wives, husbands, and children.

When the phenomena of convergence and of dispersion are tied in with the phenomenon of sequence, the result is a complex network of causes. The complexity is simplified, however, when it is remembered that causes vary in importance, and we seek first the important ones.

Guideposts on the map. In following the pattern just outlined, the following five guideposts should be observed.

1. A change is caused by another change and never by a constant. An increase in marriage is not caused by the sex instinct but by an increase in prosperity. Sex is a factor in marriage but not a cause of its increase.

2. Changes are of two kinds: those that occur (a) over time in a single group and (b) contemporaneously in a number of groups. Thus in 1950 there are variations in the causes of divorce from one state to another and from one married couple to another. But from 1900 to 1950, incompatibility has been increasingly used as a reason for divorce. These two types of change and cause are not always kept distinct. In this book our interest is in change over time.

3. Simultaneous variation does not establish causation which must be demonstrated from knowledge not observable in the variation. The correlations in the statures of fathers and sons do not tell us which causes which. Hence description and analysis may demonstrate causation in a limited sample without the measurement of statistics, and statistics alone do not demonstrate causation.

4. The causal connection between two variables may be obscured by lags. Thus the decrease of authoritarianism in the family may not follow immediately upon the change from farm to city.

5. Psychological changes, such as changes in motives, are incomplete explanations of change unless we know what social or material conditions have brought about the psychological changes, for the physiological bases of psychological traits of a people

rarely change over short periods of time. An increasing desire of wives to earn an income is not a very satisfactory explanation of the increased employment of married women unless we know the conditions that brought about this increased yearning for more money by married women.

With the help of this map and its guides as shown in the preceding paragraphs, we can obtain knowledge of the field of causation of the changing family.

PART TWO

Recent Changes in the Family

3

From Economics to Romance

If we were to ask a representative sample of recent newlyweds in the United States today why they had chosen each other as mates, probably the most common answer would be "Why, because we love each other," or words to this effect. If they did not love each other, they would be ashamed to admit it, for love is the most acceptable and respectable reason for marriage in our society today. Indeed love is regarded as a sufficient reason for marriage, outweighing all other considerations. Love conquers all, it is said. When a king of England relinquished his throne "for the woman I love," he was warmly defended by many.

If we were to press the newlyweds further and ask them why they love each other, probably the most frequent reply would be because his or her mate was a wonderful person, even the most wonderful person in the world. If we continue to inquire as to what makes him or her so wonderful, good looks, charm, attractive disposition, or strong character might be mentioned. The emphasis would be on the personal qualities.

Qualifications of a Bride and a Groom

If a man today were to say he married his wife because his parents approved of her and thought she would make him a good cook, housekeeper, and seamstress, we would think him odd. But that was precisely the kind of answer that men would have had to give a century or two ago if the truth were spoken. In earlier times, the emphasis was on the practical rather than the personal considerations.

The critical reader may ask: Was there then no falling in love in earlier times, no interest in good looks, in personal attractiveness, and in qualities of character? The answer is yes, there was an interest in these matters but the emphasis on them was different. To understand this change in emphasis we must first understand the change that has occurred in the role of the family in the selection of a mate.

Qualities of a wife in earlier times. In earlier times the parents played a larger role in the choice of a mate for their children, for the family was a more important institution in controlling the behavior of its members. An indication of this in Colonial times in New England was the offense known as "inveigling," punishable as a misdemeanor, which consisted of courting or attempting to court a girl without her father's permission. That such a law existed is evidence of the fact that young men did on occasion try to by-pass the family of the girl they were interested in, but the law also means that the family was not to be ignored with impunity. In other times and places, the authority of the parents might be extended further, even to the point of actually selecting a mate for their children, and there are cultures in which the betrothed would see each other for the first time at the wedding ceremony. Difficult as it is for us to conceive, there are even some cultures where it is customary for the couple to be absent from their own wedding. They meet for the first time after the ceremony. Obviously, in such cases there is little or no romance involved in mating. The theory underlying such marriages is that if the couple come from comparable backgrounds and are adequate to the tasks of marriage, they will be congenial, and, if love is deemed important, congeniality will foster it. It is not so important, these people think, that there should be affection between mates before marriage as after it.

A writer in the United States in 1832 reports that "it is usual for parents to choose a husband for their daughter, and to consult her only for form's sake." [1] At other times and places, in cultures where marriages are arranged by the parents, there is a good deal of variation in the respect accorded to the wishes of the young people, and generally their wishes are not ignored. But, these variations aside, if one is interested in the change that has occurred in the matter of choosing a mate, then one will note that in earlier times the role of the parents in the choice of a mate was appre-

[1] *The Lady's Book,* 4: 267-8 (Philadelphia: L. A. Godey & Co., 1832).

ciably greater than it is now, and the role of the young people correspondingly less.

In the choice of a mate, there may be many factors: family background, religion, race, education and economic status, as well as the capabilities of the persons concerned, their personal qualities, and their love for each other. In earlier times as now, all of these factors would enter in, but the distribution of emphasis has changed. One of the first questions parents used to ask about any suitor was: "Who are his people?" The status of his family was an important consideration, for a person was regarded primarily as a member of a family rather than as an individual in his own right, and marriage was a family affair, establishing new relations between all the members of the two households, not just between husband and wife, and between parents and son-in-law or daughter-in-law. Relatives on both sides would be affected, too, by the marriage and were therefore concerned about it. If the young man's family was thought to be suitable, then the question in the minds of the girl's parents was whether the young man would make a good husband. And since most persons belonged to economic classes that had to work for a living, the criterion of "a good husband" was mainly in terms of being a capable worker and a good provider. Likewise, if the girl's background was satisfactory to the boy's parents, a further question would concern her domestic aptitudes. How efficiently would she discharge her duties as a housewife? Personal attractiveness and qualities of character would of course be considered too, but within the framework of family background and domestic skills.

W. I. Thomas and Florian Znaniecki[2] have recorded how in the traditional rural society of Poland the marriage of the children is a primary responsibility of the family and how the family guides the choice of a mate in terms of (a) the personality of the partner as one which can be assimilated into the group, as regards customs, economic status, occupation, age, and, if possible, personal or family acquaintance; and (b) qualities of the family to which the prospective mate belongs and to which the considering family will be allying itself. In a society where dowries and marriage settlements are the custom, as in traditional rural society, these practices help greatly to strengthen the control exercised by the

2 W. I. Thomas and F. Znaniecki, *The Polish Peasant in Europe and America* (Boston: The Gorham Press, 1918), Vol. I.

family over the marriage of their children, for without a dowry or marriage settlement a youth would be greatly handicapped in finding a marriage partner. The twin purposes of these family aids is to assist the young people in setting up a new household from which they will get their living and to aid them in maintaining the social level of the parental family. Ordinarily both families help. The boy's family may provide land, or a master workman's facilities, and the girl's family may give money. It may be noted that in earlier agricultural times, married children continued much more often than now to live near their parents. In villages which are small, the inhabitants are well acquainted with one another and the family background and personal qualities of all the young people are well known.

That the capabilities of mates rather than love was stressed in earlier times can be seen from the following famous passages from the Book of Proverbs [3] setting forth the praise and properties of a good wife:

Who can find a virtuous woman; for her price is far above rubies . . .
She seeketh wool, and flax, and worketh willingly with her hands.
She is like the merchants' ships; she bringeth her food from afar.
She riseth also while it is yet night, and giveth meat to her household, and a portion to her maidens.
She considereth a field, and buyeth it: with the fruit of her hands she planteth a vineyard.
She girdeth her loins with strength, and strengtheneth her arms.
She perceiveth that her merchandise is good: her candle goeth not out by night.
She layeth her hands to the spindle, and her hands hold the distaff.
She stretcheth out her hand to the poor; yea, she reacheth forth her hands to the needy.
She is not afraid of the snow for her household: for all her household are clothed with scarlet.
She maketh herself coverings of tapestry; her clothing is silk and purple.
Her husband is known at the gates, when he sitteth among the elders of the land.
She maketh fine linen, and selleth it; and delivereth girdles to the merchant.
Strength and honor are her clothing; and she shall rejoice in time to come.

[3] Proverbs 31: 10–31.

She openeth her mouth with wisdom; and in her tongue is the law
of kindness.
She looketh well to the ways of her household, and eateth not the
bread of idleness.
Her children arise up, and call her blessed; her husband also, and he
praiseth her.

These words were reputedly spoken by King Solomon ten centuries before Christ but they were still popular with the American
colonists twenty-eight centuries later. Thus we find Benjamin
Franklin echoing the same sentiments in a selection from *Poor
Richard,* dated July, 1748:

> When great Augustus ruled the World and Rome,
> The Cloth he wore was spun and wove at Home,
> His empress ply'd the Distaff and the Loom.
> Old England's Laws the proudest Beauty name,
> When single, Spinster, and when married, Dame,
> For Housewifery is Woman's noblest Fame.
> The Wisest household cares to Women yield,
> A large, an useful and a grateful Field.

How large, useful and grateful a field the wisest household
cares to women yield can be seen from the following, quoted
from the diary of Christopher Marshall, a Philadelphia Quaker,
in 1778:

> As I have in this memorandum taken scarcely any notice of my
> wife's employments, it might appear as if her engagements were very
> trifling; the which is not the case but the reverse. And to do her jus-
> tice which her services deserved, by entering them minutely, would
> take up most of my time, for this genuine reason how that from
> early in the morning till late at night she is constantly employed in
> the affairs of the family, which for four months has been very large;
> for besides the addition to our family in the house, it is a constant
> resort of comers and goers which seldom go away with dry lips and
> hungry bellies. This calls for her constant attendance, not only to
> provide, but also to attend at getting prepared in the kitchen, baking
> our bread and pies, meat &c. and also the table. Her cleanliness about
> the house, her attendance in the orchard, cutting and drying of cider
> without tools, for the constant drink of the family, her seeing all our
> washing done, and her fine clothes and my shirts, the which are all
> smoothed by her; add to this, her making of twenty large cheeses, and
> that from one cow, and daily using with milk and cream, besides her

sewing, knitting &c. Thus she looketh well to the ways of her household, and eateth not the bread of idleness; yea she also stretcheth out
her hand, and she reacheth forth her hand to her needy friends and
neighbors. I think she has not been above four times since her
residence here to visit her neighbors; nor through mercy has she been
sick for any time, but has at all times been ready in any affliction to
me or my family as a faithful nurse and attendant both day and
night.[4]

The reader will note in the above the allusion to Solomon's
phrases regarding the ideal wife. But times have changed, and
today these phrases are not quoted so often or with so much approval. The diary of a modern husband would make very different
reading, unless he were a farmer whose farm produced nearly
all that his family consumed.

It is interesting to speculate on what Solomon would extol as
wifely virtues were he living today at mid-twentieth century. He
would not attach so much significance to baking bread or weaving cloth as he would to being a good companion. If Solomon
were alive today he would probably hurl his diatribes against in-
fatuation and romantic love while supporting affection and companionship, just as he extolled industriousness and competence
and condemned indolence and incompetence.

Exactly when in the history of the United States the domestic
virtues were superseded by personal ones, it is difficult if not impossible to say, for the change was gradual and not abrupt and
corresponded to the transition from the rural to the urban society.
"Among our industrious fore-fathers," we read in 1831, "it was a fixed
maxim that a young lady should never be permitted to marry
until she had spun for herself a set of body, bed, and table linen.
From this custom all unmarried women are called spinsters in
legal proceeding. What a scene of busy industry Philadelphia
would present, if all the young ladies who long to be married
were obliged to cast away the Waverley novels, and abandon all
their fashionable amusements, in order to approach the goal of
matrimonial felicity by that path of preparation which their great-
grandmothers pursued." [5]

---

[4] Alice Morse Earle, *Colonial Dames and Goodwives* (Boston: Houghton
Mifflin Company, 1895), pp. 258–260 and 314.
[5] *The Lady's Book*, 2: 165–6 (Philadelphia: L. A. Godey & Co., 1831).

As late as 1871 in a popular woman's magazine of the time[6] we find articles expressing concern over the widespread lack of domestic skills in woman. "Fifty years ago," we are told, "every woman, no matter how rich her parents, was taught systematically to cook." The theory was that even when a woman was rich enough to keep servants, she ought to know how to cook so as to be able to instruct her servants. Even beauty was not thought to be sufficient excuse for forfeiting competence in domestic affairs. "No sensible man," it was written more than 100 years ago in the fashionable Godey's *Lady's Book*, "ever thought a beautiful wife was worth as much as one that could make a good pudding." [7] It is a far cry from a situation such as this where even the beautiful are not excused for domestic incompetence to a situation such as exists in our society today where even the plain-looking are often without domestic skills. A change so extensive, one not governed merely by personal factors, would appear to be a basic change in the values of our culture related to marriage and the home.

Qualities in a wife in modern times. For clues as to the motives involved in the choice of a mate in our time we turn to several sources such as the themes of motion pictures and popular songs. Here we find that romantic love is a constantly repeated theme, almost an obsession. In one series of 115 movies, it is said that 90 per cent showed love-making, and 70 per cent intense love-making.[8] In the movies, it is claimed,[9] romantic love is made to "carry the whole weight of living," omitting other strong interests in the lives of the characters portrayed. Probably one of the most notable omissions, and the strangest in view of the dominance of the profit motive in our society, is the omission of work as a motivating influence. Where work and "making good" in a financial way are shown at all, it is usually the villain who is being depicted. This dichotomy is true not only of the movies but of most fiction and radio dramas. But even if the movies exaggerate

---

[6] *Peterson's Magazine*, 59: 242, 1871.

[7] *The Lady's Book*, 2: 166 (Philadelphia: L. A. Godey & Co., 1831).

[8] Newsweek, 28: 80, March 24, 1947.

[9] Hortense Powdermaker, "An Anthropologist Looks at the Movies," *Annals of the American Academy of Political and Social Science*, 254; 80–86, November, 1947.

reality, like stereotypes they contain an element of truth, and the truth is that in our culture romantic love is highly emphasized.

Even better than the movies as an indication of the romantic complex of our culture are our popular songs, for they are built around a single theme which makes analysis easier. An examination of the most popular songs published in 1946 shows a very large number devoted to the love theme. This can be seen from Table 2 where the theme of the song is evident in the title. Only those songs in which the love theme is evident in the title are included in this list. Examination of the words of the songs published that year showed that many of them had to do with love, although the title did not suggest it.

A theme so pervasive as romantic love naturally finds its way into advertising, especially advertising that is aimed at American women. A common sight is the appeal that says that if a woman will use the soap being advertised, her husband will think her hands are still soft; if a girl uses the toothpaste recommended, her smile will win the man of her choice.

Student opinions. No nationwide poll has ever been taken in the United States of the factors affecting the choice of a mate. Our sampling of opinion in this area has been largely limited to college students, who represent a group highly selected for sophistication. Many of them, especially those studying the social sciences, have heard a good deal about "the romantic complex," probably in a critical vein. It is highly probable, therefore, that the responses of college students on mate selection would emphasize romance less than would the responses of American youth generally. The responses of college students place emphasis upon qualities of personality rather than economic skills. Among the factors in mate selection, they attach the greatest significance to dependable character and emotional stability. Valued less highly than these factors, but still valued highly, are a pleasing disposition and mutual attraction. These findings are based on 600 students at the University of Wisconsin[10] and on 1,385 Mormon students.[11]

[10] Reuben Hill, "Campus Values in Mate Selection," *Journal of Home Economics*, 37: 557, November, 1945.

[11] Harold T. Christensen, "Student Views on Mate Selection," *Marriage and Family Living*, 9: 85–88, November, 1947.

TABLE 2

Love Songs (1946)

Tomorrow is Forever
Don't You Remember Me
If I had a Wishing Ring
Baby — What You Do to Me
My Guy's Come Back
You Can Cry on Somebody Else's
  Shoulder
Moonlight Bay
Pretty Baby
Gonna Fall in Love with You
My Treasure
It's Been a Long, Long Time
Sioux City Sue
Talkin' to Myself About You
Shy Guy
I'm Glad I Waited For You
Here I Go Again
As Long as I Live
There Must Be a Way
Prove it By the Things You Do
Just a Little Fond Affection
Here Comes Heaven Again
When the One You Love
Good Luck to You
Smiling Eyes
Talking in My Sleep
How Do I Stand with You
Love is a Merry-go-round
Broken Hearted
You can Bet Your Boots and
  Saddles
Darling, Don't you Cry
Spellbound
Somebody's Walkin' in My
  Dreams
I'll Buy That Dream
Kiss Me Hello
Sweetheart

We'll Gather Lilacs
It's Our Romance
Will You Still Hear the Beat of
  My Heart
When Tomorrow Comes
You Stole My Heart
The Letter That Never Came
This is My Beloved
Be Still, My Crazy Heart, Be
  Still
If I Loved You
Wings to Wear Upon My Heart
Embraceable You
I Held Her Hand
I Didn't Mean a Word I Said
I Fall in Love With You Every
  Day
Where Did You Learn to Love
Somebody Else's Darlin'
You May Not Love Me
In Love in Vain
One More Tomorrow
Prisoner of Love
When I'm With You
Are You Making Believe
I Knew That You Were Mine
Alone Again
Endless Love
Candlelight and Roses
I'd Be Lost Without You
There's No One But You
One Love
Let There Be Love
Right into My Heart
When I Lost My Heart To You
You May Not Love Me
Maybe I Lost Your Love
Let's Take the Long Way Home

As If I Didn't Have Enough on
My Mind
Wait and See
When the One You Love
Promises
You Are Too Beautiful
A Sky Full of Dreams
The Same Old You
I Have the Loveliest Dreams
A Little Rendezvous in Honolulu
I Love Someone and That Some-
one is You
You Haven't Changed at All
Love Will Have to Do
My Obligation
Am I the One for You
If You Cared
It's You Only You
Should I Tell You I Love You
Deep in Your Heart
Somebody Else is Taking My
Place
Side By Side
I Miss That Feeling
Fall In Love with Me
You Call it Madness
I've Never Forgotten
A Dream Each Night
Bring Back the Love I Once
Knew
I Fell in Love in the Fall
It's About Time
I've Never Forgotten
If It's Love You Want
I Just Don't Know Why But I do
My First, My Last, My Only
I Love Everything You Do
Who Told You That Lie

Dream Serenade
Anniversary Waltz
Good Night, Little Girl of My
Dreams
You'll Always Be the Same
Sweetheart
And then, You Told Me You
Loved Me
Holiday for Love
Day After Day
Don't Tell Me
Old Devil Moon
True
Good Night Sweetheart
Je Vous Aime
Stranger Things Have Happened
Tenderly
Peg O' My Heart
Do You Feel That Way, Too
I Won't Be Home Any More
When You Call
As Years Go By
As Long as I'm Dreaming
I Want to be Loved
Why Should I Cry Over You
Time After Time
If I Had My Life To Live Over
My Future Just Passed
I'm Sorry I Didn't Say I'm Sorry
Through
Stella by Starlight
Deep Down in Your Heart
Beside You
I Wish I Didn't Love You So
Heart and Soul
Lover
It Makes No Difference Now

Among these University of Wisconsin students the men are
represented as believing that the factor "good cook and housekeeper" is indispensable in the wise choice of a mate, whereas the
women think it is only barely "important." On the other hand, as

to the factor of "ambition and industriousness," which applies mainly to the men, both sexes rate it as "indispensable." In other words, men attach more significance to ambition and industry on the part of men than women do to good cooking and good house-keeping by women. Similar cultural background between mates (i.e., similar religion, education, et cetera), valued so highly by parents in earlier times, rates quite low on the list supplied by modern students. All other factors being satisfactory, 84 per cent of a group of white college women and 92 per cent of a group of white college men said they would be willing to marry a person of lower economic rank than their own; 68 and 77 per cent respectively would marry into a family they considered inferior; 70 and 74 per cent would be willing to marry a person of a different religion.[12] It should be noted, of course, that these ratings represent verbal responses which may or may not correspond very closely to the factors which operate when choices are actually made.

In earlier times, the care of the home was considered an important art and exceptionally good housekeepers were not infrequently eulogized in the pulpit and public print. The diaries of the colonial period which have come down to us contain frequent references to such capable housewives.[13] At the present time, however, really first-class housekeepers are scarce.

To sum up the discussion of the preceding paragraphs, the evidence indicates that the young people today wish to marry on the basis of personal qualities and particularly for love and companionship, rather than as in the past either for economic or utilitarian reasons.

Causes for Decrease of Domestic Economic Skills

The decline of the family as an economic institution. The trend which we have described and which we have called "from economics to romance," embodies two components. One is the decline in social regard for domestic productive skills in a wife or in

---

[12] Mirra Komarovsky, "What Do Young People Want in a Marriage Partner?" *Journal of Social Hygiene,* 32: 440–4, December, 1947.

[13] Arthur Calhoun, *A Social History of the American Family* (Cleveland: The Arthur Clark Company, 1917).

a husband, and the other is the rise in the evaluation of the sexual and affectional qualifications of a mate.

We consider first the decrease in domestic productive skills. The causes are not far to seek. When the population was largely made up of farmers and when nearly all that was consumed was produced on the farm and little was sold, the farm was a sort of factory.[14] The family was the most prevalent and generally important economic institution of the time. It was natural that productive skills would be emphasized by husbands and wives, since they determined the standard of living that the family would have. The prospective wife naturally wanted a man who was industrious and capable and often rated such qualities above personal appearance or other traits of personality.[15] The prospective husband also wanted a woman who was a good housekeeper, a good cook, and one who could spin and weave well.

As the farms came to produce crops which were sold, as more goods that were once made on the farm were bought, and as city families with husbands and fathers working away from home became much more numerous, there was a change in emphasis on productive skills as a desirable quality in a wife. In a husband, abilities to produce an income were still considered important. The new abilities of a husband in the city were, however, those which a prospective bride would know less about than the abilities of a farmer in a small community, especially when she was a farmer's daughter. The city girl has little basis for predicting what sort of lawyer or engineer a young man will become. The home industries, which were run by women, such as sewing, weaving, spinning, processing food, making medicines, et cetera, moved into factories and left the wife's duties largely cooking, caring for the house, and bringing up the children.

The removal of economic functions from the home is what we call the direct or proximate cause of the devaluation of the economic factor in the choice of a mate.

The flight of economic functions also has its causes. The causes of the departure of home industries and the replacement of the household as the chief economic institution by factories, stores,

---

[14] M. F. Nimkoff, *Marriage and the Family* (Boston: Houghton Mifflin Company, 1947), Chapter 3.

[15] Arthur W. Calhoun, *op. cit.*

banks, and other economic organizations were largely (a) the development of big metal machinery driven by mechanical power, and (b) the transportation inventions, chiefly the railroads dependent upon iron and the steam engine, which brought food to factory workers and which distributed to the homes the goods produced in the factories.

The growth of factories and railroads rested primarily upon the use of the steam engine and also iron and its derivative, steel.

Thus the recent decline in the valuation of the economic functions of women in the family is traceable to the technological developments that led to factories and railroads.[16] These technological developments are remote causes, or causes once-removed, of the changed valuation of economic factors in the choice of a wife.

These technological developments, in turn, have antecedents, but beyond the Industrial Revolution it is not profitable to proceed because the causes of these inventions were other inventions. The Industrial Revolution was mainly the bringing together, into new combinations, of inventions already in existence.

The city was the locale of the technological changes and the loss of functions of the family as a producing unit is therefore especially marked in cities.

There were, of course, cities before the steam engine and the railroad, but the early urban populations were small in comparison with the rural. These early cities were in general dependent upon boats and carts. They were largely centers of trade, i.e., of exchange of goods.

There was little production comparable to that of factories, though some mass production was had through division of labor and through some labor-saving machines even though the motive force was not mechanical. We call such techniques, handicrafts.

While there has been a change in attitude toward the qualities desired in a wife and husband with the shift from self-sufficing farming to city life, there is a lag in this change. Thus the old ideas of woman's place being in the home and the idealization of her qualities as a housekeeper persist, often for decades and, in some cases, centuries.

16 J. L. and Barbara Hammond, *The Rise of Modern Industry* (New York: Harcourt, Brace & Company, Inc., 1926).

We have said that the trend "from economics to romance" was also based upon a second component, namely, the rise in the evaluation of the sexual and affectional qualities of a mate. It is therefore desirable to chart this rising emphasis on sex, which we do in the following section.

The Emphasis on Love

Characteristics of romantic love. We have so far discussed romantic love as a basis for the choice of a mate without defining or describing it. Webster's dictionary defines love as "a feeling of strong personal attachment; strong liking; tender and passionate affection for one of the opposite sex."

Love is a strong feeling, an emotion, and like all emotion, it distorts reality, although the distortion may be more beautiful than the reality. This is implied in the folk saying: "Love is blind," by which we mean not that the lover's senses are impaired but that his judgment is impaired by his strong feelings. These strong feelings bias the lover in favor of his loved one and he is prevented from appraising her qualities fairly. Herein lies the merit of preliminary mate selection by those not emotionally involved, for they are in a position to make an objective evaluation. Then if the tentative choices of the parents are to the liking of the young people, the situation for marital happiness is favorable, for love will be mobilized in support of a congenial relationship. If the young people make their own choices without help from their elders, the problem is how to achieve the same objectivity in selection, how to make a choice on the basis of reason rather than emotion. If the choice is reasonable, their emotions can be mobilized in its behalf.

Of the many distortions caused by the highly-charged emotion of love, two may be cited here as of special importance.

The first of these is the fantasy that in mating for happiness, only one person in the world will do. This fantasy, which is evident in the titles of many popular songs, probably derives from the tendency of the lover to idealize his loved one.

At one extreme, then, is the idea prevalent in the United States today that there is only one possible mate with whom happiness is possible. At the other extreme, in cultures where the concept of romantic love is absent, there is the view that as a wife for a particular man, one woman will do as well as another if she is economically skilled. This is reported to be what the Navaho Indians believe,[17] with certain qualifications. The qualifications are that one woman will do as well as another, so long as she is healthy, industrious, and competent.

Actually, the theories stated above represent ideological extremes, from which there is considerable departure in real life. There is some selection among the Navaho, and love is not altogether exclusive in the United States, as must be evident from the fact that most persons have a series of love affairs before marriage[18] and also that many persons marry more than once. The two theories of mate selection, namely, that only one woman will do and that any woman will do, represent extreme positions to which the behavior of many individuals in the societies does not conform. Still, if one is interested in understanding the considerable difference in emphasis between societies which emphasize romance as a basis for marriage and societies which do not, then the statement of the situation in terms of "ideal types" should be helpful.

The second major tenet of romanticism is that love alone is a sufficient basis for marriage and therefore if there is love, lasting happiness is assured. The old romances, after describing the passionate feeling of the lovers for each other, used to conclude: "and so they were married and lived happily ever afterward." The increase of divorce, one might think, would have dampened this faith in the sufficiency of love. Many couples still marry on the basis of strong liking for each other, despite differences in religious outlook, standard of living, intellectual and aesthetic interests, vocational and domestic incompetence and limitations of personality.

The increased emphasis on the romantic aspects of marriage in the United States in the twentieth century, and the resulting increased dependence upon love to provide stability in family relations are related to a changed appreciation of sex and its correlated sentiments.

[17] Dorothea Leighton and Clyde Kluckhohn, *Children of the People* (Cambridge: Harvard University Press, 1947), p. 79.
[18] G. V. Hamilton, *A Research in Marriage* (New York: Lear, 1948).

The correlated sentiments are several. One is the romantic feeling found often in courtship where love is aroused with little or no outlet in primary sexual behavior. Another correlated sentiment is love with fewer romantic aspects, such as is often found in well-mated mature married couples. In any case, the trend toward romance and love as a very important factor in marriage seems to indicate a heightened recognition of the importance of sex.

Therefore, it seems desirable in describing the trend to romantic love as a factor in marriage to record the facts as we find them regarding the trends in the sexual behavior of young people. Before we proceed to do this, however, we note that love is generally an immediate cause of the interest of prospective mates in each other, and that sex is a remote cause, the cause once-removed. Marriage occurs between members of the opposite sex and the romantic interest reflects the repression of the sexual drive during courtship. Freud observed that the repression of the sexual drive led to what he called "the overestimation of the sexual object" which, as we have seen, is a component of courtship. Premarital sexual intercourse has increased in the United States in the last half-century but the relative increase has not been great. Especially for women, the sex drive is sublimated before marriage and love and romance are emphasized.

Changes in sexual behavior. With more emphasis on sex, it is not surprising that there should now be more sexual freedom and experimentation before marriage, especially for women, than was true in earlier times. Only a few studies exist to document this change, since practically all the vast literature on sexual behavior in our culture is limited to a given time and place and is therefore not useful for indicating trends. The Kinsey data indicate a trend in the direction of a single sex standard for both sexes, patterned after that of the male. Perhaps "standard" is not quite the correct word, for the evidence relates to sexual behavior rather than to the sex mores. The evidence indicates that there is more sexual experimentation on the part of females, and that their sex behavior is therefore becoming more like that of the males. There is some evidence, too, however, that there is more tolerance of the new sex patterns for women, which if established would represent a change in the sex mores themselves.

One of the few studies[19] reporting data on trends is Terman's, where the sex findings are a part of a more inclusive report on the factors associated with marital happiness. Terman, studying a sample of 793 couples heavily weighted with members of the upper occupational groups, found that the incidence of intercourse before marriage among these couples showed marked relationship with date of birth. For men, virginity at time of marriage was 50.6 per cent in the group born before 1890, as compared with 13.6 per cent in the group born in 1910 or later. For women, the corresponding figures are 86.5 per cent and 31.7 per cent. These are striking data but generalizations based on them must be drawn with caution since Terman's sample is a small, unrepresentative one.

Differences between the sexes appear in the direction of these changes. Although the proportion of men who had premarital intercourse with women other than their wives remained almost stationary for the period, there was a sharp rise in the corresponding figure for women. About five times as many of the youngest wives studied as of the oldest had premarital intercourse with partners other than their future spouses.

Kinsey's data indicate that the incidence of premarital sex intercourse on the part of men has increased somewhat in the last generation or two, and the nature of it has also changed, with unmarried men having less intercourse with prostitutes and more coitus with future spouses or other "good" girls.[20] While the number of prostitutes may not have greatly changed, the traffic with them has decreased, and the incidence of non-commercialized coitus has increased. The change for men thus appears to be in part a shift in the type of sexual outlet, whereas for women the change is more an increase in premarital coitus. In his study of women, Kinsey[21] reports that the greatest changes he found between the patterns of sexual behavior of the older and younger generations of American females were in the increase in premarital petting and the increase in premarital coitus. Among the females

[19] Lewis M. Terman, *et al.*, *Psychological Factors in Marital Happiness* (New York: McGraw-Hill Book Company, 1938).

[20] Alfred C. Kinsey, Wardell B. Pomeroy, and Clyde E. Martin, *Sexual Behavior in the Human Male* (Philadelphia: W. B. Saunders Company, 1948), pp. 411–13.

[21] *Sexual Behavior in the Human Female* (Philadelphia: W. B. Saunders Company, 1953), pp. 298 ff.

in his sample those who were born before 1900, less than half as many had had premarital coitus as among those born in subsequent decades. Since Kinsey's sample is not a representative one, his findings may be utilized with assurance only for his sample.

The question remains as to whether the changes in sexual intercourse represent a change in moral standards, or merely increasing violation of unchanging standards. There is reason to think that the standards, the mores themselves, are changing somewhat, although on this point the evidence is not so clear as it is regarding actual behavior. A Fortune survey,[22] using a representative sample of the population of the United States, asked the question: "Do you think that sexual moral standards in this country are better or worse than they were a generation ago?" Forty-five per cent thought they were worse, 17.1 per cent better, 27.8 per cent the same, and 10.1 per cent said they didn't know. A later survey [23] conducted during World War II and devoted entirely to young women between the ages of twenty and twenty-five asked the question: "Do you think that during the past two years women in general have become more strict in their morals, less strict, or stayed about the same?" The answer "more strict" was given by 11.1 per cent; "less strict," 51.4 per cent; "no change," 32.3 per cent; and "don't know," 5.2 per cent. These are of course merely opinions, not records of change. Other polls report contrary findings.[24]

A number of studies report that public attitudes toward sex relations before marriage have become less condemnatory, reflecting a change in sex ethics. The item "having sex relations while unmarried" received a slightly less degree of disapproval in 1939 than it had ten years earlier in a study involving groups of students.[25] In another study the same questionnaire was used in 1929 and again in 1936 with the entire student bodies of two church-related colleges, as well as with 200 sociology students at the University of Iowa. Analysis of the responses to the questions as to what traits they would like their mates to possess showed

[22] *Fortune,* 15: 166–68, January, 1937.

[23] *Fortune,* 28: 101, August, 1943.

[24] Henry F. Pringle, "What Do the Women of America Think About Morals?" *Ladies Home Journal,* May, 1938.

[25] Paul Crisman, "Temporal Change and Sexual Difference in Moral Judgments," *Journal of Social Psychology,* 16: 29–38, 1942.

that sexual purity declined in favor over the seven-year period.[26] In appraising these studies, it may be noted that the time span covered is relatively short, hardly sufficient to establish a trend, and the responses are responses of students, a small segment of the population likely to give less conservative responses on the subject under consideration than are other groups in the population. Other studies report fluctuations in attitudes towards sex behavior, with greater approval of premarital sex relations in 1924–27 than either before or after that period; although after what is termed "the reaction" of 1931–32, it is claimed that there was more toleration of premarital sex relations than in the period 1900–05.[27]

We conclude that the evidence regarding changing sex practices of women before marriage is more reliable and convincing than the evidence regarding changes in sex standards, although such scant data as are available suggest a gradual liberalization of attitude, with the preponderant opinion, however, still favoring chastity before marriage. A discrepancy between theory and practice is not confined to the realm of sex experience, but is characteristic of many areas of activity in our culture [28] and in many other cultures as well.

Causes for Rise of Romantic Love

The family throughout history has not only been an economic institution, but also an institution for the regularization of mating and for the rearing of children. While the family has lost many of its economic functions, it still retains functions relating to sex and the care of little children. Therefore as the economic functions were transferred from the family to outside institutions, the remaining family functions were more largely concerned with mating and with child care.

Decrease of economic functions as a cause. There are several ways of describing this change. "From authority to companionship" is one popular expression of the idea. Another is the phrase, "per-

[26] Wayne C. Neely, "Family Attitudes of Denominational College and University Students," *American Sociological Review*, 5: 512–522, 1940.

[27] Hornell Hart, "Changing Social Attitudes and Interests," in *Recent Social Trends* (New York: McGraw-Hill Book Company, 1933).

[28] Karen Horney, *The Neurotic Personality of Our Time* (New York: W. W. Norton and Company, 1937).

sonalization of the family." As the family diminishes in significance as a socio-economic institution the individual person rises in importance. Still another way to characterize this is to say that the economic functions have given way to the personality functions. In an economic institution a man is often viewed in terms of what he does, and not as an individual. Thus there are factory "hands," workers, or clerks. So a husband as producer in the rural household married a housekeeper. Any capable housekeeper would be satisfactory, it is implied.

But with the decline of the economic functions, a wife is selected more on the basis of her personality, her companionability, and her qualifications as a mother. It follows that in appraising a personality for a companionable wife, the factor of sex is important, since mating is a highly important function of marriage. Two members of the same sex do not marry. The sexual function generally comes after marriage, while the romantic interest predominates before marriage in the choice of mate.

Thus the romantic factor in marriage has become increasingly important, in part merely because of the decrease of the economic factor. Romantic factors in the choice of a mate are said to be strongest in the technologically advanced United States, somewhat less in Europe. In Asia, particularly China, where the household economy flourishes, there is little of the romantic factor in selecting mates.

But as we have seen in the preceding descriptions of changing attitudes toward sex and changing sex behavior in young people, there are also several special causes, in addition to the above-mentioned general cause of the increased emphasis upon sex.

The naturalism of sex. The focusing of attention on sex was made possible, especially for women, by bringing it somewhat out of the obscurity where a social taboo of the subject had kept it, particularly in the religious atmosphere of the United States.

One reason for the breakdown of the taboo on the discussion of sex was the spread of biological knowledge in general, and the resulting emphasis upon health which gives full recognition to our biological heritage and the ways in which it functions. In colleges and high schools, biological subject matter has been a medium for purposely explaining sex.

The discoveries in biology had their effect upon specific religious attitudes toward sex, somewhat as discoveries in astronomy had their effect upon religious views of the universe, and as discoveries in the evolution of species had their influence upon religious ideas of the creation of man. The new biological knowledge changed somewhat the conception of behavior of mankind, tending to make conceptions of moral behavior synchronize more with biological behavior.

Sex and shame with little children. The approach to sex which was more in conformity with the idea of nature was particularly pertinent to the rearing of little children. In homes where religion was of the puritanical sort, there was a certain factor of shame and prudishness attached to ideas of sex. Information coming from the children on the streets brought in addition the idea of dirtiness. The effect, especially on little girls, was to align the powerful forces of the child's mind with the repression of sex impulses, often resulting in a highly prolonged dormancy.[29] The more naturalistic approach has probably made young people more aware of the drives of the maturing sexual structure. This general cause of the heightening of interest in the sex factor in personality and in behavior, especially on the part of women, is reducible largely to discoveries in the sciences of biology and psychology.

At the same time, books on sex were more freely circulated in the United States; and in particular the writings of Freud showed how widely the sexual impulses and related emotions permeate the whole personality. And since one of the aims of marriage is the provision of sexual outlets, it is understandable how more freedom was given to the sexual and affectionate role in companionship between men and women who were contemplating marrying and who after marriage were seeking a continuing compatibility.

That this interest of young people in the sexual factors in personality should lead to more overt sexual activity prior to marriage is understandable, and has been described in previous paragraphs. The specific causes for such increased overt activity are several.

Lessening of the fear of pregnancy. One is the discovery of birth

29 Evelyn Duvall and Reuben Hill, *When You Marry* (Boston: D. C. Heath & Company, 1945), p. 140.

control with the knowledge that sexual intercourse does not necessarily result in pregnancy if the proper precautions are taken. This
conclusion is borne out by a study of 1,364 college and university
students at forty-six institutions in all parts of the country, which
reports the girls who refrained from sexual relations, although
strongly attracted to some man, as giving their reasons in order of
frequency as (1) fear of pregnancy; (2) religious scruples; and
(3) hesitation in forming serious relationships.[30] Also reports on
the distribution of contraceptives indicate a large market among
young users.[31] Further reducing the fear of pregnancy are the
methods of quickly detecting it. A recent method reports an accurate determination within two hours after conception.[32]

Lessening the fear of venereal disease. Another cause of more
sexual activity between the young is the diminished chances of
contracting and suffering for a long period from a venereal disease.
The fear of such diseases has been reported especially for men,
who give it as one of the two leading restraints.[33] Perhaps this fear
exists more among men because it is males who associate with prostitutes. There are, of course, many for whom such a fear is overcome by the strength of sexual desires. On the conquest of venereal
diseases the editor of *Science News Letter* rated as one of the ten
great discoveries of 1949 that one pill of penicillin taken not long
after exposure is a preventive of gonorrhea. It has been reported
that the first four patients to get penicillin treatment for syphilis
have now passed a six-year period without a return of the disease.[34]
The prevention of venereal diseases had made much headway long
before the late date when antibiotics came to be used. As far back as
World War I, hygienic measures and use of antiseptics shortly
after exposure reduced the incidence of incapacitating venereal
diseases in the men in the armed forces.

[30] Dorothy Dunbar Bromley and Florence H. Britten, *Youth and Sex* (New
York: Harper and Brothers, 1938).
[31] Norman Himes, *Medical History of Contraception* (Baltimore: The Williams & Wilkins Co., 1936).
[32] *Science News Letter*, Vol. 51, No. 25, 1947, p. 388.
[33] Raymond R. Willoughby, *Sexuality in the Second Decade* (Washington,
D.C.: National Research Council, 1937), Society for Research in Child Development, Monographs, Vol. 2, No. 3.
[34] *Science News Letter*, January 21, 1950, p. 48.

Lessening the fear of detection. Still another cause of increased sexual intercourse before marriage is the reduction of the chances of detection and a lessening, therefore, of the fear of having the facts known by those who disapprove. This change has been brought about by the conditions of city life which make individuals strangers to one another, and by the automobile which makes it possible for individuals quickly to remove themselves from the presence of familiars.

We have recorded several causes of the increased sexual behavior in the young and of their interest in the sexual factor in personality. Prominent among these causes are the discoveries in biology and psychology which have influenced the pressure of moral and religious codes of behavior on sex; the development of preventive medicine; and the invention of contraceptives.

To sum up the argument of the chapter as a whole, the explanation of why the emphasis in mate selection has shifted from economic skills to romantic aspects of personality lies in the technological factors, particularly steam and steel, that took the household production and put it into urban factories; discoveries in biological science; preventive medicine; and the invention of contraceptives.

4

Starting Earlier

Whether marriage occurs early or late matters greatly in society. For instance, age at marriage affects size of family: fertility is more closely related to age than to any other demographic factor. Where a woman in the United States is married before she is eighteen years old, is native white, married once, and lives with her husband throughout her married life, the chances that she will remain childless are at the present time one in thirty, whereas if she marries at twenty or twenty-one, the chances of infertility are one in ten, and they are greater than one in five if she marries at the age of twenty-seven,[1] though this decreasing fertility may be due to other factors than biological maturation or deterioration. It is also thought that sexual morality is bolstered by early marriage and jeopardized by later marriage. So society is concerned about the age at which marriage takes place.

Average age at first marriage. During the present century the average age at first marriage in the United States has been decreasing. That is, we have been marrying earlier. This statement may come as a surprise, since it is commonly said our ancestors were married earlier than we are. Such, however, is not the case since 1890, the first year for which there are marriage data for the United States. From such data a median age at first marriage has been obtained. This type of average is a midway point, or median, at which half are married.[2] In 1890 this median age at first marriage

---

[1] M. F. Nimkoff, *Marriage and the Family* (Boston: Houghton Mifflin Company, 1947), p. 537.

[2] Bureau of the Census. *Current Population Reports — Population Characteristics.* Series P–20, No. 38, April 29, 1952. For method of construction and a statement of characteristics and errors, see page 7. The Census marriage statistics do not show the ages at marriage, hence it was not possible to obtain

for males was 26.1 years, whereas in 1950 it was twenty-three years. The median age for males at first marriage declined, then, about three years during this interval of sixty years. The changes were somewhat irregular over this period, as shown in the following line of median ages at first marriage for males by decades beginning in 1890 and ending in 1950:

26.1 25.9 25.1 24.6 24.3 24.3 23.0

For one decade there was no decrease, but for another (from 1940 to 1950) the decrease was quite great. The above figures are for males.

For females the decrease in the age at first marriage was less. In 1890, half the females who were married, or would ever marry, married at twenty-two years of age, while in 1950 this midway point was 20.1 years, a decrease of about two years. Since the age for males decreased by three years, then it follows that the ages of brides and grooms were a little closer together at the midcentury than at the beginning. For two decades during this period, the age at marriage for females rose instead of falling, as is shown by the following line of median ages at first marriage for females, by decades, beginning in 1890 and ending in 1950:

22.0 21.9 21.6 21.2 21.3 21.5 20.1

Even though the median age of marriage has been decreasing, it should be noted that, of those who have or will be married, one-half of the males had not been married at twenty-three years of age, and one-half the females had not been married at age twenty.

Proportion of young people married. We have been presenting data on the average (for a median is an average) age at marriage. Averages are, however, not as good an indication of early marriage as are the percentages of the young people who are married. So we shall next consider in some detail the number of young people married at different ages, an excellent measure of early marriage. The data show that in 1890 only half as large a proportion of those

---

an arithmetic mean or a median from such data. Their data do show the marital status at the time of the Census for each age. From such data the Census rather cleverly devised a median age at first marriage, which is the age at which half of those who have married or, it is estimated, will eventually marry, are found as having married by the time the Census was taken.

between fifteen and twenty years old were in the married state as in 1950.

The above comparison is only for the beginning and the end of this sixty-year period and does not tell us what happened in between. For the intervening decades, the percentages of females fifteen to nineteen years of age recorded by the census taker as married is shown in the following line of percentages beginning with 1890 and ending in 1950:

10   11   12   13   13   12   17

The general trend is toward more early marriage, though for one decade there was a decrease and for another little change.

It may be asked, however, whether this apparent increase in early marriage may not have been due to an increase in age of the young women of these age groups, between 1890 and 1950, instead of being due to an increase in the propensity to marry. The young women fifteen to nineteen years of age in 1950 may have had a higher average age than the young women fifteen to nineteen years old in 1890. Such would be the case if there were a larger proportion of eighteen- and nineteen-year-olds in 1950 than in 1890. Should this be so, a larger per cent of the fifteen to nineteen age group would have been married in 1950 than in 1890, even if exactly the same percentages at each year of age were found married in 1950 and in 1890, since many more young women marry at eighteen and nineteen than at fifteen and sixteen. In which case the apparent increase in early marriage would have been due to increasing age and not to more marriage per year of age.

We can find out whether this apparent increase in early marriage was due to increasing age or to an increasing tendency to marry. We do this by finding out the percentage of young people fifteen to nineteen years old who would have married if the ages had been exactly the same in 1890 and in 1950 (and also in the intervening decades). Thus the influence of age is eliminated as a factor by holding it constant.

This operation, called by professional demographers "standardizing for age," can be performed, however, only for four decades, from 1910 to 1950, because of lack of marriage data for individual years in 1890 and in 1900. When age is standardized, we see there is little change from the unstandardized data in the percentages married as shown in the following two lines of figures for the decades 1910–1950:

Not standardized for age	12.1	13.0	13.2	11.9	17.1
Standardized for age	12.3	13.4	13.5	12.0	17.1

The comparison of these two lines shows for the terminal figures that the increase actually was five percentage points from 1910 to 1950 but would have been 4.8 percentage points if the age distribution had been the same as shown in the standardized line of figures. The difference was .2 percentage points. Therefore of the increase in early marriage from 1910 to 1950, only 4 per cent was due to change in age.

The slight influence due to age appears negligible indeed when we compare the decade-by-decade changes in the percentage increases in the proportions that are married. Rounding off the figures at the decimal point, the average per cent of increase by decades for the four decades is 11 per cent for the standardized and also for the unstandardized data, and 11 per cent, too, for the six decades from 1899 to 1950.

We therefore conclude that in the first half of the twentieth century young people have been marrying earlier.

This tendency to marry earlier has been presented in terms of percentages. There is some interest in knowing how many young people (not how large a per cent) are marrying earlier. Let us take the approximately 5,000,000 young women fifteen to nineteen years old in the United States in 1950. On the average, 750,000 are married. During another decade the average increase in the per cent married, if it continues, will bring the number married up to 832,500, without any increase in population being considered. In other words, if the average rate of increase continues, 82,500 will be added in a decade to those married, for better or for worse.

We have shown that for the teenage group of females fifteen to nineteen years of age there has been an increase in the proportions married. This conclusion is for the group as a whole. But this increase is true also for each single year of age. Thus the proportion of the fifteen-year-olds who have married has increased over the forty-year period, as has also the proportion of those who are sixteen, seventeen, eighteen, and nineteen years old.

We have dealt only with the young teenage group. For the

young women in their early twenties, that is, twenty to twenty-four years old, there has been an increase in the percentages married but only about half as great as for the teenage groups, for the sixty-year period. For the group in the early twenties, the average per cent increase for the six decades was 6 per cent, while for the teenage group it was 11 per cent. This increase is not affected appreciably by any change in the age distribution; and for each year of age between twenty and twenty-five years of age, there has been an increase in the percentage in the married state, for the period 1910–1950 for which data exist for single years.

Since young women are marrying earlier, it is supposed that young men are, too, though boys do not marry as early as girls. In fact, the percentage of teenage boys who are married is quite small. But are they marrying earlier, too? The data show that the proportions of those fifteen to nineteen years old who have married have increased greatly from decade to decade. The average increase for the six decades was 39 per cent. This large per cent, though, does not mean that very many married, for only about 2 or 3 per cent of the boys of these ages are married. For men in their early twenties, twenty to twenty-four years of age, the average increase in the proportion married by decades was 15 per cent. For these years of age, the percentage married is around 25 to 35 per cent of the population of these ages. Nor are these increases in early marriage due to the influence of increasing age. The increase is found for single years as well as for the age group. The increase in early marriage was somewhat greater for young men than for young women.

The increase in early marriage (that is, the per cent of young people recorded as being in the married state) was very pronounced from 1940 to 1950, the last decade of the period under review, much more so than in any preceding decade. In fact the average increase per decade in the proportions of young people married was 7 per cent before 1940 and for the decade after 1940 it was 50 per cent. The increase if any from 1950 to 1960 is not likely to be so great. This tide of early marriages between 1940 and 1950 affects the trend. In fact, the trend (as measured by a least squares straight line) before 1940 was just half as great as the trend up to 1950.

The presentation of this trend toward earlier marriage has necessitated the consideration of a good many figures, which are singularly dry and are sometimes difficult for the reader to follow. But the increase in early marriage carries much significance for human welfare. Marriage is always a great event in the life of any person and has much to do with his future happiness and career. Married persons in general live longer, have fewer mental breakdowns, commit fewer crimes than the unmarried.

Despite a surge of early marriage, it is well to remember that there were in 1950 many young people still single; 968 out of a thousand males fifteen to nineteen years old and 810 females had never married. So eight or nine out of every ten boys and girls from fifteen to twenty had not been married by 1950. Marriage implies responsibilities for which the young may not always be well fitted, although the sex drive is stronger in the teen ages than at any other time of life.

For the first half of the twentieth century, then, somewhat larger proportions of the young men and the young women have been getting married. For earlier times, data are missing for the United States as a whole. For Massachusetts, though, there are marriage data for the last half of the nineteenth century.[3] For this period from the Civil War to the turn of the century in Massachusetts, the age at marriage increased a little. The median age of marriage for men increased from 24.9 years to 26.1 years, and for women from 22.5 to 23.5,[4] or about a year, which is 4 per cent.[5]

[3] Thomas P. Monahan, "One Hundred Years of Marriages in Massachusetts," *American Journal of Sociology,* 55: 541, May, 1951.

[4] These medians are ten-year averages from 1850–59 and 1890–00. These ten-year averages with overlaps of five years show rather smooth increases from one decade to another.

[5] These increases in the ages at marriage were for total populations that were growing older, that is, populations whose average age was increasing. In Massachusetts for this period the median age of the white population increased by 3.1 years. Could this increased age of the population have accounted for the increased age at marriage? Probably not.

An increased number of old people increases the average age of the population, but not the age at marriage. But a decrease in the young people will affect both the age of the population and the age distribution of the years when most marriages occur, eighteen to thirty years. The age distribution of this marriageable age period shifted a little toward older ages in the United States from 1920 to 1950. The influence of this shift in the per cent married was only 3 per cent when the specific ages at marriage were held constant. Thus the influence of increasing age in this test of actual experience influenced the per cent married only slightly and hence the median age of marriage

While the median age of marriage was increasing in Massachusetts by about a year during the last half of the nineteenth century,
Massachusetts was industrializing; and New England was an important industrial section of the United States, more so than other
sections, which were more largely rural.

The data just discussed for the nineteenth century were for the
average age of marriage. Although this average is not as good an
index of early marriage as is the percentage of young people married, there is a relationship between the two indices. When the
average age at marriage is late, the percentage of the young who
are married is small. And conversely when the average age at
marriage is early, the percentage of the young who are married
is large. The correlation is of the order of —.9. So we conclude that
in Massachusetts there were larger proportions of the young men
and women married about the time of the Civil War than there
were at the end of the century, that is, that early marriage was
decreasing slightly.

Age at marriage in colonial times. Nearly all writers who refer to
the age at marriage in colonial times state that marriage generally
occurred at an earlier age than now. This opinion is very widespread, but it is not precise; it does not tell us how much earlier,
nor does it specify the exact dates, although we assume the period
referred to is the one before we had many cities. Experience with
similar testimony regarding the size of family in colonial times [6]
shows that the prevailing opinion is in general correct, but in error
as to details. The colonial family was larger than the family of
1950, but it was not as large as is usually claimed.

The opinion as to the early age at marriage in colonial times rests
on several grounds. The common law ages for marriage of twelve
for females and fourteen for males were in effect, whereas at the
present time higher ages are fixed by statute, the general standard
being sixteen for girls and eighteen for boys, with parental con-

even less (for the variation in the age at marriage is less than that of the
percentage married). It does not seem probable, therefore, that an increase
of three years in the age of the population over the last half of the nineteenth century could explain the increase in the age of marriage. For the
whole United States, the increase in the median age of the total population
was 3.5 years for this period.

[6] See Chapter 5.

sent. The writings of travelers from Europe frequently comment on the early age at marriage in Colonial America, even as compared with the age of marriage in the agricultural societies of Europe, where the population was older. There are genealogical records showing early marriage, but they represent a highly selected sample of the population.

We know that at the present time in the United States the chances of early marriage are greater on the farms than in the cities; in 1920, cities reduced marriage by about 10 per cent.[7] Since in colonial times community life was predominantly rural, we infer that the conditions were favorable for early marriage.

Age of marriage among preliterate peoples. Though the age of marriage among primitive peoples is beyond the scope of this book, we present some data because of the interest in the subject and because the data serve as an interesting background to the modern data. We are interested in marriage among primitive peoples because they are supposed to live a somewhat more natural biological life than do the peoples of our advanced civilizations. However, even the peoples with the simplest hunting cultures today have an organized family and regulated sex life and are far removed from the probable animal-like life of pre-glacial times.

For information on the age of marriage in preliterate cultures we have no adequate statistics, only the reports of ethnologists and others more or less trained. These reports are based either on impressions or on a very few observations. What information we have has been compiled for the authors from the Cross-Cultural Survey (Human Relations Area Files) at Yale University by the assistants of Dr. George Murdock, professor of anthropology.

In seven hunting and food-gathering societies with no agriculture or herding, the males marry at twenty-two or twenty-three years of age and the females at seventeen. These are arithmetic means; but the sample is small, the range is wide, and the reporting may not be very accurate.

There are data for twice as many societies with agriculture but without domesticated farm animals. Their average ages at mar-

[7] E. R. Groves and W. F. Ogburn, *American Marriage and Family Relationships* (New York: Henry Holt & Company, 1928), Chapter XIV.

riage were twenty and seventeen for males and females, respectively.

For eleven peoples with intensive agriculture and domesticated farm animals, the corresponding ages at first marriage were twenty and sixteen years.

The reported later age of marriage of primitive hunters may be due to the difficulty in obtaining food because of its scarcity, or the time required in learning the skills and developing the judgment needed, especially in periods of great shortage of food. But it is hardly worthwhile speculating, for the small number of cases and the possible errors in reporting do not allow us definitively to establish a later age of marriage for the male hunters than for the agriculturists.

In reflecting on the meaning of these ages at marriage, we recall that in modern civilizations the cultural age for marriage, that is, the actual age at which in our culture marriage occurs (on the average, in the twenties), is later than the biological age for marriage, which is in the early teens. Among the preliterate peoples, the cultural age of marriage is somewhat nearer the biological age for marriage, but not much nearer. Marriage and coitus are not the same. Sexual activity between boys and girls is permitted and common before marriage among many primitive peoples. Frequent coitus does not begin with marriage. Marriage even among the simple hunting cultures is an institution which is motivated not wholly by sex but also by other considerations such as the presence of children, the adequate performance of economic functions, or the transmission of property. For instance, among a few peoples, not necessarily hunters, marriage occurs in infancy; among others it occurs at puberty; and in one culture at least the marriage of males is prohibited until a long period of training and service is concluded.

Throughout the population. We have seen that for the United States as a whole, the recent trend has been toward earlier marriage. We next wish to have a quick look at some of the different peoples and regions to see whether increasing early marriage is found in these different components of the population.

The family structure is somewhat different on the farms from what it is in the cities; so it might be that the trends in age of marriage would be different in urban and rural areas. But in each area, the movement has been toward marrying younger. Thus of teenage girls, twice as large a proportion were married in 1950 as in 1910 in the cities; and in the rural areas the increase was 40 per cent, as shown in Table 3.

For young men under twenty years old, marriage is much less frequent than among young women of this age group. But the growth of early marriage has been greater among the male youth; the proportion married in the cities quadrupled, and in the country doubled, between 1910 and 1950. These data for urban and rural young people were not standardized for age; but for such great increases, changes in age distribution would have little reduction. We see, then, that the forces bringing about earlier marriages swept over both the cities and the country. The forces were not quite as strong, though, in rural areas as in cities. Since more young people are married in rural areas than in the cities, it follows that the differences in the percentages of the young who are married in city and country have become less. In many ways the farmers are becoming like the city men, that is, less set apart. So, too, the pattern of early marriage is less different.

These comparisons between urban and rural areas were not between city and farm populations, since the rural population which was compared included villages, some suburbs, and some non-agricultural towns. Since 1930 the data for farms have been presented separately. These data show that more young people have been marrying on the farms, too; but the increase was not as great as in the cities. One peculiarity was noted, however. In 1950 a larger proportion of young men in the cities were married than on the farms. All our other data have shown more marriage on the farms or in rural areas.[8]

The population of the United States is further differentiated by race, commonly distinguished by color. A substantial part of the people are not white; of the non-whites, nearly all are Negro or of Negro extraction. The trends in age of marriage among the colored population were much the same as in the total population

---

[8] By way of possible explanation, we note that the definition of cities was changed from 1940 to 1950 by the Bureau of the Census. So that some suburbs were taken from the rural category and added to the urban, and in the suburbs there is often more marriage than in the city.

from 1890 to 1950. The movement for the whole population showed a very large increase in the proportions of the young married people between 1940 and 1950, but a decrease in the depression decade of the 1930's, and not much change between 1920 and 1930. In earlier decades there were substantial increases. The non-white population, both male and female, followed this pattern.

Whatever the forces were that have been bringing about earlier marriage in the United States, they seem to have operated much alike on the different segments of the population and were not confined to any one segment. The remainder of the chapter will be an effort to find out what these forces were. But first we wish to examine some other countries to see whether the movement toward earlier marriage has been world-wide.

In other countries. Early marriage varies greatly from country to country as seen in Table 4, which shows the percentages of females fifteen to nineteen years of age who were wives at some time after the World War of 1939–1945. The great difference in early marriage is shown by the fact that in the United States the percentage of young women married is ten times as great as in Eire. We make no attempt to explain these differences, since this would be very difficult to do.

From a small sample of countries for which we have data as far back as 1900, we infer that early marriage in some countries has increased, and in others decreased. The trend in the percentage of the young persons married has been rising in Denmark, New Zealand, Sweden, and Iceland, but has been declining in Brazil, Hungary, Switzerland, and Finland. There has been little change in Portugal and Ireland. These are countries for which we have comparable data for a long enough period to show a trend. The evidence for trends in early marriage is presented in Table 5 which shows the difference between the percentage of young people married in 1900 and 1940. The plus sign in the table shows the increase in the percentage married over the period, and the minus sign represents a decrease.

The conditions affecting marriage differ in the various countries. Some are in different stages of economic development, and others have quite different customs. How varied marital conditions are in various countries is shown in Table 6, which shows the percentage

TABLE 3

Trends in Early Marriage in Urban and in Rural Areas in the United States 1910–1950, as Shown by Percentages of the Population in Each Age Group Who Are Found Married in the Census Years

Ages	Year	Males Per Cent Married			Females Per Cent Married		
		urban	rural	difference	urban	rural	difference
15–19 years	1910	.7	1.4	.7	7.7	14.3	6.6
	1920	1.7	2.4	.7	10.4	14.5	4.1
	1930	1.3	2.2	.9	10.2	15.5	4.7
	1940	1.4	2.0	.6	8.8	14.9	6.1
	1950	3.1	3.3	.2	15.1	19.9	4.8
20–24 years	1910	20.6	27.3	6.7	42.4	57.5	15.1
	1920	25.8	31.1	5.3	47.6	58.4	10.8
	1930	25.8	31.1	5.3	47.1	58.8	11.7
	1940	25.1	30.2	5.1	45.6	60.3	44.7
	1950	39.3	41.0	1.7	61.7	74.5	12.2

of females in the population fifteen to nineteen years of age and twenty to twenty-four years of age who are married. In the Irish Free State, for instance, only 12 per cent of females twenty to twenty-four years old are married, while in Denmark the figure is 40 per cent.

That there are these various factors influencing marriage is shown in the following paragraphs. We shall not be able, however, to discuss these factors for the different countries of the world. The presentation will concern only the United States during the past sixty years.

Causes

The leading facts regarding the extent of early marriage have been presented, particularly for the United States. Our concern is why there has been this trend toward marrying early. Several factors affecting marriage will now be considered.

Is the sex ratio a factor? In seeking explanations for the lowering of the age at marriage in recent decades, we consider first a pos-

TABLE 4

Percentage of Females 15–19 Years Old Who Were Wives in Different Countries in Post-World War II Years *

Country	Per Cent 15–19 Years Married	Year
United States	16.7	1951
Yugoslavia	13.6	1948
Czechoslovakia	5.8	1947
Australia	5.6	1947
France	5.6	1946
England and Wales	4.5	1951
Sweden	3.0	1945
New Zealand	3.0	1946
Norway	2.2	1946
Germany	1.9	1946
Eire	1.6	1946

* Metropolitan Life Insurance Company, *Statistical Bulletin*, May, 1953, p. 8.

TABLE 5

Trends in Early Marriage in Different Countries for Four Decades as Shown by the Differences between the Percentage Married in Age Groups 15–19 and 20–24 Inclusive at the Beginning and the End of the Period. A Plus (+) Sign Indicates an Increase in the Percentage Married. *

Country	Period	Females		Males	
		15–19	20–24	15–19	20–24
Canada	1911–41	−1.3	−1.3	−.7	−.1
Brazil	1900–40	−11.8	−2.8	−5.2	−9.9
Denmark	1901–45	+2.1	+14.4	+.2	+3.0
Finland	1900–40	−1.2	−3.8	0	−5.5
Hungary	1900–41	−2.8	−16.3	−.4	−6.9
Iceland	1901–40	+.8	+5.8	0	−.7
Ireland	1900–41	+.3	−1.0	+1.0	−1.9
Portugal	1900–40	+.1	+.4	−.3	−.8
Sweden	1900–45	+2.2	+16.4	+.2	+4.5
Switzerland	1900–41	−.3	−2.1	−.1	−2.7
New Zealand	1900–45	+1.1	+11.8	+.3	+10.5

* Metropolitan Life Insurance Company, *Statistical Bulletin*, Vol. 28, No. 2, February, 1947, p. 9.

sible biological factor, the equality or inequality in the numbers of the sexes at marriageable ages. However, an excess of males or of females does not always have a biological cause. For instance, migration or differential death rates cause variations in the sex ratio as truly as differential birth rates. Migrations and differential death rates are often the results of economic and scientific factors rather than biological ones.

It is commonly thought that the largest number of marriages occurs in communities where the number of men and women is equal. Such is not the case, however. There are more marriages in cities and in states of the United States where there is a small excess of men, say, 110 or 120 men to 100 women.[9] If the excess of males in a place is very great, the marriage rate is low. The sex ratio in a town has more effect on the marriage rate than does the sex ratio in a whole nation. Hence the sex ratio for a large country is not significant for marriage frequency unless the sex ratio is the same in smaller localities.

When we turn to the evidence, however, we find that the sex ratio in 1890 was slightly more favorable to a high rate of marriage than it was in 1950. The sex ratios for the populations over fifteen years of age were 106 in 1890 and 97 in 1950. In other words, the increase in early marriage occurred in spite of an adverse sex ratio. So this factor is ruled out as an explanation.

Earlier maturity. An interesting question is whether there has been any change in the desire of young people for earlier marriage, and if so whether this has been a factor affecting early marriage. The desire for marriage is not wholly a biological matter. Marriage is a social institution and biological cravings are conditioned by social environment.

Regarding social attitudes, some are opposed, at least to very early marriage, as illustrated by the laws restricting marriage at early ages. The newspapers carry stories occasionally of child marriage, implying in the tone of the write-up that they are to be decried. Also marriage counselors in the columns of the newspapers often advise against early marriage as well as hasty marriage.

[9] E. R. Groves, and W. F. Ogburn, *American Marriage and Family Relationships* (New York: Henry Holt & Company, Inc., 1928), Chapters XXV and XXVI.

T A B L E 6

*Early Marriage in Various Countries as Shown
by the Percentages of Young Females Married* *
(*In Different but Recent Years*)

Country	Ages 15–19	Ages 20–24
United States	12	53
Canada	6	39
England and Wales	2	26
Scotland	2	23
Irish Free State	1	12
Sweden	2	28
Norway	1	19
Denmark	3	40
Netherlands	2	25
Germany **	1	23
Belgium	4	41
France	6	49
Italy	4	31
Portugal	4	31
Australia	4	31
New Zealand	3 ***	28

* Metropolitan Life Insurance Company, *Statistical Bulletin*, Vol. 28, No. 2, February, 1947, p. 9.
** Includes Austria and Sudetenland.
*** Ages 16–19.

Among the young and unmarried there is little evidence of their attitudes; but many young people, particularly girls, are said to want to enjoy the pleasures of courtship, parties, dances, and travel before settling down to the duties and responsibilities of managing a home and rearing a family and before committing themselves to one person of the opposite sex. Many adult advisers are said to think that the problems of married life in our complex society cannot be handled by the very young as well as by the more mature. Maturity as measured by the acquisition of social knowledge and wisdom is probably being postponed as our civilization becomes more complex. Formerly in a simple agricultural society a youth became a man at twenty-one years. Now we speak of men in their twenties as youngsters. These attitudes vary perhaps by social classes, social maturing occurring somewhat earlier in the classes with lower incomes in the cities as well as on the farms.

The evidence on biological maturation indicates that girls are maturing a little earlier when maturity is measured by the date of beginning menstruation. In 1932 in Louisiana the average age for the beginning menstruation for 680 college girls was 13.6 years while for their mothers, 357 in number, the average was 14.0 years.[10] A question might be raised as to whether the reporting of the mothers is as accurate as that of the daughters, but there appears to be no obvious reason why there should be a bias for reporting a later age by mothers than by daughters.

Such a criticism does not apply, however, to college records of women students made over a long period of years. In four different cities in both northern and southern parts of the United States the age of first menstruation for those born at the close of the last century was from 14.0 to 13.7 years of age, while for those born around 1920 it was from 13.4 to 13.2 years of age.[11]

These conclusions are in harmony with the knowledge that those who grow tallest do so soonest, that retardations in growth are on the average not made up and that stature in the United States has been increasing.

The earlier sexual maturation of girls, and presumably of boys, too, may then be a factor in earlier marriage. Kinsey [12] has shown that the sex drive is strongest in males in the teen ages, probably much stronger than is realized by most adults who think of teen-agers as children.

Though earlier physical maturity be a reality, we still need to ask what has made this development possible. It could not have been a change in the hereditary mechanisms. The reasons generally given for the increase in stature are (1) the improvement in nutrition of children, and (2) the conquest of the diseases that occur during the period of growth in stature and weight.

This possible cause of early marriage then probably traces back

[10] N. N. and M. R. Grould, "Age of First Menstruation in Mothers and Daughters," *Journal of the American Medical Association*, Vol. 98, No. 16, April 16, 1932, p. 1350.

[11] Clarence A. Mills, "Further Evidence on the Reversal in the Human Growth Tide," *Human Biology*, Vol. 13, No. 3, September, 1941, p. 365.

[12] A. C. Kinsey, *et al.*, *Sexual Behavior in the Human Male* (Philadelphia: W. B. Saunders Company, 1948), Chapter 7.

to scientific discovery in regard to nutrition and diseases and to the forces of production, largely technological, which have brought a higher standard of living to the masses.

The changing evidences of age. An interesting counter-influence tending to raise the age at marriage is provided by developments which make it possible for women to conceal their true age. We are told that "Balzac's woman of thirty is haunted by the prospect of the end of her attraction as a woman: at the turn of the century this worry had been postponed for a decade, 'the fashionable age is forty, or say thirty-seven' (Shaw, *Man and Superman*) and now it is difficult to guess a woman's age by her looks at all." [13]

This achievement results from advances in the conquest of disease, better nutrition, and more leisure, as well as advances in cosmetology, costuming, and the like.

Legal requirements. As a cause of the tendency to marry earlier, we can also rule out changes in the law regarding the age at which marriage is permitted, for, as is well known, the law has raised the earliest age at which marriage may legitimately take place. In earlier times, the common law permitted marriage at age twelve for females and fourteen for males, with parental consent; whereas at the present time statutory law generally provides that the minimum age for marriage shall be sixteen and eighteen for brides and grooms respectively, with parental consent. During the period in which the median age for marriage has been lowered in the United States, namely, since 1890, the trend of the law has been to raise somewhat the minimum age for marriage. The changes in the law are then not a cause of the reduction of the age of marriage and are instead a factor tending to raise the average marrying age.

Education. It is pertinent to inquire as to the relation, if any, between the earlier age of marriage and the changes in the education of the population of the United States. It is common knowledge that considerable advances have occurred in the educational status of the population. The percentages of the population sixteen years of age attending school in the census years beginning with 1910,

[13] Charlotte Luetkens, *Women and a New Society* (New York: Duell, Sloan and Pearce, 1946), p. 42.

were 51, 51, 66, 76, and 81. For twenty years of age the percentages were 8, 8, 13, 13, and 18.[14] So larger proportions of the population are staying in schools for longer periods.

The nation-wide data presented in Table 7 reveal that for native-white women, fifteen to forty-nine years old, who have been married only once and who are living with their husbands, the median age at marriage rises from 19.6 years for those who have had six years of grade school or less, to 20.5 years for those with seven and eight years of schooling, to 21.6 for those with four years of high school, to 23.7 for those with one year or more of college.

The foregoing data are for 1940. In 1950 the same conclusion is indicated. Smaller percentages of those who complete sixteen years of schooling are married among a population over twenty-five years old than of those who have gone to school only four years, as is shown in Table 8. The more schooling a man or a woman has, the greater the chance of not marrying. However, the chances of not marrying are small. The percentage of women marrying seems to fluctuate with education more than the percentage of men. It is as though the men will marry irrespective of their years of schooling, whereas with women marriage depends more on their education; the less they have the greater their chance of marrying. However, the differences are not great. Thus of the women twenty-five to twenty-nine years old, the median years of schooling completed for single women is 12.4 and for married women (husband present) is 12.1. For ages thirty to thirty-four, the unmarried women had been to school a little longer than the married. The median years were 12.2 and 11.9, respectively. The effect of college and post-college education is to postpone marriage, and it may therefore be concluded that the influence of increasing college attendance has been to increase the age at marriage. The mean age at marriage, however, would also be raised by increasing attendance at high school.

As to the influence of education on the age at marriage, it is concluded on the basis of the foregoing evidence that increased schooling on the part of the youth of the United States in recent decades has not been a factor in the trend toward earlier marriage, but on the contrary has been a factor tending to delay marriage.

14 *Statistical Abstract of the United States, 1953* (Washington, D.C.: U.S. Government Printing Office, 1953), p. 109.

TABLE 7

Median Age of Woman at Marriage, 1940: Native White Women 15 to 49 Years Old, Married Once and Husband Present, by Education and Age of Woman at Census, for the United States *

Age of Woman at Census	Total	Grade School			High School		College
		Less than 5 yrs.**	5 and 6 yrs.	7 and 8 yrs.	1 to 3 yrs.	4 yrs.	1 yr. or more
Total, 15 to 49	21.0	19.6	19.6	20.5	20.4	21.6	23.7
15 to 19 years	...	...	...	...	...	18.5	18.8
20 to 24 years	19.6	18.6	18.6	19.1	19.2	20.2	21.1
25 to 29 years	21.2	19.4	19.3	20.3	20.6	21.9	23.3
30 to 34 years	21.4	19.5	19.5	20.5	20.8	22.4	24.3
35 to 39 years	21.5	19.7	19.8	20.8	21.2	22.7	24.4
40 to 44 years	21.7	20.1	20.4	21.2	21.6	22.8	24.3
45 to 49 years	22.1	20.5	20.9	21.6	22.3	23.4	24.6

* 16th Census of the United States, 1940, *Population: Differential Fertility: 1940 and 1910,* "Women by Number of Children Under 5 Years Old" (Washington, D.C.: U.S. Government Printing Office), p. 5.

** Includes category "School years not reported."

TABLE 8

*Percentage Who Are or Have Been Married of Those Completing
Various Years of Schooling for Ages over 25 Years in 1950 **

Years of School Completed		Men	Women
None		84	91
Elementary	1 to 4 years	89	94
	5 to 7 years	89	94
	8 years	90	93
High School	1 to 3 years	90	93
	4 years	88	89
College	1 to 3 years	88	88
	4 years	87	76

* Compiled from the Special Report P. E. No. 58, *Education*, United States
Census of Population, Education, U.S. Bureau of the Census, 1950, pp. 5B 61–62.

War. In measuring the extent of marriage of young people by
decades during the first half of the present century, it was observed
that the increase was particularly great from 1940 to 1950; indeed
about 50 per cent for those married in the teen ages. As to why
there was this remarkable increase, the answer is sought in two
phenomena. The first is the depression of the 1930's, when the
marriage rate was low. Because of this, in 1940 a lower than normal number of young persons would be found married, whereas
in 1950 a more than normal number of young people would be
found married due to the high rate of marriage just before and
after the war, the war being the second phenomenon that explains
this remarkable increase from 1940 to 1950. In 1941, the year war
was declared against Japan, the marriage rate was 127 for 10,000
persons, the highest recorded rate up to that time; and in 1942 it
mounted to 132. But with the movement of troops overseas in suc-
ceeding war years, the marriage rate decreased, only to soar after
the armistice and the return of the armed forces. In 1946, the
marriage rate reached the all time high of 164, as compared with
a usual rate of around 105. In 1948 and 1949 the rate was about
down to normal again.

World War I seems to have had a similar influence, though to a
lesser extent. In 1917, the year we entered the war, the marriage
rate moved up from around 100 to 111, the highest that had been

recorded up to that time. The next year, 1918, when our troops were fighting in Europe, the marriage rate fell below normal, but rose in 1920, when the soldiers had returned, to 120. This high marriage rate in 1919 and 1920 meant a rather large per cent of young people were found married by the census taker in 1920, which accounts in part for the small increase in those found married in 1930 as compared with 1920.

The influence of the war years and the immediate postwar years may be summarized by saying that the average annual marriage rate for the years from 1917 to 1920, inclusive, was 110 and for the years 1941 to 1947, inclusive, it was 130; both well above normal.

How is it that a war can increase marriage? Possibly because of the desire to have a mate and perhaps a child before facing the high chances of death. Sometimes perhaps to avoid or postpone being drafted into the armed forces. The marriage of returned soldiers is probably a making up of postponed marriages. But, in addition, these two world wars were periods of unusual prosperity at the time of our entry because we had had a large export trade with those countries that were later our allies; and immediately afterward the stored-up purchasing power was released and brought prosperity. Then, too, the wars were of short duration for the United States, the homeland was not bombed or invaded, and casualties were small compared with those of many of our allies. Hence, though war and war prosperity increased early marriage in the United States in the past two world wars, they may not so increase it in another; nor will war necessarily have such an influence in other countries where the conditions are different.

Hence it cannot be said from the data we have examined that war is generally a cause of more early marriage. Nor would war be a factor in explaining the increase in early marriage from 1890 to 1910.

Increased income. It is natural to think that an increase in income would encourage earlier marriage, for many young men are deterred from marrying because they are not able to support wives. Hence if incomes are increased, it is expected that more will get married. Similarly an unemployed male will not be so likely to marry as one who has a job. Consequently, if incomes are increasing and unemployment is diminishing, we should expect more young persons to marry.

We have seen that the amount of early marriage in the United States increased in the sixty years from 1890 to 1950. The income of the people also increased during this time. The increase was great; in fact, the per capita income more than doubled. The per capita income (net national product) in 1890 in dollars of the purchasing power of 1952 money was about $540,[15] whereas in 1950 the per capita income was about $1450 [16] in 1952 dollars.

But even though the income rose for the sixty years that early marriage was increasing, this concurrence does not itself establish a causal connection. In fact in the preceding half century early marriage seems to have decreased a little in the state of Connecticut, yet from 1874 to 1890 the per capita income in the United States increased about 60 per cent.[17] With so great an increase for the United States, there very probably was a substantial increase in Connecticut. In other words, early marriage decreased during one half century and increased during another when the per capita income was increasing all the while.

From such trends we are not able to show whether an increase in incomes favors earlier marriage or not, for there are many other factors affecting early marriage which are changing at the same time, as, for instance, urbanism, birth control, and social classes. On the other hand, we cannot say that changes in income have no effect on marriage. In fact, there is much evidence to show that more people marry in good times when wages and salaries and profits are rising than in bad times when income decreases as does employment.

For instance, we have seen that in 1940 following the great depression of the 1930's, the Census found no more early marriage than in 1930, though the surrounding decades showed increases of married young people. In fact, for the four years of the depression from 1930 to 1934 the average number of annual marriages per 10,000 population was 88, whereas the normal was around 105 for this period. The marriage rate was similarly low in the bad years of 1894, 1904, 1908, 1915, and 1922. So also the marriage rate has been high in the prosperous years. It is quite certain then that

[15] Simon Kuznets, and Raymond Goldsmith, *Income and Wealth in the United States, Trends and Structure* (Cambridge, England: Bowes, 1952), p. 55.
[16] *Statistical Abstract of the United States, 1953*, p. 282.
[17] Kuznets, *op. cit.*

this type of increase of income causes more marriage and, by inference, more early marriage. However, there are other aspects of
the relation of income and marriage that seem to show the opposite
effect. They indicate that higher incomes have a deterrent effect
upon marriage. Thus, groups with lower incomes are reported to
have larger percentages married than those groups with high incomes; also they are said to marry younger. Cities with higher
average incomes have slightly smaller percentages married.[18] How
can it be that if the incomes of individuals are increased, there is
more marriage; but nevertheless there are smaller percentages married among those who have high incomes than among those with
low incomes? As an explanation of these apparently inconsistent
phenomena, we advance the hypothesis that two quite different
phenomena are compared, one, differences between socio-economic
classes, and the other, differences between the income of individuals within the same socio-economic class.

The individuals within a socio-economic class will have larger
percentages married if their incomes are increased within a short
range of time. But the individuals in a class which has had high
income for a long time will have smaller percentages married
than will the individuals in a social class with low incomes. With
these income classes are associated different customs which in
turn affect the age of marriage and hence the per cent married.
Thus the young in a higher income class probably spend more
years in getting jobs with high pay. Also the expectation of a
standard of living of a bride is high in such a class; so the bride-
groom must earn more than he would if he were in a lower income
group. For these habits to develop, individuals must belong to
such economic classes for some time. In the socio-economic classes
with higher incomes, more time is spent in formal education which
postpones marriage.

Evidence that members of the upper income classes marry later
than those in classes with lower income is shown in Table 9.
Where those in the upper-upper income class have a median age
at marriage of 27.9 years, those in the lower-lower group marry
at 23.2 years on the average or nearly five years earlier. So also
Table 10 shows that members of higher socio-economic classes,

[18] Groves and Ogburn, *op. cit.*, Chapter XIX.

as indicated by occupations, marry later than those in occupations generally with lower incomes.

That stabilized income differentials show the age of marriage to be lower for those with high incomes than for those with low incomes when the socio-economic classes are different is also illustrated by the age of marriage in cities and on the farms. A larger per cent of the young are married on farms than in cities as is shown in Table 11. Yet the income in cities is a good deal higher than on the farms. Thus in urban places of over 2500 population in the United States, the median income per person in 1949 was $2162 while on the farms it was $1099, or about half as much.[19] But farm income implies more than merely money from agriculture. The recipients have a way of life on farms which is different from that of those whose income is derived from urban pursuits. So the differences in income of farm residents and city residents represent differences in customs of living as well as differences in income, and these differences in customs affect marriage.

The influence of changes of income on marriage depends, then, upon what change in customs has occurred with the increase or decrease of incomes, as is found in social classes. For a population experiencing an increase of income but remaining in the same

T A B L E   9

Income Class and Age at Marriage *

Income Group	Percentage of Population	Median Age at Marriage
Upper-upper	1½%	27.9
Lower-upper	1½%	26.6
Upper-middle	10%	26.1
Lower-middle	28%	25.1
Upper-lower	33%	24.4
Lower-lower	25%	23.2

* Adapted from W. Lloyd Warner and Paul S. Lunt, *The Social Life of a Modern Community* (Yale University, 1941), Vol. I of *Yankee City Series.*

[19] These figures do not include the money value of food raised and consumed on the farm. But the value of such food consumed would not equal in amount the value of all other income.

T A B L E   10

*Median Years of Age of Husbands at First
Marriage . . . , By Major Occupation Groups of
Husband, for the United States: Civilian Popu-
lation, April, 1948* *

Major Occupation Group of Husband	Median Years of Age at First Marriage
	Total
Total employed husbands**	24.1
Professional workers	25.5
Service workers	24.7
Proprietors	24.6
Clerical workers	24.6
Farmers	23.9
Craftsmen	23.7
Laborers, except farm	23.7
Operatives	23.4
Farm laborers	23.0

* Adapted from Bureau of the Census, Report by Paul C. Glick and Emanuel
Landau, *Age as a Factor in Marriage.*
** Includes employed husbands married once living with their wives.

social class, there is likely to be an increase in early marriage. But
for social classes with established customs, a class with higher
incomes often has less early marriage than one with lower incomes.

Causes of social classes and increased incomes. We have seen that
causes of increased early marriage may be found in increases in
income and that causes of a decrease of early marriage may be
found in the movement of people from one social class to another
with higher incomes. These are proximate causes of changes in
early marriage. But these causes are themselves the result of other
causes. We seek information on these more remote causes.

The increase in early marriage over a long period such as a half
century may have resulted from an increase in income; but we
were unable to prove it, because there were so many other factors

TABLE 11

*Percentage Ever Married 15–24 Years
Old by Single Years of Age for the
United States Urban and Farm, 1950 ***

Age	Urban	Farm
15	1.4	1.5
16	3.1	3.8
17	6.5	7.8
18	12.3	16.2
19	20.6	27.4
20	31.8	38.0
21	42.7	48.0
22	52.9	56.5
23	62.1	64.7
24	69.0	71.0

* Compiled from U.S. Census of Population, *U.S. Summary, Detailed Characteristics*, Bulletin P.C. 1, pp. 1 181 186.

operating at the same time, such as increased education, extension of birth control, shifts from farm to city, et cetera. Hence we do not inquire here what are the causes of the remarkable increase in per capita income in the United States over the past century.

We did prove, though, that increases of income in short periods of prosperity were accompanied by increases in marriage and, almost surely, early marriage. The causes of these increases of income are the causes of the variations of business in modern times which are called business cycles. The causes of the business cycle are changes in the balance of the quantity of production and the amount of effective purchasing power. Thus, when more is produced than there is purchasing power to buy at the prices offered, which are near the cost of production, a depression or recession occurs. But if costs and hence prices go down or if purchasing power is increased, then prosperity occurs. It is difficult here to be more detailed about the causes of the business cycle, but it is generally agreed that such a cycle is a business phenomenon and does not occur in a self-sufficient agricultural household economy. Therefore, it is a phenomenon of a developed capitalism which rests on extensive trade, i.e., business, which in turn depends on money (and credit) and a developed factory system of production.

As to the causes of social classes, they appear to be related some-what to income and wealth and to race in the United States. In earlier times there were religious and military classes whose rela-tion to wealth was not evident. Nor are the urban and rural classes in the United States a result solely of income. The methods of pro-duction on farms and in cities bring about different locations of residences and different ways of life. Insofar, then, as there is an economic cause of the difference between urban and rural classes, it lies more in the methods of production than specifically in in-come. But in cities and in rural areas, both, there are social classes. Thus in rural areas there are farm laborers or sharecroppers and large land owners; and in cities there are the working classes and the property owners. These differentiations seem to be rather clearly traceable to differences in income and wealth. The causes of these differences in wealth have been often sought in biological differences, that is, in inherited variations in mental ability; but without very much success. The explanation lies more likely in such factors as education, opportunity, law, government, and privi-lege, though undoubtedly individual variations in heredity do exist.

The causes of changes of income and in the development of social classes appear, therefore, in the main to be economic. Trac-ing causes further to technological or scientific factors cannot very well be done in any detail.

Employment of women. Among the economic factors affecting marriage is the employment of women. We know that the per cent of women at work outside the home has increased greatly in re-cent times, as the data of a later chapter[20] will show, but the ques-tion is how this increase has affected the age at marriage.

There are two contradictory possibilities. The one is that the working girl may postpone marriage, waiting for a good prospect. She can afford to wait, since she is economically independent and does not have to accept the first man who asks her. Or she may like for a time the independence and freedom that goes with a pay check and the life away from an authoritarian home.

Quite the opposite is the theory that, by working and helping to support their families about to be formed, girls may marry

[20] Chapter 7.

earlier than if they had to wait until their husbands were in a position to manage alone. That wives do help with the financial support of the home in order to make marriage possible, has been noted recently in connection with the marriages of veterans. Whether this represents a special case, based on the greater age and maturity of veterans and their impatience at further delay of marriage, it is difficult to say. If it is a special case, then the pattern may not be continued by girls interested in younger men who are non-veterans. There are, of course, many individual observations of where a woman works to help her husband get more education.

Relating to these conceptions, it was observed that in cities which had a small percentage of their married women young there was also somewhat more employment of women, when the sex ratio was the same for the cities. The sex ratio was supposed to be a rough indication of migration. For if employment encouraged marriage, and the brides left employment for housework, they would probably be replaced by unmarried women, some of whom migrated to the city. This tendency for cities with smaller percentages of their married women young to be cities with larger percentages of women at work, when the sex ratio is held constant, suggests that the employment of women may have a slight retarding effect upon marriage. We have found no analysis of this type of data that indicates that employment of women accelerates marrying.

If the employment of women acts somewhat to retard marrying, then the increase in early marriage has occurred in spite of this influence.

On this question, we note also that there are two kinds of employment. One is the employment of women outside the home for pay as in factory, store, or office. This is the kind of employment we have been discussing. But on farms in particular, women are employed in much economically productive work, but in general without a wage. Married women contribute to production on farms without receiving any pay. And there is very little opportunity for females to receive monetary reward on farms. In this case the economic system of farming, particularly self-sufficient farming, so different from that of the city with its many jobs for women, presents the only economic outlet for women in marriage. In the

United States it is associated with more early marriage than in the urban economic pattern.

In this case the technology of city life which became so widely spread with the railroad, factory, and steam engine has operated to postpone marriage in comparison with the technology of the farm.

In the hunting cultures the economic productivity for women lies in the family as in self-sufficiency agriculture; and the age of marriage is young.

The possible decrease in household duties. An interesting question, especially from the women's standpoint, concerns whether there has been a decrease in household duties; and, if so, whether this means that women do not have to wait as long as they used to, in order to acquire domestic skills before marrying. The evidence on the latter point is not good; but when the multifarious domestic tasks of the household economy are compared with the demands of housekeeping today, the reduction in the variety of responsibilities is quite evident. Also the housewife today has the benefit of various laborsaving devices, which gives her additional leisure and the opportunity to find employment away from the home. If labor-saving devices help women to take jobs, and jobs help women to marry earlier than they otherwise would, then the laborsaving devices are a cause, once-removed, of the tendency to marry earlier.

On the other hand, several studies have reported that wives living in cities spend more time on household duties than do farmers' wives. Such reports are a surprise when homes in cities are supposed to be somewhat less productive of economic goods and services than rural homes. When the figures are examined in detail, it is observed that wives in farm homes spend more time on care of house and preparation of meals than do urban wives, but only about half the time is spent in caring for members of the family, which means care of infants and children. They also spend less time on buying and management.[21] In towns and cities the care of infants and children, particularly in apartments, is considered to be very confining by mothers unable to have hired help. On farms, during the day, there are many household duties that can be done by a mother while at the same time keeping an eye

[21] Hazel Kyrk, *Economic Problems of the Family* (New York: Harper and Brothers, 1933).

on the child. In such cases it is the household duties, rather than the child, that appear confining. The attractions of the city possibly accentuate the feeling of confinement by a city mother. It is perhaps then the care of children rather than the care of the house that makes household duties more time-consuming for city wives. As to whether such duties act as a deterrent to marriage, the subject should be considered in connection with birth control, which is discussed elsewhere in this chapter.

It is doubtful, however, that the acquisition of the skills needed in housekeeping has affected very much the age for marriage. Most girls in earlier times acquired homemaking skills from actual experience in their homes, in the normal course of growing up, and under the tutelage of their mothers. It is unlikely that many girls had to postpone marriage for long for lack of such training, since the training would be well established by the time the girls were ready for marriage. We therefore conclude that the decrease in household duties in recent times has probably not been much of a factor in encouraging the earlier marriage of women.

The influence of the romantic conception. In an earlier chapter, we described the shift in emphasis, during the past century or so, away from economic and other practical considerations in choosing a wife, toward choice based on personal considerations, especially love. There is a growing feeling among young people that nothing matters but love. If love is the only basis for marriage, other considerations which would be barriers to marriage, and which would serve to delay marriage, are removed; and young people marry earlier, other things being equal. We have data on the growth of circulation of movies and pulp magazines and other forces which promote the romantic theory of love.

The underlying causes for the growth of the romantic conception have been discussed a good deal by sociologists; and there is general agreement as to the causes, at least part of them. Prior to the romantic conception, marriage and the family were viewed as economic and property institutions; this conception was quite comparable with the household as a miniature factory of production. This idea is discussed in another chapter. The romantic conception arises when the family as an economic institution declines in importance. This decline is due to the growth of cities and particularly to the growth of factories, which were made possible by the steam engine.

The power inventions are changing somewhat the institutional character of rural families, in that commercialized farming is not as much a family affair as subsistence farming.

Changing social contacts of the sexes. Another factor that may be noted is the increase in the number and informal nature of the social contacts of young people. Boys and girls get around more than formerly, meet more people and do so under informal conditions which encourage more thorough acquaintanceship. Observers[22] have noted that dating, and even pairing off, takes place at an earlier age than in the past; not only high school freshmen and sophomores have regular dates but even children in the elementary grades. There is, moreover, less chaperonage; and the young people have more privacy. Popenoe, studying 1181 proposals of marriage, found that 25 per cent took place in cars; 23 per cent occurred in the girl's home; 20 per cent were in public places; smaller percentages in other places.[23] It is inferred that if young people have more and freer contacts with one another, the effect would be to encourage earlier marriage.

The role of technology, especially modern transportation and communication facilities, in extending the range of social contacts and of providing more freedom and privacy is obvious. The telephone and the mail service are mainstays of romance, and the automobile plays an important part both in increasing the range of social contacts and in affording privacy.

The breakdown of sex taboos. In the earlier chapter on romantic love, evidence was presented to show the recent breakdown of sex taboos and the corresponding increase in premarital sexual intercourse. The question arises: if the breakdown of sex taboos leads to more sexual intercourse before marriage, does that increase or decrease the probabilities of early marriage? In the absence of evidence, no definite conclusions are warranted; but some speculation may be in order. In preliterate societies permitting premarital intercourse, the premarital intercourse does not discourage mar-

[22] M. F. Nimkoff and Arthur L. Wood, "Courtship and Personality," *American Journal of Sociology*, 53: 263–9, January, 1948.
[23] *The New York Times Magazine*, December 8. 1946.

riage, although we have no data on the comparative average age at marriage in preliterate societies with and without premarital sex taboos. But even if it were established that a code sanctioning premarital sexual intercourse encourages early marriage among preliterates, it would still not be valid to hold that the increase in sexual intercourse before marriage in our society in recent decades would have the same effect. For the effect of a lack of premarital sex taboos may be different from the effect of a breakdown of sex taboos. Premarital sexual intercourse among the young is generally sporadic and intermittent and hence may be more stimulating than satiating. The satisfaction of sexual cravings is easier among the married. Hence premarital sexual intercourse may lead to earlier marriage. In any case, the decrease in the age of marriage in the United States set in before the breakdown of sex taboos, which occurred at the time of the First World War and after as shown in the sales of certain types of books, and in other ways. We infer from this that the changing sex code was not an early factor affecting the age of marriage, whatever its later influence may have been.

The breakdown of taboos on sex in discussion and in action is probably related to changes in religious beliefs and especially the codes of religion which sanction moral conduct. The details of religious beliefs and of religious regulations over conduct (as for instance, as to what to eat) have been affected by the discoveries of science. The changes in moral codes have been affected by the rapidity of change itself, insofar as the codes are detailed and specific.[24] Hence old codes break down. The causes of social change are many and varied, but in the United States today inventions and discoveries in science are the causes of many changes.

Contraception. An increasing use of birth control may be a cause of earlier marriage. For if a young couple can contemplate a marriage without a baby within a year, and hence with only two to provide for, and perhaps with the bride working at a paying job, we think there would be more marriage than if a baby is pretty sure to come within a year and the mother unable to earn any money.

Against this argument is the idea held by some that a young

[24] W. F. Ogburn, "Stationary and Changing Societies," *American Journal of Sociology*, 42: 16–31, July, 1936.

woman practicing birth control could have sexual intercourse without marrying and without becoming a mother, hence she can have a man without marrying; and similarly a man can have a woman without marriage. Thus marriage might be discouraged by the spread of birth control.

It is very difficult to test these ideas with data. We do not have many statistics on the practice of contraception. It is usually assumed that the decrease in the birth rate has been accomplished for whatever reason through the medium of purposeful birth control. We infer therefore that the practice of birth control is increasing, since the trend of the birth rate is downward. Data on the use of contraceptives collected by Raymond Pearl in 1930–32 in lying-in hospitals show that the number who used contraceptives was fewer proportionally among the older women than among the younger.[25]

But even though the practice of birth control and early marriage have been increasing generally since 1890, this fact alone does not establish a causal relation. The consumption of milk and the attendance at baseball games have both been increasing over the same period without, we think, any causal relation. Other evidence than parallel trends is needed.

The following idea suggests other possible evidence. If a low birth rate means an extensive practice of birth control, then communities with low birth rates should have a good deal of early marriage, assuming that birth control encourages early marriage. On the other hand, if birth control discourages early marriage, then places with low birth rates should have little early marriage. Such is the general idea, which, however, needs to be examined more carefully.

The hypothesis back of these remarks is: there is a relationship between birth rates and marriage rates. We know, of course, that there is a relationship between marriage and births, but not necessarily between marriage rates and birth rates. We have assumed that if there is a relationship between birth rates and marriage rates that the cause of this relationship is birth rates. That is, birth rates cause marriage rates. This could be true if birth rates are a symbol for the use or non-use of birth control. But we should ask, can marriage rates affect birth rates?

[25] Raymond Pearl, *The Natural History of Population* (New York: Oxford University Press, 1939), p. 197.

The answer to this question depends on how birth rates are measured. If the birth rate is the total births divided by the total number of married women fifteen to forty-four, then high marriage rates will mean high birth rates if the high marriage rates are due to more early marriages, for the chances of birth are greater, the younger the wife.

Thus during the 1940's the considerable increase in the birth rate has been due to the phenomenal increase in the marriage rates, especially in the younger years. But if the birth rates are measured by the number of births per 1000 married women of single years of age, the marriage rate would not affect such birth rates. Such birth rates per individual year of age would presumably not have increased during 1940 because of an increase of marriage.

Therefore in comparing birth rates (per 1000 married women of all ages) between different cities, the cities should have wives of the same ages, to remove the influence of age. This we have done by statistical methods, somewhat crudely, in finding out whether cities with lower birth rates had more early marriage.

We do find that cities with low birth rates do have more early marriage when the age distribution of wives is the same. For 170 cities (studied in 1920) the correlation between the birth rate (births per 1000 married women fifteen to forty-four years old) and the early marriage (the per cent of the population fifteen to twenty-four who were married) was −0.45 when the age distribution of wives (per cent of all wives who were fifteen to twenty-four) was held constant. That is, cities with low birth rates had large percentages of young people married.[26] This correlation is a fairly high one and is not likely to have its sign reversed by holding other factors constant. This evidence then does indicate that the increasing practice of birth control does bring about earlier marriage. Therefore one of the causal factors in the increase of early marriage is the increasing use of birth control.

If we go further in the chain of causes, then the question may be asked, why is the use of birth control increasing? There are generally two different kinds of answers given. One is that a technique has been invented and is being diffused among the population. The other answer concerns the motives of couples for limiting the number of births.

[26] Groves and Ogburn, *op. cit.*, p. 269.

With regard to the first type of answer, we think the important fact is the invention of contraceptives, that is, mechanical devices or chemicals for preventing conception. These are supposed to have been put to use in the early part of the nineteenth century in certain places in Europe. Before this time there are indications that birth control was practiced to some extent without contraceptives.[27] But the knowledge of contraceptives makes the spread of birth control more rapid, as will also the scientific knowledge as to the most probable time of conception in a female's monthly cycle. The *increase* in birth control is probably mainly due to the *increase* in the use of contraceptives rather than to any increase in non-appliance methods of birth control.

A consideration of this factor traces either to a technological cause or to scientific discovery. As to why couples practice birth control, the reasons are very numerous; but they appear to be associated with city life and with religious sanctions, both of which are related to the growth of technology and the growth of science. The great increase of cities is associated with factories and railroads and hence with the steam engine. Scientific discoveries in biology and anthropology have affected the pattern of religious beliefs and hence of religious dictation over specific types of conduct.

Hence science and technology are important factors in the use of contraceptives, and therefore a cause of early marriage.

Easier divorce. Another possibility is that early marriage is encouraged by the fact that divorce is relatively easy, on the theory that young people are less afraid to commit themselves to marriage when they know that the marriage can be readily dissolved if it does not work out satisfactorily. There is no doubt that it is easier to get a divorce now than it was in earlier times, not only because the laws are easier but because public opinion is more favorable to divorce. Despite these considerations, it is doubtful that this possibility of easy divorce is often present in the minds of those about to be married; and, if it is not, the greater ease of obtaining a divorce is not a significant factor.

[27] A. J. Jaffe, "Urbanization and Fertility," *American Journal of Sociology,* 48: 58–9, July, 1942.

Conclusion. Within the last sixty years, or since 1890, the trend in the age of marriage has been downward in the United States. The percentage of the young people under twenty-five years of age who are found married by the census taker has shown a rising trend over this period. In a sample of other countries for which data are available in the present century, most of them show a trend toward earlier marriage. The trend is less marked generally from 1920 to 1940, years disturbed by wars and by depressions. But in the United States during the 1940's, very prosperous war years, there was a phenomenal increase in early marriage.

For the preceding fifty years, before the turn of the century, the data from one state, Massachusetts, indicate that there probably was a slight increase in later marriage. Perhaps in the United States our great grandfathers and mothers married earlier than the young do in the twentieth century. The primitive people, hunters, fishermen, and early agriculturists, probably married earlier also.

As to causes in the change in age at marriage, there are many different factors. Since there are so many different causes, it is not surprising that at one time or in one country the trend was toward later marriage and at another time and in a different country the trend was toward earlier marriage.

We were not able in this chapter to study these different periods nor the different countries. Attention was focused on the United States from 1890 to 1950, the period for which the Census of the United States has recorded the marital status of the population.

Of the several factors affecting early marriage which were examined, we think the increased income is an important factor. The evidence is definitive that an increase in income for the members of a given social class results in an increase in marriage. The marriage rate is correlated with business prosperity.

Another cause, the spread of the practice of birth control, was very important. There are many reasons to think that the knowledge of birth control techniques encourages early marriage. This theory is supported by the discovery that communities with the lowest birth rates have the largest percentages of young people married when the age factor is held constant.

Pushing the inquiry into causes beyond the methods of birth control, we find that the spread of birth control is encouraged by the invention of contraceptives, which may be thought of as a technological development, not of a complex nature, but a very important one. There are also scientific discoveries that have been responsible for limiting the size of families.

The increase in early marriage would probably have been greater had it not been for the prolongation of schooling and also the employment of women. The classes which go to school longer marry later, and the extension of the period of education has been quite general in the United States. Regarding the employment of women, we really do not know that the employment of women has served to delay marriage; but the data on employment of women in different communities and percentage of the young people married when analyzed in several different ways suggest very strongly that the employment of women does in general retard marriage, although of course there are many exceptions. How much weight should be given to the earlier maturation of women, perhaps half a year, we do not know. It is also difficult to say whether the breakdown of sex taboos has been an important factor in encouraging early marriage. They both may be somewhat significant. Both of these factors trace back to scientific discoveries affecting nutrition, health, and religious sanctions.

In general we think the important forces that lead to early marriage originate in technological advances and in many different scientific discoveries. Here and there these forces may be made specific, as in the case of contraceptives and the case of the steam engine.

5

Toward a Smaller Family

The knowledge that families in the United States now are smaller than a hundred years ago is not very precise. Thus, as evidence, someone recalls the name of a prolific ancestor of a century ago who gave birth to sixteen children and contrasts this fact with a family of three living in an adjoining apartment. In such an observation the illustrations are not representative. The most fertile ancestor is remembered, and not the typical one. Nor is the concept of the family the same in the two periods. In the case of the prolific ancestor the family is defined as consisting of husband, wife, and all the children ever born, whether deceased or living elsewhere. In the modern case, the family is the parent-child group living together at any one time, irrespective of age.

Family and household. To find out how much the family in the United States has decreased in size, we must know how large the family was in earlier times. But no statistics on the size of the family were collected during the nineteenth century. However, an approximate figure has been derived from the data available. These data are the number of residences or households and the total population. If the total population of the nation be divided by the number of households, then the result is the number of persons per household or average size of household. This figure is sometimes used as an approximation to the average size of the family. We need to examine how close an approximation it is.

First it may be noted that not all of the country's people live in households. Some live in military barracks, in hotels, in schools. Some are in prisons or in institutions for the disabled, the old, the feebleminded, the insane. Such places have been designated quasi-households. Because some people live in these places called quasi-households and not in family residences, the total population is larger than the household population in family residences. But not much larger, only 3.9 per cent in 1950. The population in quasi-households is not known for the nineteenth century; but we do have the 1950 figures. Hence the comparison for 1950. Nevertheless, the approximation to the size of the household is a little larger than the average size of household, because of the inclusion of the quasi-household population.

The approximation to the size of the household is also larger than the average size of the family, since some households have servants and lodgers living in the family dwelling, whereas the family as a group of relatives does not include such servants and lodgers. So from the total population it is necessary to omit these lodgers and servants, most of whom are unmarried, to get at the population in families. The total number of lodgers and servants is, however, small as compared with the total household population; in 1950 it was only 2.8 per cent.

We are trying to find out how closely the average size of household, determined by dividing the total population by the number of households, approximates the average size of family a century or more ago when there were no statistics on size of family. We have seen that the average size of household is too large because the total population includes the institutional population (quasi-households) and servants and lodgers. It is also too large because it includes persons living alone. The latter are not families and are not part of the family population. So these persons living alone must be subtracted. The number of persons living alone in 1950 was about 3.1 per cent of the household population, a small percentage.

We have now seen that the total population is larger than the family population because the family population does not include persons living alone, the institutional population, and servants and lodgers,[1] while the total population does. In 1950 the total population was about 10 per cent larger than the family population.

One more adjustment must be made, though, before we can say how close the approximation is. The approximation was made, it is

---

[1] There are a few families in the quasi-household population and a few among servants and lodgers living with families. Hence the above statement is not exact. But the difference is slight.

recalled, by dividing the total population by the number of households. But we have seen that the total population in 1950 should be reduced about 10 per cent to get the family population. But if we get in this manner the family population, it should be divided by the number of families and not the number of households, to get the average size family. Now, oddly, the number of households is larger than the number of families, since a person living alone is called a household, but is not a family. Hence the number of families is the total number of households minus the number of one-person households. In 1950 the number of one-person households was about 10 per cent of the total number of households.

Summarizing this discussion as to how good a measure the total population divided by the number of households is of the average size of family, we find that it is an excellent measure in 1950, for we find that the approximate size of household is about the same as the average size of family. The approximate size of household (total population divided by the number of households) is 3.51 persons, while the average size of family is 3.60. This close agreement in size must necessarily be so,[2] for the family population is about 90 per cent of the total population, and the number of families is about 90 per cent of the number of households. In 1940 the approximate size of household was 3.77, and the average size of the family was 3.75. We do not know that this close relationship held in 1790 or in the nineteenth century. We may, however, examine the possibility that it was so.

In the early years of our nation there may have been relatively more servants and fewer lodgers. Then, the quasi-household or institutional population may have been a smaller proportion of the population; and there may have been proportionately fewer persons living alone. Those remarks are quite speculative, since there is no numerical evidence and scant descriptive material. If these suppositions should be true, the family population would have been a little larger per cent of the total population in 1790 than in 1950; and the number of families a little larger per cent of the

---

[2] The relationship in 1950 may be shown in symbols. $\dfrac{P-Q-L-S-1P}{H-1P} = \dfrac{P}{H} = \dfrac{F}{N}$ approximately, where P equals total population, Q the quasi-households, L the lodgers, S the servants, 1P the one-person households. H is the total number of households, F the family population, and N is the total number of families.

number of households. In any case, the corrections are small. Hence any trends in the approximate size of households will probably not be very different from the trends in the size of the family. Furthermore, the numerical size of the approximate household will be close to the numerical size of the family. These conclusions are important and justify the detail of the preceding discussion. These conclusions also permit us to view with confidence the measures which we are about to present, of the approximate size of household as indications of the size of family.

The approximate decrease in the size of the household. In 1790 the approximate number of persons per 100 households was 579, or an average-sized household of 5.79 persons. In 1950 the average size was 3.51 persons. Thus in 160 years the approximate size of the household has decreased by more than two persons, exactly 2.28 persons. This decrease is a 40 per cent decline in size in about a century and a half.

The decrease was slow in the first half century of our nation. For in 1850 the approximate size of the household was 5.5 persons or a decrease of 4 per cent from 1790. This period was one when the United States was almost wholly agricultural, and little of the agricultural produce was sold except cotton and tobacco. What the family produced it consumed. There were few cities in 1850. By the beginning of the twentieth century the approximate average size of the household was 4.76. The decrease was faster than it had been in the previous half century. The decline in size was 15 per cent during these fifty years when industry and cities were growing. During the next fifty years, the first half of the twentieth century, the decrease in the approximate size of the household was at a still faster rate, 28 per cent for this period of unprecedented urban and industrial growth. How this decrease occurred by decades is shown in Table 12.

In this table, it is shown quite impressively that the rate of decrease in the approximate size of the household has been getting faster. The approximate average size of the household in 1950 was only 3.5 persons. The size is getting closer to its limit. We do not know what this limit is. Usually though, as a decreasing series approaches a limit, the rate slows up. The limit for a household is different from the limit for a family.

These data show a 40 per cent decrease in the approximate size of household in the century and a half preceding 1950. Since the approximate size of the household is very nearly the same as the average size of the family, can we assume that the average size of the family has decreased about 40 per cent in this century and a half? The downward trend in the size of the family may have been a little slower than that of the approximate size of the household.[3] But not very much slower, if at all, because of the small

T A B L E   12

*The Approximate Number of Persons per 100 Households by Decades from 1850 to 1950, and the Change in Numbers and Percentages Each Decade ***

Year	Persons per 100 Households	Decrease in Persons	Per Cent Decrease
1850	555		
1860	528	27	4.9
1870	509	19	3.6
1880	504	5	1.0
1890	493	11	2.2
1900	476	17	3.4
1910	454	22	4.6
1920	434	20	4.4
1930	411	23	5.3
1940	377	34	8.3
1950	351	26	6.9

* Data for 1850–1900 from U.S. Census, 1900, "Population," Part II, p. clviii; data for 1910–1940 from U.S. Bureau of the Census, *Historical Statistics of the United States, 1798–1945*, p. 174, H. 91.

[3] It may be that the size of the family has decreased more rapidly than that of the household, because of a possible greater decrease in the proportion of servants and lodgers, though we do not know. On the other hand, the size of the family may have decreased less rapidly than the size of the household because of a possible greater increase in the proportion of the quasi-household population. More important is the possible increase in the proportion of persons living alone. If such is the case, then the decrease in the size of the family may have been less rapid than the decrease in the size of the household. Furthermore we do not know that persons living alone were called households in the censuses of the nineteenth century. Also, the family is smaller because there is a larger proportion of elderly married couples living today than in 1790, and without any children living with them.

proportion of the factors involved. However, this research shows that the decrease in the size of the family since the founding of our nation has been of the order of, say, 35 to 45 per cent, and that the family in colonial times was only about two-thirds larger than now, and not two, three, or four times as large as is sometimes thought in comparing the so-called large family of those days with the small family of today.

The biological family. The family we have been writing about, it is recalled, is a kinship group and includes the related kin living in the same domicile with parents and children or with childless mates. This conception of the family as a kinship group is the one used by the United States Bureau of the Census in compiling its statistics in recent censuses. This conception is also used in various parts of the world. The family among the lower animals is a group consisting of parents or parent and offspring. Other kin are not considered part of a family of birds, for instance. Nor are the little birds when they have grown up and flown from the nest considered part of the family, even among those birds that mate for a lifetime. So we have a concept of a biological family, sometimes called a nuclear family. This biological family may be defined as a group living in the same dwelling unit consisting of parents or parent and offspring,[4] or a husband and wife without any children. It is observed that other kin are not included in this conception of the family, and hence the biological family differs from the kinship family as dealt with on previous pages.

There are variations in this biological conception. For instance, there are some observers who would not call a husband and wife without children a family. They would be thought of as a married couple, but not as a family until children are born. However, if children have been born but are no longer in the family dwelling, a married couple would be called a family, since they have borne children.

Another variation of the biological conception is to include in the family all children wherever they may be living and however old they may be. Thus an adult offspring living in Florida would be considered a member of the family of a married couple living in

---

[4] The few adopted children are by convention included as members of this biological family.

California, by the family in California, if not by the census taker. Certainly the task of the census taker would be difficult indeed if he were to try to classify scattered adult children, married or unmarried, as members of their parents' families. So in the statistics of families, the definition of the family is of a group living together in a single dwelling place; though data are sometimes presented on married couples or on mothers together with the number of children ever born.

Popular language on the family consists, then, of various conceptions of the biological or nuclear family. In the following discussion the particular conception of the biological family used is that of parents and children and mates without children.

In further reflection on popular usage, it seems that there are two basic ideas involved. One is economic, and the other is biological. Thus at one extreme is the household as an economic unit. This economic group was in the days of our earlier ancestors the most common unit of production, now replaced by, say, the factory. Since in most households there were none other than parents and children and kin, the term household and family were used interchangeably.

At the other extreme is the biological or nuclear family. This concept is widely used today when the economic or productive functions of a family are few. The emphasis, today, is on mating and rearing offspring.

In between these two extremes of the economic household and the biological family lies the kinship family, which seems to have some lingering aspects of an economic nature and some blood relationships suggestive of the biological family.

The size of the biological family. An attempt will be made in the pages which follow to measure the size of the biological family, and to see what can be done toward estimating trends. It should be stated though that the size of the biological family will be affected by the age of the population at different periods. The older the family after, say, middle age, the smaller will be its size. The size of the biological family will also be affected by the practice of children living at home as may be the case on farms, or of moving elsewhere. The size of the biological family does not therefore fully reflect the number of offspring living or ever born.

In 1950, the average biological family was estimated to be about 3.19 persons. We say "about" because in the census figures on family, from which we deduce a biological family, two relatives living together, such as two sisters, are called a family. Also the Census does not tabulate as two families a group consisting of a parent living with a son who is head of a family. Even though the figure is approximate, it is interesting to know that the average biological family in 1950 is only 3.2 persons.[5] This number does not mean a couple with 1.2 children, for included are widowed persons with children. It was noted that the approximate size of the household in 1950 was 3.51, just .32 persons larger than the biological family. We do not know, of course, whether this difference was the same in 1790, nor do we know what it was during the decades of the nineteenth century for which period we have the approximate size of the household.

For 1940 we have not been able with the data of the United States Census to make a satisfactory estimate of the size of the biological family following the procedure described in the preceding footnote. The estimate we reached was 3.38 persons, but there

---

[5] The size of the biological family in 1950 was calculated as follows:

Number of Families

Primary families	38,732,000
Secondary families	462,000
Subfamilies	2,369,000
Total	41,563,000

Population in Families

Primary & subfamilies	138,609,000
Secondary families	1,157,000
	139,766,000

Minus parents or heads, & relatives such as aunts, cousins, etc.	7,336,000
	132,430,000

$$\frac{\text{Population in families}}{\text{Number of families}} = \frac{132,430,000}{41,563,000} = 3.19 \text{ average size of biological family}$$

Data from "Current Population Reports," P–20, No. 33, p. 12. The number of "parents of head and other relatives" was taken to be the same percentage of the total household population as in 1940, that is, 4.98 per cent. A variation of one per cent of "parents of head and other relatives" increases or decreases the size of the family by about .03 person.

were too many assumptions involved to place much credence in this figure. We have better evidence as to how much change there was between the size of the biological family in 1940 and 1950. The size seems to have decreased between 1940 and 1950, though the very high birth rate in the 1940's might lead us to think otherwise. Though the birth rate increased, the number of young people under twenty years of age did not increase very much, 13 per cent, while the number of married couples (and widows and divorced persons) increased more, by 23 and 22 per cent. Hence the size of the biological family must have decreased during this prolific decade.

As to how much it decreased, an estimate can be made. The number of biological families is the number of married couples plus the number of widowed and divorced persons with children. If we take one-third of all the widowed and divorced persons as the number having children and add to this the number of married couples, we have a figure for the number of biological families. Even though there be considerable error in this estimate, the rate of decrease will not be affected, if the same error exists both in 1940 and 1950. The same is true of the estimate of the number of children, here defined as those under twenty years of age. On this basis our estimate of the size of the biological family in 1940 was 3.30 persons and in 1950 3.18 persons, or a decrease of 3.6 per cent. Since we already have a measure of the size of the biological family in 1950 as 3.19 persons, then the probable size of the biological family in 1940 is 3.30 persons. It is not profitable to try to estimate the size of the biological family in earlier decades.

Sizes of different types of family. We have indicated that in practice there are three concepts of the family: the household, the kinship family, and the biological family. They differ in size. In 1950, their average sizes were 3.38, 3.57, and 3.19 persons, respectively. The kinship family was the largest, and larger even than the household, for the reason that the household includes persons living alone. If one-person households be excluded, then the average multi-person household was the largest, 3.63 persons, a little larger than the average kinship family, 3.57 persons, because of the inclusion of a few lodgers and still fewer servants. The average kinship family of 3.57 persons is larger than the average biological family of 3.19 persons, because of the inclusion of kin, such as aunts, uncles, cousins, nephews, and in-laws.

Trends in the size of the biological family. The cause of the change in the size of the biological family over long periods of time is mainly the presence or absence of children. The number of parents and mates in a family does not differ very much from one period of history to another. Since our system is monogamy, the maximum in any biological family at any moment is two, and the minimum is one in the small percentage of families where the head is widowed or divorced. At the present time the average biological family has not two parents or mates but about 1.85. The changes in the size of the biological family therefore over the years is not due very much to changes in the number of mates per family, but to the number of children.

The change in the number of children in a biological family is due to changes in the birth rate and the death rate of children, and also to changes in the age of the parents, for older parents (who are more numerous now per 1000 families than formerly) are less likely than younger parents to have their children living with them; some of these older parents are living with their children. We consider first the changes in the birth rate as an index of changes in the biological family.

As for variations in fertility, we do have the number of children born in the United States by years, but only as far back as 1909. If we divide these births by the total population, we have a rate that is called the crude birth rate. In 1909 it was thirty per 1000 and in 1936 it was as low as 18.4. But since the depression, and during the period of economic recovery of the prewar and postwar years, the birth rate has increased, reaching a high point of twenty-seven in 1947. The course of the annual birth rate for the whole United States corrected for underenumeration is shown in Table 13. The trend in the birth rate as shown in Table 13 is downward, for the average for the first five years of the table is 29.8 and for the last five years it is 25.3.

Another indication of the changing number of children that extends further back than 1909, the earliest date of birth rate figures for the United States, is the record of children ever born to women ever married. These data were collected in 1910 and in

T A B L E 13

*The Annual Birth Rate for the United States,
Both White and Non-White, 1909–1950 **

1909	30.0	1930	21.3
1910	30.1	1931	20.2
1911	29.9	1932	19.5
1912	29.8	1933	18.4
1913	29.5	1934	19.0
1914	29.9	1935	18.7
1915	29.5	1936	18.4
1916	29.1	1937	18.7
1917	28.5	1938	19.2
1918	28.6	1939	18.8
1919	26.2	1940	19.4
1920	27.7	1941	20.3
1921	28.1	1942	22.3
1922	26.2	1943	22.9
1923	26.0	1944	21.5
1924	26.1	1945	20.7
1925	25.1	1946	24.5
1926	24.2	1947	27.0
1927	23.5	1948	25.3
1928	22.2	1949	25.1
1929	21.2	1950	24.6

* From "Births and Birth Rates in the Entire United States, 1909–1948," *Vital Statistics, Special Reports,* Vol. 33, No. 8, p. 141.

1940, and the women are classified by age. From these records we learn that the average number of children reported ever born to women ever married aged forty-five to forty-nine in 1940 was 3.1.[6] These women had reached the end of their child-bearing period in 1940. They probably married on the average around 1915 and the central point of their fertility was probably about 1920. Thus women married about 1915 appear not to have borne on the average more than three children, though of course some women gave birth to many more, and some none at all.

[6] This arithmetic mean is computed from Census data with two unequal class intervals and from one open-ended class interval for ten or more children. The numbers to go in regular class intervals were estimated from a freehand curve drawn through the frequency histogram.

T A B L E   14

The Average Number of Children Ever Born
to Women Ever Married of Ages 45–49 and 65–74
*in 1940 and in 1910 ***

Ages in 1940 and in 1910	About the time of marriage	Average number of children ever born
1940		
45–49	1915	3.1
65–74	1896	3.8
1910		
45–49	1885	4.7
65–74	1864	5.4

* Calculated from U.S. Bureau of the Census, "Differential Fertility, 1940 and 1910, Women by Number of Children Ever Born," Tables 1–6. Rates were calculated to give total for both white and non-white.

It is possible to obtain the average number of children ever born for earlier periods. These are shown in the preceding Table 14, where it is indicated that the women marrying about the time of the close of the Civil War in 1864 gave birth during their married life through their child-bearing period to an average of five children. There was probably very little use of contraceptives at this time. Clearly the number of children being born was decreasing rapidly during the latter part of the nineteenth and first part of the twentieth century, more rapidly than the approximate size of the household. The connection between the two is not known. But if the death rate of babies was being lowered, the decrease in the size of the family would be less than the decrease in the number of children ever born.

We do not have the birth rate in the United States further back than 1909. We think it was decreasing, though, during the nineteenth century, for the United States Bureau of the Census shows a diminishing number of little children in proportion to the number of women of child-bearing ages during this century. This ratio of children under five years of age to women twenty to forty-four years old is an approximation to the birth rate. How good its course is as an indication of the change in the birth rate is shown

T A B L E   15

Index Number of the Crude Birth Rate and of
the Ratio of Children under Five Years of Age to
White Women 20–44 Years of Age for the United
States by Decades 1910–1950 *

Year	Index Birth Rate	Index Ratio Young Children to Women
1910	100	100
1920	92	96
1930	71	80
1940	64	66
1950	82	91

* Calculated from the *U.S. Census of Population, U.S. Summary, General Characteristics*, P–B1, p. 1–93.

in the following Table 15 which gives for the census years 1920, 1930, 1940, and 1950 the birth rate and the ratio of children zero to five years to women twenty to forty-four years, each expressed as a percentage of the birth rate and of the ratio for the year 1910.

During the nineteenth century it is questionable whether the ratio of little children to women of child-bearing age was a good indication of the changes in the birth rate. For the ratio of children under five to women from twenty to forty-four as shown in Table 16 decreased from 1800 to 1940 by two-thirds. Such a decrease is hardly possible for the birth rate. For the birth rate was 19.4 in 1940 and such a decrease would have meant a birth rate of fifty-eight in 1800. Even with a favorable age distribution in 1790, the birth rate would hardly have been fifty-eight. However, the changing ratio of children under five years of age is a better indication of the changing size of the biological family than the changing birth rate.

In Table 16 there were 2.4 times as many children under five years old per 1000 white women twenty to forty-four years old in 1800 as in 1950. In 1950 we know there were about 1.34 children in the biological family, which was 3.19 persons. If the children in the biological family in 1800 were 2.4 times as many, then there would have been 3.22 children in the biological family at the beginning of the nineteenth century. And if there were 1.85 parents

TABLE 16

The Ratio of Children under Five Years of Age
per 1000 White Women Twenty to Forty-four Years
*by Decades for the United States 1800 to 1950.**

1800	1342	1880	780
1810	1358	1890	685
1820	1295	1900	666
1830	1145	1910	631
1840	1085	1920	604
1850	892	1930	506
1860	905	1940	419
1870	814	1950	552

* Data through 1940 taken from P. K. Whelpton, *Forecasts of the Population of the United States, 1945–1975* (Washington, D.C.: U.S. Government Printing Office, 1947), p. 16.   *U.S. Census of Population, 1950, U.S. Summary, General Characteristics,* P–B1, p. 90.

and mates per biological family in 1800, then the size of the biological family would have been 5.07 persons. Hence the biological family would have decreased in a century and a half 37 per cent, and the number of children per family would be 59 per cent less.

Recent changes in size. We have been trying to find out how much the family has changed since the United States became an independent nation. Data for more recent changes are more easily available. Table 17 shows for the past few decades changes in the size of the household, the kinship family, and the biological family and also in the approximation to the size of the household. From Table 17 we see that the size of the biological family decreased 3.6 per cent, while the size of the kinship family (which includes some relatives and some families of the children of the head) decreased 5 per cent. The implication is that some few relatives or married children moved elsewhere. At the same time the size of the multi-person household decreased much more, 8 per cent. This greater decrease in the size of the multi-person household was due to the decrease in the number of servants and lodgers, which was quite phenomenal. The absolute numbers of servants were cut in half during the decade, and the lodgers were reduced numerically by about one-fifth. The decrease in the size

T A B L E   17

The Average Size of the Approximate Household, the Household,
the Multi-person Household, the Kinship Family Group, and the
Biological Family in the United States in 1910, 1930, 1940, 1950.

	1910	1930	1940	1950
Approximate household *	4.54	4.11	3.77	3.51
Household *	4.47	4.01	3.67	3.39
Multi-person household *			3.94	3.63
Kinship family		4.04	3.75	3.57
Biological family *			3.31	3.19

* The approximate household is the total population divided by the number of occupied residences or the number of households. The household includes one-person households. The sizes of the biological families are estimated. Figures are calculated from Census data. The multi-person households are those with more than one person in them.

of the household from 1930 to 1950 was also greater than the decrease in the size of the kinship family for the same period.

The composition of the approximate household 1800 and 1940. From these data we can make some estimates of the composition of the approximate household at the beginning of the nineteenth century. A household is composed of parents, mates, children, and others. We can get an idea of the comparative number of children by noting the ratio of children to women in the two periods. In 1800 the children under sixteen years old per 100 women sixteen to forty-four years old were 2.3 times as numerous as in 1940. Now the children (unmarried and living at home) in 1940 per household were 1.49. Hence the children per household in 1800 would have been 3.4.

We have no information about the number of parents and mates per household at the beginning of the nineteenth century. We have calculated the number of parents and mates in 1940 as 1.77 per approximate household. This number is somewhat lower than the number per biological family, which was about 1.85. The reason for this difference is that there are more households than families. The number of mates and parents per household would not vary very much over a century and a half, since the limits of their variation are narrow. If they were the same in 1800 and in 1940, then we have an estimate of the number of parents and mates and the number of children in 1800.

There are others in the household in addition to parents and children. There are persons other than boarders and lodgers and relatives, for we are studying the composition of the approximate household, which is the total population divided by the number of households. Hence included are the institutionalized population and persons living alone. We have calculated for 1940 the number of these "others" in the approximate household (that is, those besides parents and children) and find them to be about 13 per cent of the size of the approximate household, or .51 person per household in 1940.

For 1800 we take the size of the approximate household to be the same as in 1790 or 5.79 persons, of whom 5.20 were parents, mates, and children. There were therefore .59 persons per household in 1790 called "others" as compared with .51 persons in 1940. These "others" were the relatives, lodgers, servants, persons living alone, and those in institutions (who were not parents, mates, and children). These were about 10 per cent of the population in 1800 as compared with 13 per cent in 1940.

The composition of the approximate household in 1800 is shown in Table 18. For comparison the composition in 1940 is also shown.

The foregoing composition is for the approximation to the size of the household. It did not seem feasible to obtain the composition of the household or of the multi-person household.

The number of children per approximate household has de-

TABLE 18

*Composition of the Approximate Households
in 1800 and in 1940*

	Persons		Per Cent	
	1800	1940	1800	1940
Parents and mates	1.77	1.77	31	47
Children	3.43	1.49	59	40
Lodgers, servants, relatives, etc.	.59	.51	10	13

creased in this century and a half by some 50 or 60 per cent, while the size of this household has decreased around 35 per cent. The number of "others" in this household seems to have decreased probably by about 10 or 15 per cent. More unmarried persons appear to be living outside the family domicile.

These figures, the reader needs to be reminded, are not the reports of census takers, but are estimates that have been carefully calculated. Since they are estimates, they contain some error, the exact amount of which cannot be indicated. It is hoped that other researchers will make refinements. Until then, these estimates are set forth as a contribution to our knowledge about certain aspects of the family at the time of the founding of our country, aspects about which we have previously known little. These estimates are also a contribution to our knowledge of the changes in the total household and of the elements that go to make it up.

Causes

We are next interested in inquiring into the causes of this decrease in family size. The decrease is of two classes; one is the decrease in the number of children in the family, and the other is the decrease in the number of lodgers, servants, and relatives.

Lodgers, servants, and relatives. The latter class concerns the members of the household who are not in the biological family of the head of the household. The number of lodgers and servants living in the family dwelling decreased from 1930 to 1950, as we have seen, but there were no data for prior decades.

In searching for the causes of any possible decrease in the number of servants living in the family dwelling, we should think separately of urban and of farm families.

In urban houses, particularly where gas and electricity and running hot and cold water are available, there have for many years been household appliances available which would appear to have brought technological unemployment to servants. These same utilities and appliances are becoming available also to farm houses. The movement for shorter hours of work among household servants has probably tended to reduce the effective demand for them. This factor was not operative during the first part of the twentieth century or in the nineteenth century.

On farms and in homes of farmers there was a difference between a household servant and a "hired hand" who worked in the field. The latter was not classified as a servant, and when he lived in the dwelling he was sometimes classified by the Census as a lodger. These farm laborers are being replaced by farm machinery, and large specialized commercial farms are coming to depend on a migratory labor force to harvest crops.

The causes of these changes in the number of servants and of other farm employees appear to be technological.

We turn next to the cause of changes in the number of lodgers, who appear to be a smaller proportion of the population of households in 1950 than in 1930. These lodgers are largely unmarried — that is, single, divorced, and widowed — about 88 per cent in 1950. Hence any decrease in the percentage of the single, divorced, or widowed in the population is likely to decrease the number of lodgers, *ceteris paribus*. We know that the percentage of the single in the population has been decreasing since 1890. The decrease in the number of single persons has been particularly great from 1940 to 1950, when the decrease in the proportion of members of households that are lodgers was also great. The number of divorced has been increasing, though they are a smaller number. The causes of the increase in marriage and hence of the decrease in the number of single persons have been discussed in another chapter.

On the other hand, the relatively greater increase in the urban population than in the farm population has probably meant an increase in lodgers per household, for there are more lodgers to a household in cities than on farms, about three times as many in 1940 and in 1950. This greater number may be due to the migration of young people away from their families to the cities.

We can see, then, factors that bear upon the increase or decrease in lodgers, even though over a long period we do not know whether they have increased or decreased per household.

With regard to kin in the household, though we do not have the data as to their increase or decrease per household, we do know something about the factors affecting their presence or absence in the home. In general we know that in the rural household economy the tie of the kin to the family head was closer than it is in the city. This responsibility may not have changed much for, say,

the father or mother of the husband or wife, but it is said to be weaker for collateral relations like cousins or nieces and nephews in cities. The migration to distant areas brings a separation from relatives and for that reason some lessening of responsibility, particularly in regard to collateral relatives. For women kin in cities, especially of younger ages, there are more jobs of different kinds open than is the case in rural areas. Hence there is possibly less dependence upon relatives for support than was the case on the farm in earlier days. These causes affecting the family care of kin are due in part to the growth of cities and to transportation inventions.

Children. The greatest decrease in the approximate size of the household has been the decrease in the number of children living at home. We have also indications that the biological family has decreased greatly since 1790; and, of course, its decrease has been due to fewer children. There may have been some variation in the tendency for children to leave or stay at home, and there has been a very great reduction in the death rate of young children; but the outstanding reason for the decrease in the number of children living at home has been the reduction in the birth rate, for which we have good evidence since about 1865 and approximate estimates since 1790. The evidence has been presented in the preceding section of this chapter.

What have been the causes of the reduction in the birth rate? This is a subject which has been investigated and discussed for many years. There has been no evidence discovered to indicate any hereditary change in the fecundity of the population. Nor is there much suggestive evidence that there has been any loss of fecundity during a lifetime due to constitutional changes. Incapacitating venereal diseases are now being lessened, and there is probably more Vitamin E consumed now than formerly. There may have been some tendency to marry later during the nineteenth century. Since 1890 the trend is toward early marriage, and during this period the birth rate declined rapidly until 1986. We conclude, therefore, that the influence of biology and change in the age of marriage have had little or no effect in producing the decrease in the birth rate.

Birth control. On the other hand, the practice of birth control has been increasing. Some methods of birth control have been known for a long time. Indeed, some use of them is found among various preliterate people before contact with whites, though no doubt the use was very slight. Cities, whose populations appear not to have made much use of any of the contraceptives in early times or in parts of the world distant from western Europe and the United States, have lower birth rates than the surrounding rural communities have.[7] It is inferred that in these cities some practice of birth control occurs without the use of contraceptives. The practice of birth control without contraceptives is based upon knowledge. Knowledge, of course, is the objective of science. Primitive peoples have much such knowledge, though it is usually obtained by a trial and error method rather than by any systematic scientific methodology used by scientists today, which reduces the time and effort employed by the trial and error method. More recently birth control is practiced according to knowledge of the date of ovulation of women. This knowledge like modern invention is the product of good scientific procedure.

Contraceptives, on the other hand, are inventions and may be referred to as products of technology, although the technology is in most cases rather simple. Neither the names of the inventors nor the early dates of their invention are known. But the use of contraceptives in any appreciable manner began around the first part of the nineteenth century, particularly among the upper and middle classes of the cities of France. From there the use of these inventions has spread to these groups in other countries and has recently been diffused to the lower income groups in towns and cities and to the farming population.

Since the non-appliance method of birth control appears to have been known and used before the era of appliances, it seems reasonable to assume that most of the decrease in the birth rate has been due to the increased use of contraceptives rather than to the increased use of non-appliance methods. It is the decrease in the birth rate, not the birth rate, for which we wish to find causes. There may have been some increased use of the knowledge of the time of the fertile period in the menstrual cycle in lessening the

[7] A. J. Jaffe, "Urbanization and Fertility," *American Journal of Sociology,* 7: 48–60, July, 1942.

number of births, but its use has probably been relatively slight.

The question of causes in the decrease of the birth rates may therefore be sought in the factors that lead adults to use these appliance methods; and where birth rates have not decreased, we seek the factors that lead to resistance to their use.

Causes of the use of contraceptives. These factors, which bring the use of birth control, are of two kinds, or at least have two aspects. One kind is sought in the human motives that lead a person to use contraceptives or to reject their use, and the other kind is the conditions that are found associated with their use, irrespective of motivation.

An illustration of the latter kind (that is, a situational factor) is cities, where there is more use of contraceptives than on farms. Thus in the United States the gross reproduction rate (the sum of the age specific birth rates) for urban areas in 1942–47 was 1177 and for farming areas 2029.[8] Urban life is thus a cause of the practice of birth control, though not expressed in terms of motives.

An illustration of the first kind, that is, of the motivational factor, is the desire not to undertake the costs of rearing a child or a large family. This motivation may operate more in the city than on the farms, though we do not know that it does.

It is somewhat easier to designate with assurance situational factors than motivational ones, for motives are difficult to ascertain accurately. To many persons, motives are the end product in the search for causes. Thus they want to know the motives, the subjective forces, that made a person commit a crime.

To others, on the other hand, motives are not the end product in the search for causes; they want to know the objective situation that produced these motives. They want to know what are the conditions that make a boy want to steal. The desire they know. But the conditions they do not know without investigation. These may be bad companions, or a broken home. Here the end product in the search for causes is the situation.

In searching for the causes why married couples do or do not practice birth control, the quest for motives is not very satisfactory. For if it is the love of pleasure, for instance, the pursuit of which

---

[8] *Statistical Abstract of the United States, 1953* (Washington, D.C.: U.S. Government Printing Office, 1953), p. 48.

is interfered with by child care, and if this cause is determined by evidence, it still remains unsatisfactory because it does not tell us, for instance, why birth control was widely practiced, let us say, in the United States in the first half of the twentieth century and not in the first half of the nineteenth. Biologically the people were the same. Nor do motives, in this case pleasure-seeking, in the absence of information on the situation tell us why there are fewer children born in the cities and more on the farms. We have knowledge, for instance, that cities "cause" the birth rate to be lower than on farms without any reference to motives.

Situation and motives affecting the use of birth control methods. A good clue to the situations affecting the changes in the birth rate is in the factors that facilitate or retard the information on birth control and the purchase of contraceptives. Ignorance or knowledge is one such factor; and poverty or wealth another.

Obviously the spread of an invention or of a specific piece of knowledge is dependent upon communication which necessitates contact, whether face-to-face or through the mails, or by telephone or by some other means as, for example, advertising. Communication is very easy in cities, and it is in cities that the greatest use of birth control is found. In rural areas, the farming districts nearer to a city have been found in many states to have lower birth rates than the more distant farms.[9] There are, however, exceptions where for some distance up to, say, fifty miles the birth rates neither increase nor decrease with distance. There is indication that the correlation is higher in the areas where the farming lands are less good and where the income appears to be lower than usual for farming. There is thus an economic factor that must be considered in relating distance from city and birth rates.

Distance alone is not always a good index of contacts. For instance, in cities where all live relatively close together, the areas with low rental values for residences have higher birth rates and larger families than in areas where higher rents prevail. This relation of birth rate to income has been shown in many studies.[10]

[9] P. K. Whelpton, "Geographic and Economic Differentials in Fertility," *Annals of the American Academy of Political and Social Science,* 188: 7–9, November, 1936.

[10] Bernard D. Karpinos and Clyde V. Kiser, "The Differential Fertility and Potential Rates of Growth of Various Income and Educational Classes of Urban

Though the poor and the rich may live close together, the custom may be that intimate conversation about birth control does not occur.

In the course of time, however, those who pay low rents for homes come to know about birth control. Yet knowledge may not result in lower birth rates. Housing conditions may be an obstacle. So also the cost of contraceptives, though the price of contraceptives is not as great as the expense of rearing a child. In rural districts of India, China, Java, Ceylon, and Puerto Rico the costs and inaccessibility of contraceptives might be an obstacle even though there was knowledge that they existed.

Another social condition affecting the practice of birth control is education. Several studies of American cities have shown that in the areas where the residents have more schooling the birth rate is lower than where the years spent in school are less.[11] In one study of small urban areas in Chicago,[12] the correlation between ratio of little children to married women and the years spent in school was higher than the correlation between this ratio and the median rental paid in the area for a home. Furthermore, the correlation between this fertility index and educational status with rent held constant was greater than the correlation between the fertility index and rent with educational status held constant. Apparently one way of increasing the practice of birth control is to improve the general education of the people.

Religion is another factor affecting the spread of birth control. The official organs of religions do not actively work to promote birth control, though sometimes religious organizations do. On the other hand, some organized religions oppose the use of contraceptives.

Couples adhering to the Roman Catholic Church have long been known to have larger families than Protestants, but it was not clear whether the difference was wholly due to religion, since the Catholics were supposed to have lower incomes than the Protestants. But in 1941, a study in Indianapolis showed that while

Populations in the United States," *Milbank Memorial Fund Quarterly*, Vol. 17, No. 4, October, 1939, p. 376.

11 Whelpton and Kiser, *op. cit.*, pp. 252–3.

12 Richard O. Lang, *The Relation of Educational Status to Economic Status in the City of Chicago by Census Tracts, 1934* (Ph.D. Thesis, University of Chicago, 1936), p. 38.

Protestant couples had 147 children born to 100 wives fifteen to forty-four years of age, the Catholics had 173.[13] The median rental value of dwelling unit for the Catholics was slightly higher, $33 a month, than for the Protestant, $30 a month. The age of marriage of Catholic wife was a year later. The comparisons were standardized for age. For the Jews the number was 110. The Mormons are said to have the highest birth rate of any religious group in the United States. Attitudes on birth control appear to vary by religious groups. Yet families of the same religion which disapproves the use of contraceptives have birth rates that vary according to the rent paid for dwelling unit. For instance, in the Indianapolis study the births for 100 wives fell as the rents increased until a rental of $50–$59 a month was reached. Catholic families paying $60–$79 and more than $80 had higher birth rates than those of smaller rentals where the birth rate increased with lower rentals.

Birth rates also vary by broad occupational groups, but it is difficult to separate the income factor from the purely occupational influence.

Another situation that is related to birth rates is business fluctuations. In prosperous periods the birth rate is higher than in years of business depression.[14] This correlation is much greater for the first born or second child than for, say, the fourth or fifth. The reasons seem to be economic.

These social conditions are then correlated with a low or a high birth rate. It would be desirable in some cases to trace the link of causes one step further back. But the task is difficult and extensive.

Such a tracing to other underlying factors is especially desirable in the cities, where the birth rate is well-nigh universally lower than on farms or even in small towns. The reason for this desirability is that a city is a composite of so many factors. We have only mentioned one, namely, the large number of easy contacts between its citizens.

---

[13] P. K. Whelpton and Clyde V. Kiser, "Social and Psychological Factors Affecting Fertility 1. Differential Fertility Among 41,498 White Couples in Indianapolis," *Milbank Memorial Fund Quarterly*, Vol. 21, No. 3, July, 1943, pp. 221–380.

[14] W. F. Ogburn and Dorothy Thomas, "The Influence of the Business Cycle on Certain Social Conditions," *Quarterly Publication of the American Statistical Association*, 18: 324–340, September, 1922.

Of the underlying factors in cities, prominently mentioned and sometimes recorded statistically, is the cost of rearing children. In the Indianapolis study of 1941,[15] previously cited, of the reasons given for not having more children, the most common reason by far was the economic costs. Half of the wives and two-fifths of the men gave costs of children as the main reason. Other reasons of a financial nature were "Not sure of a steady income," "Parents had a hard time rearing children," and "Sharing house." All these economic reasons were given by two-thirds of the wives and three-fifths of the husbands. Yet strangely the families with low incomes have more children than families with large incomes.

Also rearing a child satisfactorily is somewhat difficult in an apartment house; and the number of children in a sample of apartment homes in Chicago was fewer than in separate dwellings with yards.[16] City streets are more hazardous than country roads. Transportation vehicles and stores in cities are built for adults rather than for children, with or without their mothers.

The city has many attractions outside the home which appeal to adults, many more than are found near farms in the open country. Those who must stay at home to care for children are thereby prevented from enjoying these attractions. As to how much of a deterrent this "love of pleasure" is to child-bearing, there is some evidence from the Indianapolis study.[17] Only about 2 per cent of the husbands and wives gave the desire to "avoid being tied down" as a major reason for not having more children.

One of the problems in measuring motives is the difficulty respondents have both in knowing their motives and in stating them frankly. Often reasons are given which sound well to the inquirer.

One-fifth of the husbands gave the poor health of the wife as the main reason why they, the husbands, did not want any more children. This was the main reason for one-sixth of the wives.

We have been discussing motives and situations that might explain the differential practice of birth control in farming and in

15 Clyde V. Kiser and P. K. Whelpton, "Social and Psychological Factors Affecting Fertility, XI. The Interrelation of Fertility, Fertility Planning, and Feeling of Economic Security," *The Milbank Memorial Fund Quarterly,* Vol. 29, No. 1, January, 1951, pp. 41–122.

16 Joseph B. Gittler, *Society's Adjustment to a Mechanical and a Social Invention* (Ph.D. Thesis, University of Chicago, 1941).

17 Kiser and Whelpton, *op. cit.*

urban areas. Another very common differential is by income classes. Generally speaking, families with small wages have more children than families with larger salaries. The motives back of such a differential have seldom been adequately examined. Indeed one might guess that the poor would have fewer children than the rich, in view of the reported reason of the economic burden of child care. Various theoretical explanations come to mind, particularly those concerned with ambition and with class standards. But this is not the occasion to speculate on these reasons. It is desirable to have some evidence.

The diffusion of birth control. It is recalled that an inquiry of the causes of the diminished size of the family led to the conclusion that the practice of birth control is the main cause. Birth control was seen as an invention or a scientific discovery which spreads from its place of first use to other lands and to other classes. Its first introduction led to wide differentials, particularly by income groups, as shown by studies in England. As time passed and the invention spread, it was to be expected that these widened differentials would lessen. We wish then to inquire what the evidence shows in regard to lessening differentials.

In the United States in 1934 Raymond Pearl wrote that in United States cities "among the well-to-do and rich white women over 78 per cent had practiced birth control . . . and that among the very poor and poor classes of whites . . . only a few more than one-tenth of the women practiced birth control really intelligently." [18] In London, differentials in the birth rate by social classes existed as far back as the middle of the nineteenth century but became accentuated in the latter half of the century.[19] But for the intercensal period in England from 1921 to 1931, the birth rates in some of the lower classes had dropped so much that they were lower than those in occupational classes with higher incomes.[20] In Sweden, the highest fertility was also found, in the period from 1917 to 1930,

[18] Milbank Memorial Fund Press Release, March 14, 1934.
[19] David Heron, *On the Relation of Fertility in Man to Social Status During 50 Years.* Drapers Company Research Memoirs. Studies in National Deterioration, No. 1. 1906.
[20] J. W. Innes, "Class Birth Rates in England and Wales, 1921–31," *The Milbank Memorial Fund Quarterly,* 19, January, 1941, pp. 72–96.

to be in the upper classes.[21] In the United States there are many studies indicating a lessening or a reversal in the differential rates between income groups. In New York City in 1929 the difference between the highest economic group and the lowest in number of births per 1000 white population fifteen to forty-four years of age was sixteen. In 1942 it was two.[22] In Indianapolis in 1941, home owners with rental values over $60 a month had more children born than those with values from $50 to $60. This fact was true of both Protestants and Catholics,[23] standardized for age. As to religious differentials, Stouffer, published in 1935 a report of a study which showed that the confinement rate for Catholics had declined more than for Protestants in Milwaukee families. Hence the differential was less.[24]

From these reports it appears that the practice of birth control is spreading from the higher to the lower economic classes and also to the Catholics. Indeed in Europe, the birth rate of the poor is often less than that of the well-to-do. This fact suggests that the reason for the differential may have been ignorance. If it was housing or poverty or lack of education, then these barriers seem to have been removed.

There is not much evidence on the trend in rural-urban differentials. We would like to know if birth control is spreading to the farmers. In a previous paragraph, it was observed that the birth rate or its equivalent was higher in farming areas distant from a large city; but that in good farming areas the birth rate did not become greater for some distance away from the city. Better evidence is from the gross reproduction rate for farming and urban areas for the first half of the twentieth century.[25] In the period 1905–10, the rate in urban areas was 49 per cent of what it was on farms. In 1942–47 it was 58 per cent. The rate on the farms

[21] K. A. Edin and E. P. Hutchinson, *Studies in Differential Fertility in Sweden* (London: P. S. King & Son, Ltd., 1935), p. 89.

[22] Paul H. Jacobson, "The Trend of Birth Rate Among Persons on Different Economic Levels, City of New York, 1929–42," *The Milbank Memorial Fund Quarterly*, 22, April, 1944, pp. 131–147.

[23] Whelpton and Kiser, *op. cit., The Milbank Memorial Fund Quarterly*, 21, July, 1943.

[24] S. A. Stouffer, "Trends in Fertility of Catholics and Non-Catholics," *American Journal of Sociology*, 41: 143–166, September, 1935.

[25] *Statistical Abstract of the United States, 1950* (Washington, D.C.: U.S. Government Printing Office, 1950), p. 26.

had decreased a little more than the rate in cities. But the differential between the farms and the cities was still very large. It looks as though it will be a long time before the birth rate on the farms will be as low as it is in the cities. Perhaps the farms are more favorable areas for rearing children. It should be remembered though that the income is a good deal lower for the farm family than for the urban family.

Conclusion. The conclusion of this inquiry about the size of the family, largely from data for the United States, is in two parts. In the first part it was shown that the approximate size of the average household in the United States in 1790 was 579 persons for 100 households, of whom probably 177 were parents with about 343 children and the remainder, about fifty-nine, were relatives, servants, lodgers, and others. By 1940 the number of children had been reduced to 149 and the others to fifty-one, with a total of 377 per 100 approximate households. In other words, the decrease in the size of the household is due largely to the decrease in the number of children, a decrease of about two per household in some 150 years.

The second part of the inquiry concerned the reasons for this reduction in the number of children. They appear related to the spread of the practice of birth control, which is of two kinds, one based on a mechanical or chemical invention, and the other based on knowledge of conception. The first direct cause of the decrease in family size is therefore due to science and technology. The spread of these inventions and discoveries is due to knowledge, contacts, income, and difficulties in rearing children. Barriers to the spread are religious attitudes, poverty, and lack of education. The spread to the farming areas is rather slow. The spread is somewhat more rapid to the low income groups in the cities.

The more remote causes are education (not easily traceable to technological factors), the decrease of religious sanctions (in part due to the impact of science), and various locational and economic factors traceable in general to technological changes.

6

Shrinking Functions

The family, like the church, or industry, or government, engages in many different activities. The family may worship together, engage in play, and extend help to relatives; homemakers may sew for other members of the family. These activities are performed by members collectively or by individuals operating in the name of the organization, or as members of it. Any organization is important for what it does, or for what it does not do. The significance of the structure of an institution lies in how it functions. We therefore wish to chart what modern families do.

Since we are also interested in studying family changes, we want to describe what the family has done in the past and record what changes have taken place in family functions.

Families of the household economy. We take as our starting point the rural family of, say, one hundred fifty or two hundred years ago in the states of North America. This farm family was called the self-sustaining family, because it produced nearly all that it consumed of food and various other items. The economic life of this time was called by economic historians, very appropriately, the household economy. There were then not very many cities, and the towns and villages were small. In the United States in 1800 there were only thirty-three places with more than 2500 population each, and all the population in these places was only 6 per cent of the total population of the United States. The urban population in other lands was similarly small in comparison to the rural population. In other countries, the farming population generally lived in villages and went out some distance to cultivate their lands, while in the United States farmers lived more often in scattered farm houses not clustered in villages. Where the farmsteads were isolated, as in the United States and Norway, the individual farm family was more or less self-sustaining. Where the farmers lived in small villages, the village was more or less self-sustaining. The household economy was characteristic of most of the world during the period of written history. It is appropriate, therefore, to use it as a unit of comparison with the modern urban family.

There were variations from this modal family, of course. For instance, Chinese rural families differed from Anglo-Saxon families in Colonial America. There were also variations among the Chinese families and among American colonial families. These variations relate, for instance, to marriage customs, to kinship, and to manifestations of authority. Differences existed, too, between the families of peasants and those of the rich landlords. There were also some cities on the rivers and coast during the household era in various countries, and probably the urban families were quite different from the modal rural family of the household economy, though we do not have very good data on these early urban families. Nevertheless, there are similarities that mark off such a family of the household economy from that of a modern city apartment-dweller.

Primitive families. If, prior to the household economy, we look further backward to families of preliterate peoples existing in economies based on the hoe culture and on hunting, we see that there are many more varieties of family organization and customs in the different hunting and hoe cultures than are found in the household economy of the plow cultures. The population in these simpler cultures live in communities from, say, a dozen to a couple of hundred persons. Hence families are found in communities too small to have many social organizations. The collective affairs of life are carried on mainly through these two groups, the family and the local community. Therefore the primitive family must have very many different functions. A striking variation of the family unit in the small primitive community, as in the plow culture, is the strength of the kinship tie as between grandparents, parents, children, grandchildren, uncles and aunts, et cetera, as compared with the strength of the tie between husbands and wives.[1]

[1] Ralph Linton, *The Study of Man* (New York: D. Appleton-Century Company, 1936), Chapter X.

Modern family functions. If we look forward from this family of the household economy with its plow and domesticated animals, we see the family of the modern cities and, in the rural areas, of commercial farming. These are the two main types, though there are variations within farming areas.

If we start with the family of the household economy for the purpose of seeing what it does, we need some classifications into which to assort the different activities in which these family members engage. Families have been either centers for or have engaged as families in most of the activities common to mankind. These more or less universal activities of man may be classified broadly into such categories as working, loving, playing, governing, fighting, protecting, and worshiping. It is possible then to summarize the functions of families into such a set of categories and to trace the changes from the family of self-sustaining farmers in the era of the household economy to that of the modern family.

Economic functions. Of basic importance is the work we do. The family is the supplier of various goods and services to its members; and the house and land where a family live have been the locus of much economic activity of its members.

In the United States before the coming of factories and railroads, many families produced nearly all they consumed, as for instance, thread, cloth, clothing, furniture, leather, raw food, processed and preserved foods, liquors and wines, meals, medicine, shoes, brooms, toothbrushes, and other small objects. There were some goods produced in excess of consumption, notably cotton, and tobacco in the United States, but also lumber, meat, and grain. From the sale of the products money was obtained to buy guns, powder, utensils, iron plows, harness, salt, nails, axes, shovels, vehicles, carpets, shoes, medicine, et cetera.

What a family consumed from production or purchases depended upon its wealth and income, which in turn rested upon the size and quality of its land, and upon the number of workers. The search for wealth and income then became a struggle for land and more land, though the supply in any area is limited. But there were always some large landholders, who sometimes in earlier times and countries acquired their lands by force. To operate large agricultural holdings, it helped to have a large family, expanded laterally as well as vertically, as is the case in China, where brothers-in-law and sisters-in-law and aunts and uncles become part of the same household. In other cases there were slaves or serfs. Often families were allowed to work on a rich man's land, if they gave part of the crop to the land owner.

The family thus expands beyond the biological family of parents and children, to become a household including kin, slaves, serfs, sharecroppers, and servants. The expansion of the family among the rich landholders was very great indeed. With the help of a private army, the land acquired became a province or even a kingdom. The pattern of political power over a kingdom was indeed much like that in a household. The king was like the authoritarian father, and the kingdom was passed on at death to the ruler's child or children, much as the family property was inherited.

In Colonial America and in western Europe the amount of goods purchased from outside the farm household depended on the wealth of the family. When the plane of living was simple and low, the family did not buy silks, lace, china, carpets, shoes, and furniture. They either did without these commodities or made them on the farm. But gradually as the industrial arts progressed, families bought proportionately more of what they consumed, and produced proportionately less. Trade thus increased, and trading places grew.

Within the past century or so, families have ceased spinning and weaving, as earlier they had stopped preparing leather and making furniture. Many handicrafts moved from the home into shops of specialists, like cobblers, wheelwrights, blacksmiths, potters, tinkers, et cetera.

Observations of very recent times indicate that this process of the removal of economic production from the home and the household has not ceased.

Looking first at the preparation of food, we find that most meals are eaten at home, although there is a tendency in cities, especially the larger ones, for the midday meal to be eaten away from home, particularly by those who, like suburbanites, travel long distances to work. In 1941, in a sample of United States cities 18 per cent of all food expenditures went for eating outside the home.[2] On

2 Margaret G. Reid, "The Economic Contribution of Homemakers," *Annals of the American Academy of Political and Social Science*, 251: 61–9, May, 1947.

farms the percentage was three. In cities where the income of the family was over $5,000, 38 per cent of all food expenditures was spent on eating away from home. To meet this demand for serving city workers with lunch, the drug stores and soda fountains, ten-cent stores and big department stores have begun serving light meals, since it is difficult for a restaurant to prosper if it serves only one meal a day at noon for five or six days a week. The amount spent in eating places in the United States from 1929 to 1948 increased 52 per cent (in money of the same purchasing power) while the number of families increased 39 per cent.

For food served at home more processing is done outside the home. Food from delicatessen stores, from deep-freeze lockers is almost wholly ready for consumption; and the products from chain groceries are often quite highly processed. The president of the American Can Company says the average person in the United States opened about 200 cans a year in 1950 compared with twenty-five in 1900. The patronage of bakeries in cities is shown by the fact that 230 pounds of baked goods in 1940 were bought for every 100 pounds of flour and meal (reckoning a pound of bakery products to two-thirds of a pound of flour).[3] On farms the number of pounds of baked products purchased was seventeen, much less than for the city. Yet farmers are patronizing bakeries increasingly. For instance, in 1949 in four counties in Kansas 94 per cent of the families bought some bread at a store or bakery.[4] In 1936 only 67 per cent did so, though it should be remembered that 1949 was a more prosperous year for farmers than 1936. The trend toward less preparation of food at home still continues.

What is saved by the use of processed foods is time, not money, although the time of the wife may have a cash value, especially if she has a job. It takes the homemaker one-fourth the time but costs over one-third more money when she feeds her family from ready-to-serve foods instead of home-prepared foods.[5] This cost

[3] *Ibid.*
[4] Gertrude S. Weiss, "Farm Family Spending," an address at the 28th Annual Agricultural Outlook Conference, October 31, 1950, a release from the United States Department of Agriculture.
[5] These results are reported by home economists of the United States Department of Agriculture, based on experiments with a family of four, including two children. For one day, home-prepared meals cost $4.90, took 5.5 hours to prepare, whereas partially prepared meals cost $5.80, took 3.1 hours to prepare; and ready-to-serve meals cost $6.70, took 1.6 hours to prepare. *Science News Letter,* November 7, 1953, p. 296.

factor probably results in more use of processed foods by the middle class than by lower-class families.

The reduction of time spent in preparing food at home is also accomplished in part by the use of many labor-saving devices such as electric and gas stoves, running hot and cold water, machines that wash dishes and dispose of refuse as well as frozen lockers and mechanical refrigerators. The appearance of the kitchen is quite different from what it was in the days before stoves one hundred and fifty years ago when cooking was done in the open fireplace.

The production of clothing outside the home has recently extended to women's dresses, as earlier the tailoring of men's suits was transferred from the home. From 1935 to 1943 the production outside the home of women's and misses' clothing increased about 30 per cent, while the production of men's and boys' clothing remained about the same.[6] There is still some knitting, done in the home, of sweaters and socks; and the sewing machine and needle are used in repairing, sewing on buttons, altering, making some children's clothing, curtains, et cetera, consuming about four or five hours a week around 1930.[7]

The cleaning of the house and of dishes and utensils still remains an economic activity of the home. The cleaning of outer clothing is now an extensively established business, showing an increase of over 300 per cent from 1919 to 1939 in the number of establishments reporting receipts over $5000 a year. The increase still continues at a rapid rate. There was an increase of slightly over 100 per cent from 1939–1948 (these figures include smaller establishments than the figures for 1919–1939). The use of laundries to wash clothing has not been increasing as rapidly as in earlier decades probably because of the invention of the electric washing, drying, and ironing devices. The number of power laundries actually decreased in the United States from 1929 to 1939, while their receipts, adjusted for the value of money, were almost the same. Fom 1939 to 1948, however, the amount of money spent for laundry service per household in money of constant purchasing power increased 17 per cent.[8] This increase may represent an increase in

[6] J. Frederic Dewhurst and Associates, *America's Needs and Resources* (New York: The Twentieth Century Fund, 1947).

[7] *The Time Cost of Homemaking*, Bureau of Human Nutrition and Home Economics, United States Department of Agriculture, 1944, 10 pp.

[8] U.S. Bureau of the Census, *Census of Business, 1948*, "Service Trades," United States Summary.

the standard of living rather than a transfer of an economic service away from the home. During this period the income per household in constant money increased 54 per cent. In 1941, 40 per cent of the families sent their laundry out in cities, and 10 per cent on farms.[9] The new electric washing machines may be used not only in one's own kitchen or basement, but also in a nearby building for a small rental. Thus a woman may take the soiled clothes to a launderette to wash them, as she formerly took them to a running stream on the outskirts of the village, with a considerable change in the labor involved, however.

To gain further knowledge as to how much of an economic institution the family still is, we may ask what economic production is still carried on by the family. The answer is cooking and preparing meals, housecleaning and decorating, some laundering, a little sewing and marketing. By contrast, there is a great proliferation outside the home of economic organizations, including not only the great economic enterprises such as factories and banks, transportation lines and stores, but also a large number of smaller miscellaneous undertakings such as beauty shops, bootblack stands, and cleaning and dyeing establishments, as well as restaurants and hotels.

The causes of the decrease of economic functions of the family. The reason for the departure of economic production in general from households is the development of the factory, as is seen in the case of the cotton and woolen mills. The word factory is used to symbolize a large center of production with labor-saving machines run by mechanical power. Spinning and weaving went directly from the home to the factory almost within our memory. Similarly washing recently has gone, in part, to laundries. Prior to the factory system, many industries requiring special skills, for which home production was infrequently needed, such as the making of metal pots or horseshoes or wheels, had been developed outside the household.

The "factory" was able to win out over the household in production for several reasons, chief of which was the economy of mass production resting upon specialization and division of labor as well as upon mechanical power. More resistant to transfer from home to factory was the activity that could be done more cheaply or

9 Margaret G. Reid, *op. cit.*

conveniently at home, such as sweeping and the making of ice. In these two cases people took power-driven machines into the homes rather than taking these services outside. The invention of power machinery does not, therefore, automatically transfer an economic activity from home to factory. The outcome depends upon economy, convenience, and preference. Those services that require a large capital outlay, that are cheaper outside the home, or that are performed infrequently in the home tend to be the first to go.

The shrinking economic functions of the family have been viewed simply as a withdrawal from the household. They may be also viewed relatively, by comparing the economic production in and at the household with the production outside. Thus our cotton factories and steel mills and automobile companies represent great concentrated aggregations as compared to the economic production of any one family. A modern factory requires more workers than any one family or household can supply; though there were some plantations in the southern states that used many hundreds of slaves. By comparison, the shrinkage of the economic factors in the family seems very great indeed. It should also be remembered, in making this comparison, that not all the economic functions that have developed outside the home are transfers from the household. There has been a great proliferation of economic activities outside the home that were never in the home, such as banks and telephone exchanges.

We have been speaking largely of production. Consumption is also an economic function. The consumption of a single family as viewed by what the housewife and the husband purchase for the family is much increased for the average modern family over what it was for a pre-Industrial Revolution family.

Though the cause of the loss of economic functions by the family is technological, this influence is facilitated by the economic and social organization of urban life, that is, the city, and also by the organization of commercial farming.

Recreation. Play may be considered an essential activity. A life with only work and rest would be an abnormal one.

In very small communities of the past, if play was indoors it occurred in family dwellings since these were the only buildings. In other communities there was a clubhouse, a church, stores, and a school. But some recreation was out-of-doors, such as hunting, fishing, picnicking, et cetera. There appears also to have been a recreative factor in religion as in religious festivals or camp meetings of a religious nature, when there were no buildings big enough to hold the special congregation. But much recreation consisted of family visiting, particularly on Sunday. Travel was not considered recreation because of its discomforts. Children spent a good deal of time in play, and there was much visiting by children at one or another's home where they played in and around the dwelling place. There was also team play in vacant lots and also play in nearby fields and woods.

In modern cities the provision of recreation has become a business for profit with advertising appeals to take the members of the families as individuals to other places than home for recreation, as to motion picture houses, to ball parks, to sporting events in indoor arenas, to race tracks, to public dance halls, to museums, and to concerts. In crowded towns and cities, the government has tried to create in parks and playgrounds and in public school grounds the space that was available to families living in the open country or in small villages.

However, there remains family visiting and entertainment at meals or with refreshments at other times. No doubt some conversation over the telephone is recreational. There is cardplaying, also, in the home.

From these observations it appears that of the total time spent by the members of a family in recreation, proportionately more of it is spent outside the home than was true for the country homes and the village dwellings of a century or so ago. It may also be that more time is spent in recreation than formerly, for the need for recreation may be greater since much work is repetitive and monotonous for many hours per day in factories where there is the assembly line and minute division of labor. On family farms there was less speed and more diversification and perhaps less need for recreation. Also, the shorter work day and work week mean more time is available for recreation. Around 1910, 3 per cent of total consumption expenditures went for recreation, while in 1940 it was 4.5 per cent. This comparison does not distinguish between recreation at home and outside, but very probably most of the expenditure was for recreation away from home.[10]

However, these observations, while probably accurate a quarter

10 Dewhurst, *et al., op. cit.,* p. 280.

of a century ago, do not take into consideration the recent electrical developments in the communication inventions. Many of these are particularly suitable to the home; and, while they are also adapted to commercial establishments, they are most often found in homes. Especially important are the phonograph, the radio, and television (which brings the motion picture into the home). Then, too, the home with air conditioning winter and summer becomes a pleasant place in which to recreate.

The invention of the automobile has made some travel in private automobiles, especially for short distances, a recreation away from home. Some automobiling for pleasure still remains a family recreation, insofar as more than one member of the family goes on automobile pleasure trips.

We conclude, therefore, that in modern cities the function of family provision of recreation has lessened somewhat but that during the last few decades there has been a revival of some home recreations due largely to the electrical inventions, especially those in the transmission of sound and vision.

Recreations outside the home continue to grow faster than the number of households, as is shown in Table 19 which gives the percentage increase and decrease in the expenditure for recreation, in money of equal purchasing power, from 1929 to 1941. Of this list of recreations, twenty-five increased and seven decreased. Of those that increased over this period, all but three increased more than did the number of households, which increased about 17 per cent. Of this list, not all are recreations engaged in outside the home. Those that represent home recreations wholly or in part are book rentals, photography, magazines and newspapers, and nondurable toys, all of which increased. The ranking in this list is on the basis of the amount of money spent. A ranking based on number bought or time spent would probably not be greatly different except in the case of radios. The price of radios fell sharply during this period, so that a ranking based on number bought would show a higher ranking for radios. The reader should also be reminded that the table represents extent of increase or decrease and not extent of adoption. For instance, the theater is a recreation of long standing, while gambling machines are a new type of recreation.

T A B L E   19

*Increases and Decreases in
Consumer Recreational Expenditures, 1929–1941 ***

Class	Per Cent Increase Adjusted By Price Index
Gambling machines	1149.4
Horse and dog racing	779.0
Professional football	442.6
Stamps, coins	340.4
Sightseeing buses and guides	144.6
College football	98.0
Book rental and repairs	79.5
Photography	76.4
Billiards, pool, and bowling	74.5
Luncheon clubs	68.0
Professional hockey	64.5
School fraternities	61.9
Wheel goods, durable toys, sports equipment	44.9
Magazines and newspapers	43.3
Amusement devices and parks	42.3
Professional baseball	41.5
Dancing, riding, shooting, skating, and swimming	34.8
Pet purchases and veterinary care	26.4
Boats	25.5
Sports supplies, nondurable toys	25.2
Entertainments — nonprofit organizations	23.1
Motion pictures	20.7
Camp fees	13.9
Boat and bicycle rental, storage, and repair	8.8
Pianos and other musical instruments	6.9
Books	−2.9
Fraternal, patriotic, and women's organizations	−12.4
Golf fees and instruction	−19.0
Radios and phonographs	−20.3
Private flying operations	−23.2
Athletic and social clubs — dues and fees	−42.8
Theater and opera	−60.7

* J. Frederic Dewhurst & Associates, *America's Needs and Resources* (New York: The Twentieth Century Fund, 1947), p. 284. The percentages of increase or decrease in the above table were calculated from Dewhurst's figures to take into account the differences in the cost of living index between 1929 and 1941.

Causes of the lessening of the recreational function. The causes seem to lie in the growth of cities, that is, of populations living in close enough proximity to reduce play space around the dwellings and in large enough numbers to provide attendance at places of recreation. The power inventions seem to have had little to do with providing the new, appealing forms of recreation except as they have led to the growth of cities and have provided (a) transportation to and from places of recreation and (b) the manufacture of sporting equipment. Of course, the great growth of modern cities is a derivative effect of the power inventions used in factories and railroads. Nor is there very much machinery in many recreations, such as football, concerts, and the theater; though technology is employed in the motion pictures and in travel. On the other hand, technological developments associated with electricity are bringing some recreation back to the home.

Combat functions. Fighting, like playing, is a frequent activity of humans and other animals. It also occurs between groups. Combats between families are described by a special term, feuds, which have been very widespread. Though sometimes personal in origin, feuds are fed by rivalries and are related to family status. Not all such rivalry resulted in force and bloodshed. Often in feudal society the wars between local nobility stemmed from wars between families. The wealthy landowner had armed forces recruited from the families that worked on his land. But family wars in feudal times expanded quickly into wars of one group of families against another group. In the United States we had no feudalism; but in the early American colonies family households at times had to fight marauders such as Indians or lawless white men.

The combat function of families seems not to have been developed very much among the small families of the hunting era and during the times of agriculture based on the hoe or digging stick. The clan, which engaged in some rivalry, was based on a kinship system much larger than the biological family or the household.

The combat function was most highly developed in rural areas with the union of large landed property owners with a small private military system, before the rise of a strong central government with sovereignty over a large area, and national armies.

The family in modern cities has ceased altogether to be a warring group.

Causes of the disappearance of the combat function. The growth of the state as a law-enforcing body has been an important factor controlling combat between families. Law enforcement became possible with armies and police. With more populous settlements wars really outgrew the private forces that a family might command. Large populous communities seem to be unfavorable to the family combat function.

The strengthening of the judicial system was also a factor in the settlement of grievances between families, which had formerly been settled by violence.

The growth of the state which took over the function of warring is not readily traceable to any direct technological development, though the material factors affecting increased production and trade through transportation provided a basis for a larger aggregation of population over an extensive area. Modern rapid communication and transportation facilities help the government to exercise social control over large areas. There has been much written about the role of war in developing the state and government. In a sense big wars between states outlawed little wars.

The protective functions. Closely allied to the combat functions are those of protecting the members of the family in general and not merely against attack from a hostile family. This meant in a pioneer society protection from wild animals and in America from the Indians. The women and children were particularly thought of as needing protection. The aged required protection against want. Indeed, the family assumed toward its members and its kin who were in need as in sickness or poverty the services that in modern terminology are classed under the term "social work."

For the modern family these protective functions have been taken over in part by the government and in part by private charities. Thus the various social insurances for old age, for unemployment, for sickness, and for widows with children at home, are in large part governmental functions, though sometimes these services are rendered by private economic organizations outside the home, as insurance companies. Also the responsibilities of a family appear not to have as wide a coverage over kin as formerly.

Causes of the weakening of the protective functions. The protective functions of the family are several, and an inquiry as to causes can best be made by considering the functions one at a time. The care of old people by families in their homes is made difficult in cities by the pressure for space, the high cost of living in cities, and the absence of tasks which on farms old people can do to help pay for their support. When homes were, like small factories, centers of production, opportunity could be found for the labor of old people. Furthermore, the prestige of the elders was often rather great, and filial piety was stressed. Then, too, about 10 per cent of all men and women now reach the age of forty-five without ever having married and so have no children to look after them. In addition, it seems probable that with the great mobility of labor of modern times, children scatter to different cities; and the ties with older parents are lessened to a somewhat greater extent than if children lived near their parents.

Most of these conditions are traceable to the conditions of life in cities, though also to some extent to commercial farming in areas with good highways and not too far from cities. The increasing scarcity of children to care for old people has been discussed in other chapters and is due to a large degree to birth control.

The extension of the protective family covering to various kin is limited by these same forces of mobility that scatter the kin. Then, too, in the household economy, relatives could be given employment, especially in the United States where farms were large and labor was scarce. Relatives had rather close ties in sparsely settled areas. In cities the ties of friendship may often be much closer with persons who are not kin.

The weakening of family protective functions is also due to the fact that adequate protection is more readily furnished by organizations other than the family, as for instance, government or private charities or insurance companies. Thus police are often a better protection against robbers than is the head of the house. Governmental organization may furnish health protection better than members of the family. The growth of the welfare functions in the government and elsewhere offers a competition which perhaps encourages a lessening of these protective functions in the family.

The augmentation of each of the different functions of the welfare state has its separate cause. For example, unemployment insurance is historically connected with the incidence of great business depressions, which are one phase of business cycles. We do not know what causes business cycles, but they are a phenomenon of the businesses which followed upon the Industrial Revolution and are not found in the self-subsistence household economy, though famines may have produced worse fluctuations in rural areas.

In general the welfare state has grown because government has the coverage, the authority, and the ability to obtain funds and because the voters can vote for themselves these welfare assistances (though social insurance originated in Germany, which was at the time of Bismarck not a very strong democracy). It is questionable whether these democratic and executive functions can be traced back to significant technological inventions. The state has developed these protective functions partly because of the decline in the family and partly because government is a more effective social organization for performing them than is the family. Also the government wants the loyalty of the citizens, especially in periods of crisis.

Governmental functions. The family performs other governmental functions than those of combat and of protecting its members. The family disciplines its members, for instance. Such discipline is a correlative of child rearing; and husbands have also had the authority to punish their wives. These governmental functions are centered in the father and husband as head of the household. His authority in the household economy was somewhat like that of the manager of a factory, who is, so to speak, the head of a private government.[11]

In the modern city family this governing authority of the male head and of parents is much curtailed. For example, families are not permitted to do with their children as they like. The children cannot without acceptable cause be kept at home and away from school, nor are they permitted to work outside the home for pay if they are under a certain age. Wives are also protected by the police and the courts from physical violence. However, the government of children still remains with the family, except that it is shared in part by school teachers, truant officers, and juvenile courts.

[11] Beardsley Ruml, *Tomorrow's Business* (New York: Farrar & Rinehart, 1945).

Causes of the decline of family governing functions. Probably the greatest cause of the decrease of authority of the male heads of the household lies in the decrease in the economic functions. When the household was an economic enterprise, authority to give orders and insist on obedience was natural. But with the disappearance of these enterprises, authority and government in the family were not so much needed. Also as members of the family spent more time in schools and in places of work, the government of these members was shared with other institutions.

Lessening of religious functions. In the family life in the household economy, there were certain religious practices such as family prayers, reading aloud from the Bible, the saying of grace at meal time, and family attendance at religious meetings on Sundays. The centers of religious activities were generally outside the home in churches. In European countries the churches had a considerable organization that extended over different countries. There were cases, however, when a rich family had on the estate a chapel which was used by the servants, laborers, and nearby neighbors, and the priest was financed from the family funds. It was also considered highly desirable that husband, wife, and children all have the same religious faith.

In modern city families in the United States there are fewer of these religious practices and observances, particularly family prayers, family Bible readings, and grace at meals. It is still held undesirable for marriage partners to belong to different churches with widely divergent faiths, and most marriages are still performed by men of the cloth. It is difficult to obtain statistics on family attendance at church, but no doubt many husbands and wives continue to attend church together.

Causes of the reduction in religious family practices. The most probable hypothesis for the diminution in religious practices in the family is that it is part of a general secularization movement in the Western world which has been going on for centuries. At one time many activities were religious in character. Such were education, healing, government, art, philosophy. Prayers were used sometimes for economic success; consumption, including, for instance, what one could not eat, was under religious supervision, as were many customs regarding play, buying, and selling. Morals and religion were considered more or less the same.

The withdrawal of religious authority as such from many activities of life included the family. The secularization movement has been much discussed, and its explanation is complex. The movement was affected in many cases by scientific achievements which added knowledge that was different from the ideas held by organized religion, many of which belonged to pre-scientific times. Thus scientific medicine has proved generally more effective than many religious healing practices, such as visiting holy shrines, though religion still may have considerable efficacy in certain mental and psychosomatic ills. Specific religious attitudes and practices have been changed by discoveries in astronomy, anthropology, archaeology, biology, and psychology, even if these discoveries have not affected the religious spirit.

Mechanical invention does not appear to have been as closely associated with changes in religious customs as scientific discoveries, though in quite recent times, the automobile and the radio may have affected Sunday observance, and the activities of city life depending upon technology may have offered some competition to religious leaders.

The shifting of the educational function. In the household economy vocational education for boys and girls was on the farm and in the home. The teachers were the parents. Similarly, physical education was acquired in the tasks of daily life as well as by play in the yard. More formal learning as from books was not very extensive for many young people; and we have the school curriculum characterized by the expression "reading, 'riting, and 'rithmetic." Small one-room schoolhouses where children attended school were apart from the homestead. In wealthy families, school teachers called governesses or tutors were brought into the family; and formal instruction occurred in the family setting. Moral instruction and character training were duties of the parents.

At the present time, formal instruction from books is given outside the family. Children generally leave the family for school at six years of age, though (1950) about one in five attends school at five years of age. Nursery schools are probably growing in number, though the percentage of little children in nursery schools or kindergartens is quite small. Almost all children of elementary school age attend school. There is little physical or vocational education in homes except in rural areas.

Causes of the lessening share of the family in education. The transfer of physical production away from the homestead led to a reduction of vocational education in the family, a derivative result of the power inventions. The move of families from farms to towns and cities reduced the opportunities for physical education in the family.

For formal education the development of schools, particularly the widespread school system supported by the government, meant an organization that could perform the educational function better than the family could do it. Hence successful competition helped to lessen this function. The need for teaching outside the home resulted from the accumulation of knowledge, in large part a result of the growth of science.

The provision of schooling for every child was a social invention, but the extensive use of schools rested upon the existence of populous communities of some density, which were a derivative result of economic and technological factors. Also schools were dependent upon printing, which provided a great storehouse of learning and furnished the materials for instruction. Automobile transportation has helped to bring education to farming areas of low density.

Another cause of the reduction in the educational function of families is birth control. Families with no children do not exercise this function at all, that is, for children; and those families with few children exercise it quantitatively less than families with many children.

The change in the family function of adult education is due largely to the need for it which arises from the accumulation of knowledge, the complexity of social issues in a democracy and from the social change which makes some older substantive learning quickly out of date. These conditions are derivative in good part from the growth of science and technology. The introduction of adult education into the home is aided by the communication inventions, namely, the printing press, the radio, television, facsimile transmission, and the various transportation inventions.

Conclusion. Among primitive hunters and food gatherers, communities were quite small, often merely bands wandering slowly over a limited area. The population of such a band or community varied from a half dozen or score to perhaps two or three hundred persons, not all adults. In such a society, there could not be many different social organizations. In fact, the family was the outstanding one. Hence the many different functions by which people lived were performed by the family. In large cities today there are many special organizations to perform particular functions, such as recreation, worship, production, protection, and education. There are also in large communities many one-purpose organizations such as a bridge club, a child study group, or a camera club.

The performance of some of these functions that were in early times centered in the family is facilitated by the development of material culture. Thus the multiplication of the hand tools of the farmer or of traps and hunting implements of the hunter augmented production, though the religious function was little affected. With the growth of property, the adoption of the plow, and the domestication of animals, the economic activities of the family were many; and yet the families lived in places too small in population for many special purpose organizations to develop outside the family. For several thousand years the families of much of Europe lived in such a household economy. The family was thus an institution of power; and this power affected the other functions of protection, recreation, et cetera.

With the techniques of production improving and with transportation becoming better, communities were increasing in size, trade was growing, and some economic functions were being specialized outside the average family such as blacksmithing, metal working, et cetera. The process was speeded by water transportation, which created cities with large populations on rivers and the shores of seas, where there was a tendency after a lag for the family to lose functions.

The inventions of the steam engine and steelmaking gave a great impetus to the growth of large size communities, and these increased enormously the shift of functions from the family to other organizations. At the same time, new activities never carried on in the home have developed; and there has been a proliferation of special functions not found in the homestead of the household

economy. In short, there have been two noteworthy changes:
(a) a transfer of functions away from the family; and (b) an independent growth of functions outside the family.

Across the long stretch of time, the growth of material culture,
the development of transportation and trade with division of labor,
and the coming of large, densely populated communities led to
changes in family functions, though there may have been occa-
sional special exceptions.

In recent times, from the later stages of the household economy
to the era of large cities, most of the functions exercised by the
family, except the affectional function, have diminished in size or
activity, though not in importance, and are being performed by
other social organizations. These transfers are particularly observed in cities. There is reason to think that a diminution of family
functions of farm families is occurring more rapidly as commercial
farming develops and as the isolation of farming areas is lessened
by the facilities of transportation, though few studies have been
made which point this out.

Some of the family functions which are continuing to be transferred from the household are the processing of foods, sewing, the
protection of the members of the family, and possibly recreation.
At the same time, the economic function of consumption, as illustrated by marketing, appears to be increasing as a family activity.

The causes of these changes are the same as those that led to
the loss of functions such as spinning and weaving shortly after
the steam engine was put to use in factories, that is to say, technological invention and mass production, though there are various
other special factors, as for instance, the growth of the welfare
state and the influence of discoveries in science effecting changes
in protection and religious family practice, respectively.

The growth of factories means that the city has been an influential factor in family change. The large and dense population
in the cities has led government to assume responsibility for sani-
tation, housing, and other functions formerly exercised by the
family. Large populations are also a factor in many kinds of urban
recreation. The cities are thus a proximate cause of many family
changes; while back of the cities are the "once-removed" causes of
family changes, the transportation and communication inventions
which, together with the factories, made our urban society possible.

Some functions, minor expressions of a general category, may be increasing as family activities. Such are some recreations, as for example, those brought in by the electrical inventions of radio, television, phonograph, and electric light. For all recreations, it is difficult to strike a balance. Perhaps the trend may still be outward from the home. Some electrical inventions are either keeping a few economic activities in the home or are slowing up their departure, as for instance, laundering. The making of ice is a new productive invention brought into the home by electricity. The electrical and printing inventions are also retarding the departure of some educational functions from the family. The home continues to be the major center of affectional life, even though divorces are increasing.

As to the future, technological invention will be a factor in family change and particularly the economic advantages of mass production. Even so, some services such as the preparation of food and housecleaning are peculiarly adapted to the home. No dramatic changes to modify the general trend are foreseen at present.

7

More Working Wives

A century ago, when the United States was largely rural, the farmer and his wife formed an economic partnership, a joint productive team; and it would have been difficult to determine the precise contribution of each member to production, although the husband was the head of the household and the manager, so to speak, of the joint enterprise. This partnership was disturbed in industrial society because production was transferred from the home. In the early days of the Industrial Revolution in the United States, single women were employed in the textile mills in New England, but at marriage the women almost invariably stopped working and devoted themselves to the management of the home. The saying developed that a woman's place — that is, a married woman's place — was in the home. The farm wife's place, it may be noted, was not exactly in the home; it was in and about the home, since the homestead was on the farm.

In the last century, and especially during the last half-century, the economic role of married women has undergone further change as an increasing number have entered the labor force for pay. There has been for women a return in part to the conditions existing under farming. It is true that in contemporary America the usual arrangement is that the male head of the household provides the major portion of the family support. About three-fourths of all husbands in the middle of the twentieth century are the sole providers for their families; and where the wife adds to the income, her contribution is usually less than her husband's. But if one is interested in the changes that are taking place, one will emphasize the marked increase in the number of wives working for pay. Whereas the farmer and his wife jointly produce food and other goods, the trend is for husbands and wives to produce a joint income, although not from a joint enterprise.

144

One way of noting the change that has occurred in the last half century is to observe the increase in the per cent of the female labor force that is married. In 1890 married women comprised 13.9 per cent of the total female labor force; in 1940 the proportion had more than doubled (36.4 per cent); and during the 1940's the number of married women in the labor force grew to the point where it for the first time exceeded the number of single women, the proportion being 52.1 in 1950.[1] During the decade of the 1940's the proportions of single and married women in the labor force were just about reversed. The 1940's were years of unusual prosperity which led to early marriage and an unprecedented increase in marriage. In 1946 the marriage rate reached an all-time high. There were also about two million men in the armed forces, accentuating the demand for the labor of women. The 1940's constitute, therefore, in part at least, a special situation. But for the whole half-century under review, the trend of the employment of married women is unmistakably upward.

In the preceding paragraph the unit was the labor force, and we were interested in knowing what proportion of the total female labor force was married. If now we take the married female population and ask how many are employed outside the home, we find that in 1890 the percentage of married women engaged in gainful occupations was 4.6,[2] whereas in 1940, the figure was 16.8 per cent; and in 1950, 26.8 per cent.[3] About one in every twenty-two married women had a job in 1890, while sixty years later better than one in four had a job.

Factors in the Increased Employment of Married Women

Our principal concern in this chapter is the exploration of causes. Most women work because they want more income, whether it be

[1] The figure for 1890 relates to women fifteen years old and over in the labor force. *Abstract of the Fourteenth Census of the United States: 1920* (Washington, D.C.: U.S. Government Printing Office, 1923), Table 37. The figures for 1940 and 1950 pertain to women fourteen years of age and over in the labor force. *Current Population Reports-Labor Force*, P-50, No. 29, May 2, 1951.

[2] *Abstract of the Fourteenth Census of the United States: 1920* (Washington, D.C.: U.S. Government Printing Office, 1923), Table 36.

[3] *Current Population Reports-Labor Force*, P-50, No. 29, May 2, 1951, Table 4.

because they need more income or desire a higher standard of living. Some women take jobs in order to be engaged in interesting work; and a relatively few, mainly in the professions, work also because of a desire for prestige. There is an inverse relation between the percentage of employed married women and the income of their husbands. In urban areas in the United States in 1951, about one-third of the wives whose husbands had incomes under $3,000 were in the paid labor force, as compared with about one-seventh where the husbands' incomes were $10,000 or more.[4] At the lowest income levels, the wife's wages more than double the family income, whereas at the higher income levels her contribution is proportionately much less.

Women work mainly for the same reasons that men do: because they have to, or because they want to enjoy a higher standard of living, or because they enjoy their work, or because they want prestige. The reasons for working are in part the same for both sexes but not the number who are motivated by such reasons. More men work because they must, because they are expected to be the breadwinners. A woman is more likely to work before she marries; a man afterwards. In the middle of the twentieth century, every other single woman was a worker as compared with less than one in four married women. On the other hand, better than nine out of ten married men are in the labor force as compared to about three out of five single men.

The foregoing discussion tells us why women work, but it does not tell us why the proportion of working women has increased. Economic need and the desire for a higher standard of living are factors in employment, but they are not factors in the increase in employment. Among wives who now work for pay, the factor of financial need is less acute than it used to be. This inference can probably be drawn from the facts that (a) there has been an increase in employment and real wages for men in recent decades and (b) there has been an increase in the number of families with both husband and wife employed. Both partners were employed in 11 per cent of all normal families in April, 1940, whereas in February, 1946, the figure was 18 per cent, and by the end of the

4 Bureau of the Census, *Current Population Reports-Consumer Income,* Series P–60, No. 12. "Family Income in the United States: 1951," June, 1953, Table D.

1940's it was about 20 per cent.[5] Also labor force participation increased among married women at all income levels from 1940 to 1952.[6]

The increase in working wives cannot then be explained in terms of increased financial need. Can it be accounted for by an increase in the desire for a higher standard of living? If more married women work because of a desire for a higher standard of living, is this a new factor? Have not married women always wanted better homes, better clothes, better food, better education for their children, more money for travel, and the like? The desire for a higher standard of living probably has not varied much and is a relatively constant factor. If it is a constant factor, it cannot be a cause of the change in the employment of married women.

What has changed is (a) an increase in the opportunities for jobs open to married women and (b) a decrease in the ties that bind married women to the home, making it easier for them to take work outside the home. The jobs may be regarded as positive factors, as attractions that exert a pull, taking married women out of the home. The responsibilities that married women have at home may be regarded as negative factors (from the standpoint of outside employment), as obstacles to employment. The removal of obstacles makes it easier for married women to respond to the appeal of the paying job. In addition, there may be certain annoyances in the situation of the household which constitute a push from behind. In the paragraphs that follow, we wish to examine in more detail these classes of causes: the pulls, the pushes, and the obstacles to be overcome. We turn first to a discussion of the obstacles to the employment of married women.

The Removal of Obstacles

Smaller families. One of the most effective obstacles to the employment of married women is the presence of small children in the

[5] Bureau of the Census, *Employment Characteristics of Families in the United States: February, 1946. Population*, Series P–S, No. 20, March 12, 1947. Paul C. Glick, "Family Life and Full Employment," *American Journal of Sociology*, 54: 528, May, 1949. In March, 1950, wives were in the labor force in 20.9 per cent of the cases where the husband was also in the labor force and employed. *Current Population Reports–Labor Force*, P–50, No. 29, May 2, 1951, Table 6.

[6] Bureau of the Census, *Family Income in the United States: 1951*, p. 4.

home. Therefore, the reduction in the size of families in recent decades is an important factor in the increased employment of wives. To trace the change that has occurred in the working role of women is instructive. The dominant pattern in the past was for a girl to work from the time she left high school until she married. With marriage she gave up her job and concentrated on managing her home and raising a family. Later, when her children were in school, she might return to the labor force, or she might return to work because of divorce, widowhood, or economic necessity. The new pattern that is developing is somewhat different. More women continue to work after marriage. That is to say, marriage does not so often interrupt the work experience. The arrival of a child does so, but not marriage itself. The chances (1950) are about fifty-fifty that a girl who marries will also have a job, and continue to keep it. At the end of the first year of marriage, the chances are one in three that she will be working; and they are one in five if she has been married two to nine years.[7] A large majority of the latter are at home, caring for young children. A wife is most likely to work, if she does, between thirty-five and forty-four years of age, because her children are in school or have grown up and left home. For the above reasons, the main increase in working wives in the past decade or so has been in the middle and older age groups. Only a relatively small increase has occurred in the employment of married women in their twenties and early thirties, for these are the ages of child-bearing and child-rearing.

The working of women is closely related to the number and age of their children. As the number of children increases, the per cent of wives in the labor force decreases. The age of children is an important factor, especially if they are of pre-school age. In normal families in 1950 (women living with their husbands) the chances were about one in eight that the mother would be working if she had children under six, whereas the chances were a little better than one in three if she had no children under six. If mothers have children of school age, this tends to cut down their chances of employment somewhat as compared with mothers having no children of school age living at home, but the difference is

<hr />

[7] Paul C. Glick, *Population Changes: Their Effect on Children and Youth* (Paper presented at the Midcentury White House Conference on Children and Youth), Washington, D.C., December 4, 1950.

not great. The per cent in the labor force is about the same for wives in normal families with children under eighteen but none under six as it is for wives with no children under eighteen.

The increase in the proportion of married women employed is, we conclude, made possible in part by the decrease in the size of family. This decrease was described in an earlier chapter, where the reasons for the decrease were also set forth.[8] Prominent among these reasons we noted the growth of an urban society, which in turn has depended on developments in technology. The decrease in the size of family is, then, an immediate or proximate cause of the increase in working wives; the growth of cities is a once-removed cause; and technological changes which gave us more cities is a twice-removed cause. Birth control is also a direct cause of the decrease in family size and therefore a once-removed cause of the increase in working wives.

We have evidence that married women do not now have as many children as previously and they more often take jobs. The argument of the preceding paragraphs was that married women who want to work more often do so than in the past, whether because of need, desire for a higher standard of living, or satisfaction in the work itself. But young children, where present, constitute an obstacle. The obstacle is removed by reducing the size of the family.

The above argument implies, perhaps, that married women tend to want to work and do not tend to want a larger family; or they want work more than they want more children. It might be argued by some that married women actually prefer children to work, and work only because they do not have more children, as a compensation or secondary satisfaction. If so, we would still have to account for their not having more children. The evidence suggests that they do not have more children because they want a higher standard of living for self and family, and a job makes this possible. In which case they do work and do not have more children for the same reason, namely, the desire for a higher standard of living. The desire for a higher standard of living is probably a relatively constant factor and hence cannot be a cause of the change in the employment of married women. What is new is the reduction in the size of the family which makes taking a job easier.

[8] Chapter 5.

Removal of obstacles: less work at home. When the responsibilities of married women at home are reduced by virtue of their having fewer babies, the mothers are freer to take jobs. Each child that a modern mother does have, moreover, may require less of the mother in the way of time and attention for physical care than was the case, say, a century ago. Processed foods for the child can be purchased, as can the child's clothes. They do not have to be made at home as was true in earlier times. There are machines which make the washing of the child's clothes a simpler chore than if the clothes have to be washed by hand. How much saving in time modern technology affords, where there are young children, has not been determined; but the gain would seem to be offset by the greater personal attention accorded children in our time. Studies [9] show that the conception of the good mother held by the lower class emphasizes physical care whereas that of the middle class emphasizes companionship. The general feeling is that mothers of pre-school children should not work outside the home unless required by financial need. This is in fact the official position of the Children's Bureau of the United States Department of Labor,[10] which even during World War II discouraged the employment of mothers of pre-school children. Still, if mothers of young children have to work or wish to work, the decision is made easier by virtue of the fact that the physical care of the children has been simplified by modern technology. Also there may be day nurseries or nursery schools to help look after the children. In the latter innovations the technological factor is not great.

The reproductive function is only one of several family functions which have been curtailed in recent times. There is now less production in the home, less protection by family members, less schooling, less religious education than before. This means there is less to do at home and more time and energy for outside activities, including jobs for married women. Those with small families or no children at all obviously have more free time than the women of a century or so ago with their large families. But since functions have been transferred from the home, even those with large families today have fewer demands made upon them by the home

[9] Evelyn Duvall, "Conceptions of Parenthood," *American Journal of Sociology,* 52: 193–203, November, 1946.

[10] See Release CB42–523, *Policies Regarding the Employment of Mothers of Young Children in Occupations Essential to National Defense.*

than was the case in earlier times. The causes of the reduction of household functions were examined in the preceding chapter, where it was shown that the technological influence was great, especially in the transfer of economic activities from the home.[11]

The decline in the economic functions of the home was due to the growth of factories, stores, offices, banks, and the like in the community. These new services outside the home meant, of course, the opportunity for a great many new jobs. So the transfer of functions from the home to outside agencies is in part responsible for the employment of women. Women have jobs because there is more work to be done away from home and less work to be done at home. They do not have less to do at home because they have jobs. The economic organization and the technological developments of modern times came first and led to the diminution of home tasks.

How much simpler housekeeping is today than it was a century ago is not always appreciated. We are told that Boston in 1860 with a population of 175,000 had only 31,000 sinks, 4,000 bathtubs, and 10,000 water closets.[12] Nearly a century later, in 1950, 85.4 per cent of all urban occupied dwelling units in the United States had hot and cold running water inside the house, 92.4 per cent had flush toilets, and 88.7 per cent had a bathtub or shower.[13] It is particularly in the cleaning tasks (laundering, ironing, dishwashing, sweeping, and cleaning) that the burdens of the household have been lightened. In this emancipation the role of electric power has been striking. Most of the modern appliances were available, at least in crude form, a century ago. It is claimed that the modern-type washing machine was mechanically developed in simple form as early as 1869, but what held back its widespread use was the lack of a cheap and dependable source of power.[14] The invention of the small-sized, small horsepower electric motor which we find in household appliances and the development of the electric utility industry relate, of course, to technological factors.

[11] Chapter 6.

[12] Edgar W. Martin, *The Standard of Living in 1860* (Chicago: University of Chicago Press, 1942).

[13] Bureau of the Census, *1950 Census of Housing — Preliminary Reports,* Series HC–5, No. 1, February 17, 1951.

[14] Siegfried Giedion, *Mechanization Takes Command* (New York: Oxford University Press, 1948), Part IV: "Mechanization Encounters the Household."

An interesting question is whether married women have more leisure time because of labor-saving devices and whether this makes it easier for them to take jobs outside the home. The amount of time saved by labor-saving devices in the home need not be great. A study in the 1920's among rural and farm housewives found that those without labor-saving devices spent only about two per cent more time in doing their household chores than those with such devices.[15] The explanation is that the standards of performance may be raised when new equipment is used; the speed of work may be slowed down, and help previously given by other members of the household may be dispensed with. It may take less time and energy to do the family wash in an electric washing machine than to do it in a tub by hand; but if owning the machine means that the wash is done more often, there may be no net saving of time and energy. This may be the significance of a Bryn Mawr finding that the average city housewife spends more time in housekeeping than does the average farm woman.[16] The report indicates that in a typical farm family housekeeping activities consumed 60.55 hours a week; in households in cities under 100,000 population, 78.35 hours; and in households in cities of over 100,000 population, 80.57 hours. The farm woman has more varied household and out-of-the-home duties and might therefore be expected to devote less time to housekeeping.

That the standard of housekeeping has, in certain respects, been raised is suggested by the report that in colonial times "the household wash was allowed to accumulate, and the washing done once a month, or in some households once in three months."[17]

While most married women may not use household appliances to effect a net saving of time and energy, the fact remains that the appliances can be so used. If she wants to, a woman can use the appliances to save time and energy. In this connection it would be interesting to compare a matched sample of working and nonworking women in respect to the use they make of household appliances. It is likely that those who work use the appliances to effect a saving of time and effort.

15 Margaret Reid, *Economics of Household Production* (New York: John Wiley & Sons, Inc., 1934).
16 Margaret Mead, *Male and Female* (New York: William Morrow & Co., 1949), p. 332.
17 Alice Morse Earle, *Home Life in Colonial Days* (New York: The Macmillan Company, 1898), p. 255.

Among the inventions that save labor for the housekeeper, we must not overlook central heating (especially automatic heating of houses and water), and aids in cooking such as pressure cookers and concentrated and frozen foods. It is said that the relative lack of such facilities in England makes housekeeping in that country more often a full-time job.[18] In England and in many other countries, the heating of rooms individually rather than by a central system is still the usual practice, whereas in the United States in 1950 every other occupied dwelling had central heating.[19] What part household conveniences play in the employment of married women has not been ascertained, but the greater abundance of such facilities in the United States is doubtless a factor in the high rates of employment of married women in this country. Since household conveniences make it easier to take a job, an increase in facilities tends to increase employment of women. Household conveniences, however, are only one of a number of factors influencing the employment of women, and may be offset by other factors.

Removal of obstacles: public opinion. Unfavorable public opinion toward the employment of married women is an obstacle to the employment of married women. Therefore, any change in the direction of a more favorable opinion, such as has occurred in recent times, tends to increase the employment of married women by removing an obstacle. The traditional attitude toward women working was hostile, expressed in the saying that woman's place is in the home. This traditional attitude has undergone several modifications. The first was to permit women to work before marriage. This modification of the traditional attitude has progressed to the point where many feel that it is not only permissible but desirable for a woman to work before marriage. "A woman should work before she marries" is the consensus of a sample of college students and their mothers.[20] The reasons for holding this position are not given; but presumably it is felt that working before marriage helps to mature a woman, gives her a keener appreciation of the man's role in the workaday world, and gives her experience

[18] *Marriage Guidance* (A monthly bulletin published by the National Marriage Guidance Council, London), Vol. 3, No. 10, April, 1950, pp. 6–7.

[19] Bureau of the Census, *1950 Census of Housing: Preliminary Reports,* Series HC–5, No. 2, June 10, 1951.

[20] Arlene Sheeley, Paul H. Landis, and Vernon Davies, *Marital and Family Adjustment in Rural and Urban Families of Two Generations* (Bulletin No. 506: The State College of Washington, May, 1949), p. 25.

in managing money. The traditional view that woman's place is in the home is modified by some of the exponents of the foregoing view to read that woman's place is in the home if she is married. But the more recent trend, as we have seen, is for more married women to work. So the traditional position has been still further modified to read that woman's place is in the home if she has small children. That seems to be the current view. A woman may, with approval, work after she marries and until she has children. The developing pattern is for the wife to drop out of the labor force when the baby comes, then return to work after the children are grown up, if she can find a job. Less than one-fifth of the wives are at work after five years of marriage. Working may help to make early marriage possible and the reduction in the size of family makes it easier to return to work. A consequence of these changes is that there are more older women workers, and a larger percentage of all older workers are women. In 1900, 7 per cent of women in the labor force were forty-five years of age and over; and in 1950, 31 per cent, as the accompanying chart shows.

As to the reasons for these changes in public attitudes toward working women, it appears that an important cause is the increas-

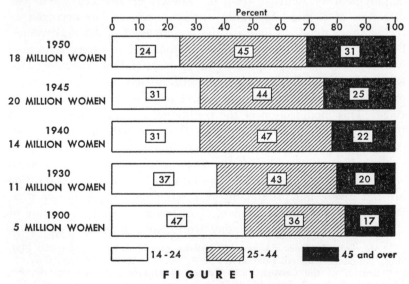

FIGURE 1

Age of Women in the Labor Force
(Source: Women's Bureau, United States Department of Labor)

ing impersonalization of human relations, which results in a more indifferent attitude toward the behavior of others. This impersonalization is, of course, associated with the urban community and results from the great density of population. In a simple community where numbers are few, the members of the group are well acquainted with one another. They know who is married and who is not, and they know who works and who does not. In a large city, neighbors are often strangers to one another and therefore indifferent to one another's behavior. The city brings more freedom, and one of the freedoms is the right to work. The city itself is, of course, mainly the product of technological influence.

We need to pursue a bit further the notion that changing ideologies are a factor in the greater employment of married women. It is apparent that if the public sentiment toward married women's working is more favorable, it will be easier for married women to work; and, all things being equal, more married women will work. A change in ideology is therefore a cause of increased employment. But this statement is not entirely satisfactory, for we still have to account for the change in sentiment. Why the more favorable public opinion? This must be because of a change in the social situation. The increase in working women who are unmarried led in the main to no unfavorable consequences. This encouraged the employment of more married women. So there is a greater acceptance of the employed married woman, despite the lag in the ideology that holds that woman's place is in the home.

The greater freedom in cities and the reduction in the size of family are not the only reasons for the more favorable public opinion regarding the employment of women. Jobs and working conditions have become more attractive, and these changes have not been without influence on public opinion. For there is a good deal of public concern about protecting women, which has been enacted into legislation; and if the jobs open to women become more attractive, there is less apprehension about their working. On changes in women's work, more later.

The employment of married women is bolstered by the recent findings of social science research that working after marriage does not seem to interfere with marital happiness. No significant difference was reported between the marital adjustment of wives who are engaged in full-time employment and those who are engaged in full-time homemaking. Nor was any difference found in the marital adjustment of the husbands of the two groups of wives.[21] An earlier study [22] reported that what seems to matter is not alone whether or not the wife works but whether she wants to work or not. Married women who work and want to, and those who don't work and don't want to, make better marital adjustments in general than those who work but don't want to, and those who don't work but want to. These research findings are probably not widely known and have not exerted much of an influence to date.

Push from Behind

Dissatisfaction with domestic roles. The decision to take a job is made easier, if, in addition to the pull from ahead — by virtue of the attraction of the job — there is a push from behind because one is dissatisfied with what one is doing. A push, it should be noted, differs from an obstacle, which is something that stands in the road that one would like to travel. A woman may not be able to take a job because she has a child to look after, in which case the child is an obstacle. This is true even if she enjoys looking after the child, if the mother wants to work. But if she dislikes caring for the child, her motivation is different; and she has a push from behind, which may prompt her to seek some way of avoiding the responsibility of child care. A job may be the way out.

There is evidence of widespread dislike for household chores on the part of middle-class women in modern industrial societies. A study [23] of the English housewife's working day reports that the jobs which occupy the greater part of the day are cooking (30 per cent), cleaning (30 per cent), and washing (13 per cent). Cleaning and washing are the most objectionable chores, especially clothes-washing and dish-washing.

The question arises as to whether dissatisfaction with housekeeping is a constant factor, in which case it could not be a cause of a change, namely, the tendency of more married women to take jobs. But dissatisfaction with domestic duties is probably a changing

---

[21] Harvey J. Locke and Muriel Mackeprang, "Marital Adjustment and the Employed Wife," *The American Journal of Sociology*, 54: 536-38, May, 1949.

[22] Ernest W. Burgess and Leonard S. Cottrell, *Predicting Success or Failure in Marriage* (New York: Prentice-Hall, Inc., 1939).

[23] Reported in *Family Life* (Los Angeles: The American Institute of Family Relations), Vol. 8, No. 3, March, 1947, p. 5.

factor, and there is more discontent than there used to be over having to keep house. When there were few or no jobs available to women, women were probably more reconciled to their domestic roles. But with more jobs and better jobs available, the domestic roles are sometimes thought to suffer by comparison. The possibility of dissatisfaction is increased where choices exist between domesticity and a job. In a similar vein, Bertrand Russell [24] has observed that democracy and opportunity lead to envy.

The relatively low social esteem accorded housekeeping is reflected in the status of domestic service, the largest single occupation for women. The occupation carries little prestige and is often among the most poorly paid. There has been an increase in pay and recognition of domestics in recent years, in connection with the attempt to organize the field and to set up standards of employment and performance. But it is doubtful that the position of domestics relative to other employed persons has changed much. This may be a factor in the decline in the number of women employed as domestic service workers, a decline which amounted to 21 per cent from 1940 to 1949, the largest decrease recorded for any occupational group. During the same interval, the number of women employed in all occupations increased 37 per cent.[25] That women tend to leave jobs as domestic servants when other jobs become available is shown by the experience of the war years of the 1940's when the demand for labor was great. The percentage of women workers who were domestics dropped from eighteen in 1940 to nine in 1945, the peak war year, and rose only to ten in 1950 when jobs were still plentiful.

The dissatisfaction of women with housekeeping as a full-time activity is probably associated in part with the education of women in schools. In public schools offering instruction in home economics, about three-fourths of the girls are enrolled in such courses in the seventh and eighth grades. The rate falls off progressively as we go up the educational ladder, until less than one-fourth of the girls in grade twelve are registered in home economics courses.[26] It may be noted that in the process of ascending the educational

[24] *The Conquest of Happiness* (New York: Liveright, 1930).
[25] Women's Bureau, *Handbook of Facts on Women Workers,* Bulletin No. 237, p. 3.
[26] *Home Economics in Public High Schools* (U.S. Office of Education, Vocational Division Bulletin No. 213, Home Economics Education Series No. 24, 1941), p. 39.

ladder, certain other subject-matter begun in the early years is not discontinued: for example, English. It is argued that instruction in the liberal arts makes for wives who are good companions, and this may be so. The question under consideration here is: does the type of education we furnish girls make them better satisfied or less satisfied to "just keep house"? On the college level, homemaking skills are even less emphasized, and the number of young women attending college has greatly increased in recent decades. Most women, college and non-college, become homemakers. But, as Margaret Mead has acutely observed, their attitude toward homemaking is often apologetic; and when asked what they are doing, many will say they are "just keeping house" or "just staying home" or even that they are "not doing anything." "If a woman has a doctorate and is a homemaker," says Margaret Mead, "she will definitely say that she is not doing anything. She may be taking care of four children in the country and doing all the family washing, but she will still say that she is not doing anything." [27]

It has been observed that among the possible roles that married women may play in our culture, the more conspicuous ones are those of glamour girl, domestic, and good companion. [28] The domestic role is the traditional one, and the good companion represents the newer trend. But if the observations of the preceding paragraph are correct, and modern women, when asked what they are doing, say they are "just keeping house," it would appear that they are less mindful of their role as "good companions" than they are of their domestic role and they are not particularly happy over the latter.

The Pull from Ahead

Jobs. It has been noted that the increased dissatisfaction with household duties stems in no small measure from the increasing availability and appeal of jobs for women. Moreover, it is obvious that if no jobs were available, regardless of the attitude of women toward their homemaking responsibilities, there would be no

[27] Margaret Mead, "What is Happening to the American Family?" *Journal of Social Casework*, Vol. 28, No. 9, November, 1947, p. 327.

[28] Talcott Parsons, "Age and Sex in the Social Structure of the United States," *American Sociological Review*, 7: 604–16, 1942.

women at work. The increased employment of women is made possible then by the existence of more jobs that are open to them. It is illuminating to compare the situation in earlier times with the situation today. Consider the situation before the opening of the factories in the United States. A distinguished visitor to the United States, Harriet Martineau, recorded that there had been but three resources available to women: teaching, needlework, and keeping boarding houses or hotels. "Now (1836)," she wrote, "there are the mills; and women are employed in printing offices as compositors as well as folders and stitchers." She also spoke of women in domestic service and shoe binding. Some other types of occupations provided jobs for women, but the number was not large.[29] Today, instead of Harriet Martineau's brief list, women may choose from among nearly all of the 451 types of jobs that are listed by the Bureau of the Census. The nine occupations in which women were not employed, according to the Census report of 1940, were the following: railroad conductors, baggagemen, locomotive engineers, locomotive firemen, railroad and car shop mechanics and repairmen, railroad brakemen, railroad switchmen, firemen in fire departments, and soldiers, sailors, marines, and coast guards. By 1951, women had penetrated all but two of these occupations, namely, locomotive engineers and locomotive firemen.[30] In addition to these new fields, certain traditional fields of work for women have shown considerable growth; for instance, the number of school teachers who were women increased from 57 per cent in 1880 to 81 per cent in 1948.[31]

Jobs for women are not only more numerous but also more attractive, from the standpoint of both pay and working conditions; and this is probably an additional factor in the increase in working women, since there is in our culture a tradition against exposing women to hazardous and/or unhealthful work. Shorter hours of work, better pay, and more comforts at work are shared by women along with men; but they are probably greater incentives to women. In these gains, labor unions have played some part, and the per cent of all union members that are women increased

[29] Women's Bureau, *Women's Jobs: Advance and Growth*, Bulletin No. 232 (Washington, D.C.: U.S. Government Printing Office), 1949.

[30] Information supplied by the Women's Bureau, United States Department of Labor, in letter to the authors dated October 17, 1951.

[31] *World Almanac*, 1951, p. 580.

from 3.6 in 1910 to 21.8 in 1944.[32] There is still room for improvement according to standards set up by the Women's Bureau of the United States Department of Labor. The Women's Bureau, for instance, has recommended maternity clauses in union contracts to protect the rights of married workers by guaranteeing them leave for childbearing. Surveys by the Bureau during World War II showed that scarcely one war plant in twenty made such provision for motherhood.

The availability of more jobs for women helps to explain why more women work, but it does not tell us why there has been a relatively greater increase in employment among married women. A decrease in the proportion of single women to married women in the population might have been expected to result in a decline in the size of the labor force. The only demographic factor working the other way was the decrease in fertility of married women, freeing them for jobs. Since 1900, the increase in the female labor force has been mainly in the age group of forty-five and over; and there has been a decrease in the percentage of women fourteen to twenty-four years old who are employed. The population, both male and female, has been getting older; but the change has more significance for the employment of women, since the decline in fertility means that the birth of the last child now generally takes place in the late twenties, so that women over forty-five are freer to take jobs. It appears that demographic factors have not been mainly responsible for the increase in working women, and that the gain must be charged instead for the most part to socio-economic factors like those we have been considering in this chapter.[33]

Modern war as a special pull. Because it takes fathers, husbands, and sweethearts away, war is abhorrent to most women, yet war is one of their best friends in opening up jobs to them, as shown in Table 20. The reason for this is the greatly increased demand for military goods and the decreased supply of male workers who are recruited for the armed forces. The demand for civilian goods and services also remains high because of the prevailing prosperity. Because of the scarcity of labor, there is a relaxation of taboos

[32] Gladys Dickason, "Women in Labor Unions," *Annals of the American Academy of Political and Social Science*, 251: 70–78, May, 1947.

[33] S. L. Wolfbein and A. J. Jaffe, "Demographic Factors in Labor Force Growth," *American Sociological Review*, 11: 392–6, August, 1946.

against the employment of women; new jobs are opened up to them and old jobs are multiplied. Wives are motivated to take jobs during wartime by (a) financial need, especially in the case of servicemen, since the rate of remuneration in the armed forces is in many instances below that which was earned in civilian life; (b) the psychological need for activity, particularly on the part of wives of servicemen away from home; and (c) the appeal to patriotism.

The relaxation of the taboos against the employment of married women during wartime means that in such a crisis there is often a contradiction between the official ideology as to woman's place and the reality. Thus under Hitler, woman's place was supposed to be in the home: the three "K's" for women were listed as Kinder, Kirche, and Kuchen (children, church, and kitchen). Actually the demands for labor were so great, and the shortage of males so great, that a larger percentage of married women was employed in Hitlerian Germany than in the United States, despite the more favorable ideology in the latter country.[34] The ideology regarding woman's place is a factor that limits her employment, but the ex-

T A B L E 20

Women in the Labor Force before, during, and after World War II *

	Total Number (Millions)	Per cent of all women 14 years old and over	Per cent of total labor force
March, 1940	14	29	26
December, 1941 (Attack on Pearl Harbor)			
July, 1944 (War peak)	21	39	36
September, 1950	19	34	29

* Data from Women's Bureau, *Women as Workers* (*A Statistical Guide*), September, 1950.

34 Clifford Kirkpatrick, *Nazi Germany: Its Women and Family Life* (Indianapolis: The Bobbs-Merrill Company, 1938), p. 204.

perience of Nazi Germany shows that ideology may give way before material conditions.

After a war, there is some reduction in the per cent of married women workers, but the number does not return to the level that existed before the war. Following a war there is ordinarily some lessening of prosperity, hence a lessened demand for goods and workers, while demobilization releases additional men to the labor market. Some jobs are wiped out and, in others, opposition develops to the employment of women. But as Table 20 shows, the level of female employment is likely to remain above its pre-war level because (a) many women who took jobs during the war are loath to relinquish the higher standard of living that the jobs make possible and (b) many employers prefer to retain the women because of lower labor costs and more efficient production in certain types of work. Other changes in the situation of the male laborers make it easier for the females to be retained, such as the retirement of males from the labor force at an earlier age and enrollment of more males in educational programs of various kinds. As an illustration, a recent survey of bank officials — jobs traditionally held by men — showed that in 1950 there were 6,013 women bank officers in the United States and its possessions. During the war years the number of women bank officers increased spectacularly from 4,605 in 1944 to 5,656 in 1945.[35]

Urbanization and jobs for women. Jobs for women are located for the most part in the cities, and so we look to the cities for an explanation of the increase in the employment of women. There we find the growth of factories, shops, stores, offices, and other places of work furnishing an increasing number of jobs. On farms, women are mainly unpaid family labor; and there are only a few paid jobs like housekeeping and teaching school. In 1949 there were, in addition, on farms in the United States, about half a million farm heads and farm workers who were women. Compare this with more than four and a half million clerks and kindred workers, and with more than three and a half million operatives and laborers who were women.[36] In 1900, when the nation was less

[35] *Women in Banking,* compiled by the Association of Bank Women from the 1950 edition of the Rand McNally *Bankers' Directory.*

[36] *Current Population Reports, Labor Force,* P–57, No. 103, February 16, 1951, p. 11.

highly urbanized, the paid occupations with the greatest numerical importance for women were agriculture and domestic and personal service.

How urbanization is related to occupations for women may be shown as follows. In 1870, the year of the first federal census of occupations in the United States, there were only 13,369 women who were employed as clerical workers. In 1950, less than a century later, there were more than four and one-half million, about a 340-fold increase. More than a quarter of all employed women (26.4 per cent) are clerical workers, that is, stenographers, typists, secretaries, file clerks, bookkeepers, cashiers, telephone and telegraph operators, and office machine operators. An additional 18.7 per cent in 1950 were operatives or semi-skilled factory workers mainly engaged in the manufacture of textile and food products. Service workers other than domestic servants (mainly waitresses and beauticians) constituted 12.6 per cent of the total, and professional and semi-professional workers comprised 10.8 per cent. What produced these changes was (a) the great growth of industry, requiring mass production, extensive written and oral communications, and accurate record-keeping, (b) a corresponding growth of government, and (c) a commensurate development of service occupations and the professions. The typewriter, the office file, and the telephone revolutionized the opportunities for women, for they created jobs in which the greater physical strength of men was not a factor, while putting a premium on finger dexterity and verbal facility in which women excel. The growth of government gave considerable impetus to the need for clerical workers, and in addition, through the extension of public education and public health programs, increased the demand for teachers and nurses, who together account for over three-fourths of all professional and semi-professional women workers. The growth of industry and government has been mainly in urban areas, and it is here that jobs for women have multiplied.

There is another way in which the city serves to facilitate the employment of married women, and that is through the rendering of extensive social services. Residents of an urban area get certain facilities in modern times as a kind of unearned increment, that is, merely because of their residence in an area of concentrated population. Families with the same amount of income in rural areas do not to the same extent have the benefits of such facilities as paved streets, sewer systems, piped-in water, electric lights, public transportation, and telephone lines, which make it much easier for married women to combine housekeeping with jobs. For example, out of every 100 dwelling units in the United States in 1950 only about three lacked electric lights in urban areas as compared with about twenty-two on farms. Many of these public services are furnished gratis by the city, or at reduced costs, since they are supported through taxation; and not all the recipients are taxpayers, nor do they always pay their proportionate share. In addition, the city makes available restaurants, delicatessens, laundromats, cleaning and dyeing establishments, which lighten the burden of housekeeping and make easier the taking of a job.

The technological basis of cities is obvious. Many cities depend on manufacturing, but even where trade and services are the mainstays of urban life, technological developments make the large-scale operations possible; and large aggregations of people cannot live together in a limited area without transportation and communication.

From household economy to factory economy. The significant change in the situation we have been considering is not so much that, over time, more married women are gainfully employed as that they are employed outside the family. Women have long had work to do other than their domestic duties; but the work was centered in or about the home, and the family was the locus of these activities. In a farming economy, women are generally unpaid family labor. In the period of middle industrialization, the work of women is an important factor; but the work is centered in the home. In Japan, for instance, in recent decades, the family has been the nucleus of much industrial and commercial activity. In 1930, 47 per cent of the married women were reported as gainfully employed, with 95 per cent of these working in family shops, household manufacturing, or agriculture, and about one-third of the total number consisting of unpaid family help.[37]

The significance of the change in the locus of women's employment as it has occurred in the Western world is that the family is less the mainstay of economic support. This change has the effect

[37] Irene B. Taeuber, "Family, Migration, and Industrialization in Japan," *American Sociological Review,* 16: 149–56, April, 1951.

of weakening the authority of the family. Women may marry less for economic reasons and more for reasons of affection and companionship. Since they may help to provide income, they can also marry earlier. These changes have already been noted in preceding chapters. In a later chapter, we shall consider as an additional consequence the greater fragility of marriage and the greater ease in getting a divorce.

Some observers have pointed out that modern middle-class wives have less well-defined roles than their husbands, and less clearly defined roles than women in the past.[38] There is some opposition to work outside the home for married women, and women are not so serious about careers as men. If they work, they often expect to stop work sooner. The difficulty appears to lie in the conflict between the feminine and masculine components of women's roles. Much of the difficulty, however, can be accounted for in terms of lag, that is, the failure of our thinking to keep pace with the changing situation. If we focus on the trend toward the greater employment of married women, our conception of the new role of married women will be increasingly clarified, fuller social provision will be made to facilitate the working wife's adjustment to the new demands upon her, and over time the lag in our thinking will diminish.

Summary. Our object in this chapter has been to trace the causes of the increase in the employment of married women in the United States during the last half-century. Married women work because of the desire for (a) more income, (b) more interesting activity, and (c) prestige. These reasons are pulls from ahead. In addition there may be certain pushes from behind, as in the conception that housework is drudgery and that it is socially isolating. These are reasons why married women work; but insofar as they are constant factors, they are not reasons why more married women work. There is no evidence that the desire of married women for more income was any different in 1900 than in 1950. The view that housekeeping is drudgery may not, however, be a constant factor. The idea may originate by contrast; that is, because of the attractiveness of the alternative, namely the job. When there are no

[38] Arnold M. Rose, "The Adequacy of Women's Expectations for Adult Roles," *Social Forces*, 30: 69:77, October, 1951.

jobs or prospects of jobs, the satisfaction with housekeeping routines may be greater. The effective pull, then, is the increase in the number of jobs open to married women.

In addition, certain obstacles to the employment of married women have been removed. These changes have been brought about by (a) smaller families; (b) lighter housekeeping duties; and (c) more favorable community opinion. These three factors, together with more jobs, are the immediate or proximate causes of the increase in working wives.

An important reason for the reduction in family size, we saw in an earlier chapter, is the economic liability of the child in the urban community. The child is a liability because the machinery in factories is too complicated for him to operate efficiently and because compulsory education laws keep him in school. The machines and the laws are causes twice-removed of the reduction in family size and causes thrice-removed of the increase in working wives.

Lighter housekeeping duties result from (a) labor-saving devices in the home as well as smaller homes and (b) the transfer of functions of economic production from the home to industry.

The more favorable attitude toward the employment of married women stems in part from several changes: (a) lighter work provided by new and improved machines; (b) social legislation regarding the employment of women, which was a revolt against the long hours, low wages, and unsanitary working conditions of selfish employers; and (c) the favorable experience with increasing numbers of unmarried women workers. Since no harm came to the unmarried women workers, there was less objection to the employment of married women.

The causes of the increase in married women in the paid labor force are seen to be numerous and diverse. But particularly partinent among the direct causes is the spectacular increase in jobs. In turn, the increase in jobs has been the result of (a) the transfer of economic functions from the home to industry, substituting paid jobs for unpaid family jobs, and (b) the vast expansion of new jobs by industry.

8

Away from Authority

Authority in the Home

More than 100 years ago, a minister officiating at a wedding gave the bride the following advice, which was printed in *The Lady's Book* [1] (later, *Godey's*), a favorite periodical of the time.

> Bear always in mind your true situation and have the words of the apostle perpetually engraven on your heart. Your duty is submission — "Submission and obedience are the lessons of your life and peace and happiness will be your reward." Your husband is, by the laws of God and of man, your superior; do not ever give him cause to remind you of it. If he be an honourable man, he will never exert his authority, but rather seem to yield submission. But mind this, never accept such submission — never exert authority over him, but remembering the wayward nature of man, still act and demean yourself according to the duty of a wife. Your husband will love you more for that denial, and your happiness will proportionately increase. Milton has defined the duty of a wife in the following beautiful poetry, which I quote, from an address by Eve to her partner, Adam:
>
> > "My author and disposer, what thou bidd'st
> > Unargued I obey; so God ordains;
> > God is thy law, Thou Mine; to know no more
> >
> > Is woman's happiest knowledge and her praise.
> > With thee conversing, I forget all time;
> > All seasons and their change, all please alike."
>
> Let all your enjoyments centre in your home. Let your home occupy the first place in your thoughts; for that is the only source of happiness. Let all your endeavours be directed towards the promo-

1 (Philadelphia: L. A. Godey & Co., 1832), 4:288.

tion of your husband's welfare, and he will reward your faithful zeal. May heaven prosper those exertions and bless your union with perpetual felicity; that after years may witness no diminution of the happiness which has been inspired on this — your *weddingday*.

> "Happy then will be the man that hath made you
>   his wife —
> Happy the child that shall call you mother."

The minister's statement tells us what was expected of a good middle-class wife. That was more than 100 years ago, and times have changed. Ministers today seldom mention obedience to brides, let alone discourse upon it. The word "obey" has virtually disappeared from the marriage vows.

A century ago, America was a man's world. When a woman married, she lost her separate legal status and became as it were a ward of her husband, as the following commentary on the common law by the eminent jurist, Blackstone,[2] discloses:

> By marriage the husband and the wife are one person in law; that is, the very being or legal existence of the woman is suspended during the marriage, or at least is incorporated and consolidated into that of her husband. . . . Upon this principle of a union of person in husband and wife depend almost all the legal rights, duties and disabilities that either of them acquire by the marriage. . . . For this reason a man cannot grant anything to his wife, or enter into covenant with her; for the grant would be to suppose her separate existence, and to covenant with her would only be to covenant with himself; and therefore it is also generally true that all compacts made between husband and wife when single are voided by the inter-marriage.

Marriage destroyed the woman's separate legal identity. At marriage any personal property she owned, even clothes and jewelry, became her husband's. Real property she could retain, but her husband acquired control over it and received the rents or other benefits. She could not sue alone or be sued, or execute a deed without her husband's approval. He was the sole guardian of their children. She did not vote or serve on juries or hold public office. The divorce laws favored her husband.

Today conditions are greatly different. The married woman retains full control of her separate property owned by her before

---

[2] Sir William Blackstone, *Commentaries on the Laws of England* (21st ed., London, 1862), Book I, Chapter XV, p. 441. In M. F. Nimkoff, *Marriage and the Family* (Boston: Houghton Mifflin Company, 1947), p. 79.

marriage or acquired by her after marriage. Twelve states, the so-called community property states, give her an equal share of all property acquired after marriage by her husband or herself. She has full contractual rights. In thirty-four states she is co-guardian of her children; and if the marriage is broken, in theory neither parent has an advantage, and the determining consideration in the eyes of the court is the best interests of the child. In actuality in divorce cases mothers are usually awarded custody.[3]

In colonial times the husband had the right of "moderate correction" of his wife but could not use violence. Today he has no legal right to chastise his wife, or to restrain her by confinement, or to compel obedience.

In a few particulars the law now favors women. They have more grounds for divorce open to them. For instance, a wife may charge her husband with non-support, whereas he cannot bring action against her on the same ground. The husband's earnings are primarily liable for family support, but the wife's not. Many of the present differences in the law may be temporary, representing a kind of lag; the changes in the law have been rapid in recent years in the direction of the removal of legal barriers to women in the several states, and the Women's Bureau has referred to the recent changes as "a clean-up period." On the other hand, equality of the sexes before the law does not mean identity or similarity in every regard because of the differing nature and needs of the sexes. The minimum age for marriage, for instance, is naturally lower for females.

The trend toward equality of the sexes extends beyond the law to behavior of various sorts. Wives have gained more freedom not alone from their husbands' authority but from their parents' as well. A study[4] of changes in courtship among 200 college-trained women,[5] their mothers, and their grandmothers, reported that the

[3] There is always a lag in reporting data on the legal rights of women because of the difficulty in assembling material from the several states. The data given here are the latest reported by the Women's Bureau, *The Legal Status of Women in the United States of America* (as of January 1, 1948), Bulletin No. 157 (Revised), Washington, D.C., 1951.

[4] Marvin Robert Koller, *A Statistical Study of Changes Occurring in Selected Aspects of Courtship among Three Married Female Generations, Central Ohio, 1949.* Abstracts of Doctoral Dissertations, No. 63 (The Ohio State University Press, 1952).

[5] Native-born, white, urban, Protestant Ohioans.

first generation showed more conformity to parents' wishes as to their male companions, less parental disapproval of the boys dated, more chaperonage, fewer dates per week, and fewer gifts to men. The present generation had more freedom of choice and action.

Increasing similarity in behavior as between men and women has been shown[6] to extend to sex, which because of the traditionally strong taboos involved is a good indication of the fundamental character of the change in women's behavior. The Kinsey studies show that American women of the present generation who are not prostitutes resort to more premarital and extramarital sex intercourse than did women of earlier generations. This accounts in part at least for the fact that American men now frequent prostitutes less often than they used to. There is a growing belief that sex in marriage should be equally satisfying to wives and husbands, and that infidelity is equally bad for men and women.[7]

There is some evidence that the behavioral differences between the sexes are narrowing as women become more aggressive. It is reported[8] that women who commit suicide are resorting to more violent methods. Firearms and hanging, used in 1921–25 in less than one quarter of the suicides among white women, accounted for two-fifths of the total in 1946. On the other hand, the more passive means of self-destruction such as asphyxiation and poisoning dropped from 56 per cent to about 40 per cent. These reports are consistent with the findings of a more extensive investigation[9] that educated women are becoming more and more masculinized. The authors add that educated men are becoming more and more feminized. So the gap between the sexes is being narrowed from both sides.

The accent on women's rights has led obstetrical and gynecological societies concerned with stimulating public interest in problems pertaining to the welfare of women to draw up a "Mother's Charter" demanding for every mother certain rights such as "The

[6] Alfred C. Kinsey *et al.*, *Sexual Behavior in the Human Male* (Philadelphia: W. B. Saunders Company, 1948). *Sexual Behavior in the Human Female* (Philadelphia: W. B. Saunders Company, 1953).

[7] "Women in America," *Fortune* Survey, August, 1946, 34: 5, 6.

[8] Metropolitan Life Insurance Company, *Statistical Bulletin*, May, 1947, pp. 9 ff.

[9] Lewis M. Terman and Catherine Cox Miles, *Sex and Personality* (New York: McGraw-Hill Book Company, 1937).

inalienable right to protection from disease and harmful influences during infancy and childhood; the right of proper and adequate care during pregnancy," and so forth.[10]   Although this Charter has not been accorded the publicity and prestige of the several Children's Charters formulated at White House Conferences, a Mother's Charter may be taken as one more indication of the growing independence of women.

So far as family life is concerned, the decline in the dependence of women on men is two-fold: (1) women have less need to marry for economic reasons and (2) if married, they have less need to depend upon their husbands for economic and other support. In earlier times, women were not able so comfortably to envision a choice between marriage and spinsterhood because as Jane Austen has put it, "without thinking highly either of men or matrimony, marriage . . . was the only honourable provision for well-educated young women of small fortune, and however uncertain of giving happiness, must be their pleasantest preservation from want."

Authority Outside the Home

The gains in the status of women extend beyond the home. Women may serve on juries in thirty-five states, and the nineteenth Amendment to the Constitution, added in 1920, guarantees women the right to vote. Formerly a rigorous distinction was made between man's work and woman's work; now, as we saw in an earlier chapter, only a handful of occupations are closed to women.[11] Women attend the same types of school as men, and the trend is toward increasing co-education. Common recreational facilities are available to both, and the sexes tend more and more to engage in the same leisure-time pursuits.

We are concerned in this chapter with the increasing equality of women outside the home because it contributes to greater independence within the home. Common civil rights, work, schooling, and play make the sexes increasingly similar in behavior. One close student [12] of the changing role of women observes that the

10 *Family Life Education* (Bulletin of the American Institute of Family Relations), Vol. 6, No. 1, January, 1946, p. 2.

11 Chapter 7.

12 Charlotte Luetkens, *Woman and a New Society* (New York: Duell, Sloan and Pearce, 1946), pp. 78–9.

earmarks of differences in secondary sex characters have been reduced, what with the shorter dresses, the sweaters, the slacks, and
the bobbed hair. Increasing mobility and the demands of the job
have led to emancipation from what Elizabeth Barrett Browning
called "the foot-catching robes of womanhood." It is pointed out
that the press-stud and later the zipper was a great emancipator
for women, who no longer had to depend upon a maid or mother
or husband to manage the innumerable and inaccessible hooks and
eyes.

It is significant that the trend toward the increase in the legal,
political, and economic rights of women is world-wide, suggesting
that similar forces are everywhere at work. A few countries have
long accorded the ballot to women. In New Zealand, women have
voted since 1893, in Australia since 1902; and in Finland they have
voted and stood for election since 1907. At the middle of the
twentieth century, fifty-six countries permitted women to vote in
all elections on an equal basis with men; three countries permitted
women to vote in all elections but under different and generally
higher qualifications than those applicable to men; five countries
allowed women to vote only in local elections; and in sixteen countries women were denied any political rights (in three of these,
men had no electoral rights either).[13]

The above report was made in 1950. A year later, the Secretary
General to the UN General Assembly reported that two additional
countries had extended the suffrage to women: the women of Leb-
anon were granted municipal voting rights, and the new constitution of Haiti embodied the principle of full political rights for
women.[14]

What we have here is an acceleration of the trend in recent
decades to accord equality of status to women. This is interestingly
reflected in a comparison of the old League of Nations and the new
United Nations, as they relate to the status of women. When the
constitution of the League of Nations was first drafted in 1919, it
made no provision for women's eligibility for positions in the
League, a situation that was remedied after the intervention of

[13] Report submitted by the Secretary General to the UN General Assembly,
covering women's status as of September 1, 1950, under political laws in
eighty countries throughout the world.
[14] Reported in Women's Bureau, *Facts on Women Workers*, October 31,
1951.

large international women's organizations. Even so, the subject of the status of women was not considered in the Assembly until the eleventh year (1930) and not until the eighteenth year (1937) was a committee of experts appointed to study the legal status of women throughout the world. On the other hand, an agency to consider the status of women was created immediately by the United Nations, and the subject was debated at the first General Assembly. Also in contrast is the service of women in responsible positions in the two international agencies. In the League of Nations, no woman was a full delegate to the annual assembly until the tenth year (1929); only eight countries ever sent a woman in this capacity during the entire existence of the League; and only ten women were ever appointed full delegates, although twenty-nine countries used women as substitute delegates and technical advisers. In the United Nations, five countries sent women as full delegates to the first General Assembly.[15]

An Associated Press survey in Europe, Latin America, and the Far East in April, 1949, listed 685 women legislators, a phenomenal change in a field where women had little or no position before World War II. The changes were particularly striking in France, Italy, and Japan.[16]

Authority of women in earlier times and in other societies. We are concerned here with the changes in the status of women which have occurred in the United States during the last century and which point in the direction of equality. It is significant, however, to note that the trend is world-wide, symbolized by the decision of the United Nations General Assembly on December 4, 1950, to include explicit recognition of equality between men and women in the draft covenant on human rights.

An interesting question that arises is: What was the situation in the United States and in England in earlier times? We have seen that in colonial times the legal, political, and economic status of women was very low. But it is sometimes claimed that in the early centuries in England the status of women was much higher

---

15 Women's Bureau, *International Documents on the Status of Women* (Bulletin No. 217, Washington, D.C., 1947).

16 Erwin D. Canham, *Awakening: The World at Mid-Century* (New York: Longmans, Green & Co., 1950), p. 21.

than it was in the eighteenth and nineteenth centuries; that it was, in fact, quite comparable to that today. The suffrage movement, according to one writer,[17] should be described as an effort to reinstate women in the high estate they formerly occupied. This writer cites Tacitus' record that "The Teutons neither scorned to consult their women nor slighted their advice." But this statement suggests that the men made the decisions; the women may have been consulted, but consultants are not policy-makers. The same writer adds that the Celts referred disputes with other peoples to their women and that, with the Picts of Caledonia, succession to the throne was by the right of the mother. There is some evidence that among our Germanic and Anglo-Saxon ancestors in the ninth century, community property existed; that is, wives shared equally with their husbands all wealth acquired after marriage and had equal rights of inheritance. The evidence, while suggestive, is fragmentary and quite generally limited to the upper class, and sometimes even only to women of rank. From such spotty and selected data it is unsafe to generalize regarding the status of the mass of women of the time. Another observation is that women, even when their formal status has been low, have often been the power behind the throne.[18] We all know individual women who by force of personality sometimes dominate their husbands and are the principal policy-makers in the family; but this is a psychological phenomenon, a matter of inter-personal relations in given instances and does not tell us anything about the rights and duties of the sexes prescribed by a given culture.

Another error is to confuse the informal status enjoyed by women within the home with their legal status in the larger society. Thus a student [19] describes the private life of the Roman matron as follows:

> With her marriage the Roman woman reached a position not attained by the women of any other nation in the ancient world. No other people held its women in such high respect; nowhere else did women exert so strong and beneficent an influence. In her own house the Roman matron was absolute mistress. She directed its

[17] Ethel Mary Wood, *The Pilgrimage of Perseverance* (London: National Council of Social Services, 1949).

[18] Mary Beard, *On Understanding Women* (London: Longmans, 1931).

[19] H. W. Johnstone, *The Private Life of the Romans* (Chicago: Scott, Foresman and Company, 1903), pp. 72–3.

economy and supervised the tasks of the household slaves, but did no menial work herself. She was her childen's nurse, and conducted their early training and education. Her daughters were fitted under their mother's eye to be mistresses of similar homes, and remained her closest companions until she herself had dressed for their bridal and their husbands had torn them from her arms. She was her husband's helpmeet in business as well as in household matters, and he often consulted her on affairs of state.

Yet we know that no more extreme expression of masculine authority has ever existed among Western peoples than existed in Rome up to the close of the Punic Wars. The Roman household was governed by the paterfamilias, usually the eldest male, who had *potestas* (power) over its members. In him resided all religious rights, all legal rights, all economic rights pertaining to the family. He had complete control over the property and earnings of all the members of the family. As chief priest, he officiated at the ceremonies of ancestor worship; and his place might not be filled by another. He could sell his children, banish them, even kill them if he chose. His children remained under his control during his lifetime, even after their marriage, which might be arranged or dissolved without their consent. This was the theory of the role of the paterfamilias, although in practice his role may have been different.

While the evidence on the status of women in early times in Western society is not clear, there is no denying the fact that women enjoy a high status in some societies without benefit of modern technology. There is evidence from primitive societies showing varying degrees of female authority and submission, ranging from the Todas of India, where a woman, on meeting a man, greets him by touching his feet with her forehead, to the rare situation among the Iroquois, where political power was in the hands of the women, who nominated the holders of titles. Superior status for women is usually found in matrilocal and matrilineal societies associated with hoe culture, in which the women play a larger and more important economic role than they do in plow culture, where the heavier work favors the more muscular male. Mead [20] has shown that the status, roles, and personality of women vary

[20] Margaret Mead, *Sex and Temperament in Three Primitive Societies* (New York: W. W. Morrow and Company, 1935), *Male and Female* (1949).

greatly in different primitive cultures, from extreme submissiveness to extensive dominance.

The inference to be drawn from the foregoing discussion is that the status of women in Western society has not been unilinear. Women's status does not begin at a low point and rise by slow, regular stages to the present high level that women occupy. The status of women at any given time is a relative matter and has meaning only in terms of the status of men. It is unlike material culture, which accumulates and is progressive, since each new invention is an outgrowth of old inventions. So we can say of a new invention if it survives that it is better for certain purposes than its predecessors and that the whole course of material culture represents systematic progress. But the status of the sexes, being relative, may vary as the circumstances vary, especially the roles of sexes in production, which we shall discuss later. The status of women may be enhanced by changes in the means of production that give women a more important economic role than they had before, only to be lowered by further developments that lessen woman's economic contribution. So in the earliest cultures, hunting favored men; later the discovery of how to grow food gave women an advantage in the simple hoe culture, an advantage which they lost in more advanced agriculture requiring the plow. Likewise in pastoral culture the care of the flocks is almost exclusively a male function, and the status of women is very low. So the status of women has risen and fallen and, with the advent of industrial civilization, has risen again.

How far has the trend toward equality gone? There is some loose talk of a matriarchy in the United States, especially on the part of men and women who find in the trend a threat to their ego and a violation of what they think are the laws of nature.[21] Actually, if there is a modal type in the United States at the present time, it is probably semi-patriarchal [22] with the male still retaining certain advantages. When a woman marries, she takes her husband's name and the children bear their father's name. When the census

[21] Ferdinand Lundberg and Marynia F. Farnham, *Modern Woman: The Lost Sex* (New York: Harper and Brothers, 1947).

[22] Reuben Hill, "The American Family: Problem or Solution?" *American Journal of Sociology,* 53: 125–30, September, 1947.

enumerator calls, he records the husband as the head of the household, if he is present. These are formal distinctions and may not seem of much consequence, but there are functional distinctions of greater import. Wives are required to live where their husbands work and elect to live, and not vice versa; and refusal to do so on the wife's part can be construed as desertion. Husbands are liable for the support of their wives and children, and wives are not generally liable for the support of their husbands.

Women in the United States at the midpoint of the twentieth century are not as free as men to do what they would like to do. Woman's dilemma results in large measure from the fact that she is less emancipated from her family of orientation (her parental family) than her brother is.[23] Sons are provided with earlier and more frequent opportunities for independent action, a higher degree of privacy in personal affairs, and a less exacting code of filial and kinship obligations. Also women have less freedom to transgress than do men. When 3381 college students of both sexes at Syracuse University [24] were asked whether immoral acts were intrinsically worse for a woman to do than for a man, 39 per cent replied that they considered certain acts worse for a woman and 5 per cent considered all immoral acts worse for a woman. The women were more liberal in their attitude toward their own permissible behavior, 69 per cent of the women believing in moral equality as compared with 50 per cent of the men. Some of the acts that were considered to be worse if committed by a woman were murder, drinking, immoral sex behavior, cursing, telling obscene stories, and gambling.

Some of the lags in the status of women seem to be temporary and are in the process of being taken up quite rapidly. This appears to be true, for example, with respect to the guardianship of children. Fourteen states still favor the father, but the trend toward co-guardianship is strong. Other limitations faced by women are more difficult to cope with, and to the lifting of some there is considerable resistance. Probably the two most substantial lags have to do with (1) income and (2) political leadership.

[23] Mirra Komarovsky, "Functional Analysis of Sex Roles," *American Sociological Review,* 15: 508–16, August, 1950.

[24] Daniel Katz and Floyd Henry Allport, with Margaret Babcock Jenness, *Students' Attitudes: A Report of the Syracuse University Reaction Study* (Syracuse: The Craftsman Press, Inc., 1931).

We saw in an earlier chapter that women have made their way into nearly all occupations, and only a handful are closed to them. The pay they receive, however, is often very much less than that of men for the same amount and quality of work. All women who had an income in 1951 received an average of $1,045 for the year, which was 35 per cent of the men's average of $2,952,[25] but there were, of course, differences in occupations by sex. The amounts represented income from all sources and not just earnings. It has been argued by the Women's Bureau, which has waged a campaign in behalf of equal pay for women, that is, pay based on the job and not on the sex of the worker, that when the butcher, the baker, and the candlestick maker sell their wares, the asking price is the same for all persons. Yet when women go out into the working world, they often find that a job carries one salary for a man, another for a woman, although in many instances the jobs are comparable. In 1952 equal-pay legislation was in effect for private employment in thirteen states and Alaska.[26] Laws requiring that men and women teachers be paid the same compensation for comparable services were in effect in sixteen states and the District of Columbia; and many school systems provide for equal pay through school-board action. The Federal Government by the Classification Act of 1923 established a uniform salary for each grade and class of work and prohibited variation because of sex.

On another fiscal front, equality has been achieved by women. At least it is reported [27] that fully half of all the country's investments in stocks and bonds are owned by women. This is so in part because women generally outlive their husbands and are generally the chief beneficiaries of their estates. The stock and bond-owning public is a relatively small group. As we have seen,

[25] Of the women, 49 per cent, and of the men, 18 per cent had income below $1,000. At the other end of the scale, 37 per cent of the men and 5 per cent of the women had incomes of $3,500 or more. The income covers all sources — earnings, rent, own business, pension, et cetera. Of all women in the population, 44 per cent had some income; of men, 90 per cent. Women's Bureau, *Facts on Women Workers*, October 31, 1952, p. 4.

[26] The laws of Illinois and Michigan covered manufacturing only; those of the other states (Maine, New Hampshire, Massachusetts, Rhode Island, Connecticut, New York, New Jersey, Pennsylvania, Montana, Washington, California) applied generally to most types of private employment.

[27] Maxwell S. Stewart, *Women — and Their Money*, Public Affairs Pamphlet No. 146.

the median money income from all sources in 1951 was for women $1,045, or 35 per cent of the $2,952 for men. In 1944, women's median money income from all sources — earnings, rent, own business, pension, and so forth — was 44 per cent of men's.[28] The average income from 1944 to 1951 increased for both sexes; but the gain for men was appreciably greater, hence the relative loss for women. There are no comparable data for prior years,[29] hence we cannot generalize as to the trend of the relative economic status of the sexes.

The biggest lag in the status of women is probably in the area of political leadership, and it is here that there would seem to be the greatest obstacles to taking up the lag. The difficulties are particularly great at the higher levels of political leadership. An interesting analysis of the Soviet Union[30] — interesting because the Soviet Union has a guarantee of sex equality written into its Constitution — shows that Soviet women are well represented at the lower political levels and become progressively less numerous at the higher levels. There is not nor has there ever been a single woman in the Politburo, the highest governing body. In the United States the President is and always has been a man. There are several federal judges who are women but none on the Supreme Court. In recent administrations there has never been more than one woman in the Cabinet.

Causes

It has been said that under the English common law that governed the relationship of the sexes in earlier centuries, when a man and a woman married, they became one; and that one was the husband. Authority was vested in the husband, and so the cardinal virtue in a wife was obedience. Today in middle-class America, authority in matters economic and familial is shared by husband and wife, decisions are made jointly, and the accent is on companionship. The patriarchal family is being replaced by the equalitarian family. We want to know why.

---

[28] Women's Bureau, *Facts on Women Workers,* October 31, 1952.

[29] Letter to the authors from the Women's Bureau, July 22, 1953.

[30] Amram Scheinfeld, *Women and Men* (New York: Harcourt, Brace & Company, Inc., 1943).

Biological factors. Man's dominance over woman originates in biological factors. Men are bigger and heavier and stronger than women, and men are by nature more aggressive. The greater aggressiveness of males is evident at a very early age, before environmental influences can have had much effect. Since the status of women has risen in the last century, we want to know whether there has been some change in the physiology of the sexes which might help to explain the change in status. It is doubtful that men are now relatively less big and heavy and strong than they were 100 or 200 years ago. If genetically determined, aggressiveness would be a constant factor and so could not account for the change in status. If the relative aggressiveness of men and women has changed in the last century or two, the causes are cultural and have to be sought in the changed social situation. We conclude that inherited biological differences between the sexes are constants and are not responsible for the changed status of women. The biological factors are, however, probably important elements in the resistance to change.

The human male is biologically dominant over the female, but culture has progressively diminished the significance of this biological differential between the sexes. In the beginning, before man developed a culture, he had to depend altogether on his muscles, and later muscles were applied to tools like the throwing stick and the bow. Still later came tools that depended less on human muscles and more on power from non-human sources: animals, wind, and water. And now we have semi-automatic and fully automatic machines that make little or no demand on muscles. These changes in technology have been highly beneficial to women in their competition with men in the labor force. They are among the basic changes which are responsible for the remarkable increase in the jobs available to women, which we discussed in an earlier chapter and which we shall consider below in terms of the significance they have for the status of women.

Another physical factor in man's natural dominance is the handicap under which women operate in child-bearing and child-rearing. Men do not take paternity leaves and therefore have an advantage in the competitive process. Still what we want to know is whether there has been any change in the child-bearing and child-rearing situations, for if there has been no change, these factors cannot be considered causes of the improvement in the status of women. As to child-bearing, no significant change seems to have occurred. It still takes nine months. Modern drugs make the experience easier, especially during the period of labor. The new methods of "natural childbirth" probably affect only a very small percentage of expectant mothers. More important for woman's status are the changes in child-rearing, especially the increasing provision of social services for mothers of small children, like day nurseries, clinics, and nursery schools. For mothers of older children there are schools, playgrounds, summer camps, motion picture theaters, and all the other facilities which help to relieve the mother of the care of her children and free her for paid employment. The reduction in size of family is, of course, another highly important change which has greatly affected the opportunities of women for employment.

Biological factors: the sex ratio. Another biological factor which needs to be considered for its possible bearing on the status of women is the sex ratio, technically defined as the number of men per 100 women. Many co-educational colleges recognize the importance of the sex ratio and make the campus attractive to coeds by maintaining a ratio of males to females of, say 2:1. It has often been observed that the scarcity of women on the frontier in Colonial America helped to explain the status of women, which was high in comparison with that of Europe. Also, woman suffrage was first developed in the western states, not in the more highly industrialized eastern states. It is thought that a factor was the favorable sex ratio, for there were fewer women migrants to the west coast than men. The West, moreover, was a new society, less bound by tradition. But the status of women in the United States as a whole has risen while the sex ratio has dropped; that is, there are more women than there were formerly; and actually in recent years the number of women has exceeded the number of men. So the changes in the sex ratio cannot be a factor in the changed status of women.

Jobs for women. It is easy to see why an increase in the number and kind of jobs for women would be perhaps the most important single factor affecting their status. Indeed, occupation and income are the principal indices of status. We judge a man's status mainly by his occupation and the amount and source of his income. We have seen how, from the time of the household economy when there were few or no paid jobs for women, women's jobs have multiplied until they cover hundreds of different occupations and only a few are not represented. The Women's Bureau of the United States Department of Labor likes to publicize the gains made by women in jobs traditionally held by men. Thus the number of women bank officials increased from 4,605 in 1944 to 6,013 in 1950. The number of women employed on Wall Street as customers' brokers nearly doubled from 1946 to 1951, when the number was 385.[31] The gains during the war period were spectacular because of the shortage of labor, but after the war, while the pace slackened, the gains continued.

One way to show the importance of jobs for status is to take the jobs away and see what happens. During the winter of the depression years, 1935–36, fifty-nine families on relief in a large industrial city outside New York City were interviewed to ascertain the effect of unemployment upon the unemployed man and his family.[32] It was found that there was in one case in five a breakdown of the father's status after his loss of employment and that this took three patterns, depending to a great extent upon the relationship between husband and wife before the loss of employment: crystallization of an inferior status; undermining of the husband's coercive control over his wife; and lowering of the status of a husband who enjoyed his wife's love and respect prior to unemployment. The father more often lost authority over older children than younger children and most often lost authority where adolescents were involved.

What are the crucial elements in jobs for women that affect their status? Women had work to do in the household economy, essential work without which the farmers would have been greatly handicapped. The women helped in the fields in addition to doing the housework and caring for the children. Women had more work to do than they do now, and their economic contribution was more

---

[31] Women's Bureau, *Facts on Women Workers*, October 31, 1951.
[32] Mirra Komarovsky, *The Unemployed Man and His Family* (New York: Dryden Press, Inc., 1941), Chapter II, "The Breakdown of the Husband's Status."

ample. So the decisive factor is not the amount of work done. The work of the farmer's wife was done in and about the home; and she depended on her husband, that is, upon marriage, for the opportunity to have work to do and to receive economic support. Today women's work is away from home, and they receive a money income. This makes them independent of their families. Women, like men, are employed as individuals and not as members of a family. The family situation accordingly is usually extraneous to the job and does not affect it; so that conflict between husband and wife need not mean loss of job. Money income, rather than payment in goods and services, further enhances the independence of the working woman, for the income enables her to secure goods and services from sources of her own choosing and not just from her family. Independent employment and a money income are, it appears, the two new factors in the economic role of women contributing to the rise in their status. Jobs not only make it possible for women to buy goods and services but also to secure deference from their husbands.

In earlier times, the work of man and wife was a joint enterprise, whether in farming or in the handicrafts; and the significant point is that joint production requires a manager or a head, as in a modern factory. So the husband as the head of the economic household had authority. Still earlier, in the hunting culture, the husband had authority because of the hazardous nature of his occupation. The subservience of a wife to her husband is, as it were, an expression of her appreciation of the special risks he runs in satisfying her economic needs, as well as his own. Among certain Eskimo tribes, for instance, the sex ratio among the young children is in fair balance, whereas in the late teens and early twenties when the hazards of the hunt take their toll, there is an excess of females. The life of primitive hunters is often one of feast or famine, and the dependence on the males for survival is great. When an Eskimo returns from a hard day's hunt, his wife gives him a fresh set of clothes. To make his frozen garments supple again, she chews the leather. This is repeated so often that the teeth are worn to the gums. The wife is obedient and does not often question her husband's authority. The Eskimos have the custom of wife-lending; and a wife will, at her husband's bidding, go to live for a time with another man, even when she would rather not.

Where the family income is in the form of money rather than goods, authority tends to reside in the member of the household who holds the purse strings. For instance, the Negro family in small towns in the South was commonly matricentric, with the mother the central figure, because Negro women have a virtual monopoly of jobs as domestic servants and have much less difficulty in finding work than the Negro males, who must compete with white men for jobs.

The residue of power in the families of the United States is in the hands of the males for these reasons, among others: that they are usually the sole breadwinners; they devote their lifetime to paid work as their wives usually do not; and they generally earn considerably more. But if one is interested in the changing aspect of the family situation, one will emphasize the increasing economic contribution of wives, and the accompanying increase in their authority.

The new pattern of jobs for women, having been established, has come to be valued and preferred by most men. Earlier when women first entered the labor market, men were not as favorably disposed toward women's working as they are now. Woman's place, we were told, was at home. In a 1946 *Fortune* poll,[33] men were asked which of three girls equally good-looking a man would prefer to marry: a girl who had never held a job, a girl who had held a job and been moderately successful at it, or a girl who held a job and had been extremely successful. The balloting ran: 33.8 per cent for the moderately successful, 21.5 per cent for the extremely successful, and only 16.2 per cent for the girl who never held a job. Most men, then, want their women to work, which increases the authority of women; but they do not so often want their women to be more successful than they are. As a rule, working women do not compete directly with their husbands, and where they do, the stage is set for difficulty.[34] In the *Fortune* Poll, the replies of the women were also of interest: 42.2 per cent thought men would prefer a moderately successful girl, only 12.1 per cent thought men would prefer a girl who had never held a job, and only 17.4 per cent thought they would prefer the highly successful. The sexes see pretty much eye to eye on this matter.

[33] "Women in America," Part I, *Fortune* Survey, October, 1946.
[34] Robin M. Williams, Jr., *American Society: A Sociological Interpretation* (New York: Alfred A. Knopf, Inc., 1951), pp. 55–61.

Education for women. In the mid-nineteenth century, when most educational facilities were for boys and men, the problem of feminine education was one of the widely discussed topics of the time, with much dispute over the "sphere" of woman and her mental abilities. With improving technology and increasing individual wealth, women had a narrowing range of activity within the home, which probably accounts for the prosperity of the "finishing" school, which emphasized a veneer of refinement. Reformers, who found such schools frivolous or otherwise displeasing, stressed the need for a more substantial liberal education for women.

Somewhat similar to the finishing schools, but offering women more in the way of academic work, were the larger seminaries founded by such pioneers as Emma Willard, Mrs. Lincoln Phelps, Zilpah P. Grant, and Mary Lyon. Academies for boys and seminaries for girls gave a general education, including languages and literature, mathematics, history, sciences, drawing, and singing. Religion and ethics were often included for boys, but not for girls.

By far the larger part of all educational facilities was under private auspices. For boys there were the Latin grammar schools and the academies, the latter being slightly less exclusive. In a few of these, coeducation was instituted; and occasionally might be found an academy which received some public support.

As suffrage was extended in the early 1800's, public education came increasingly, though slowly, into vogue. It is estimated that in the 1860's only one pupil in twenty continued school beyond the "common" or grade school. High schools for boys were under public auspices; and the first advanced public school for girls was the Philadelphia Normal School in 1848, which became in 1859 the Girls' High School.[35]

At the middle of the nineteenth century, few girls were graduates of high schools. But at the middle of the twentieth century, for every 100 men who graduated from high school, there were about 110 women.[36] At the college level, the ratio of men to women for the recent non-war years was about two to one, but a college education is available only to a small minority.

Another trend in American education influencing the relation-

---

[35] Eleanor W. Thompson, *Education for Ladies, 1830–1860: Ideas on Education in Magazines for Women* (Morningside Heights, New York: Kings Crown Press, 1947).

[36] *Statistical Abstract of the United States, 1952*, p. 121.

ship between the sexes is coeducation. While it is not essential to coeducation that the sexes be educated alike, this is actually the outcome in large measure. It is interesting that this should have been given by the Russians as a reason for abandoning coeducation in 1943, not only in the secondary but in the elementary grades. The explanation was given that, although sex equality was still said to be an undisputed principle in the Soviet Union, the war had shown the desirability of differentiating the occupational roles of men and women. The men must become soldiers; so boys should be trained for service in the Red Army while still at school. Girls will become mothers and so should have knowledge of human anatomy, hygiene, and domestic science. Another reason given for abandoning coeducation was that girls mature earlier than boys and have different interests from boys of the same age.[37] Whatever the motives of the Soviets, it would seem that when boys and girls study and play together over long periods of time, they have greater likelihood of learning the same things and therefore becoming companionable. If one were to devise an educational system to foster authority in the male, certainly it would not be coeducational on the American pattern of free choice of curriculum.

We have had then as emancipating factors more education for women on the same grounds as men, in both senses of that term. Besides, there are those who claim that the conditioning of growing boys by women school teachers has in recent generations led to their feminization.[38] Until 1830 virtually all teachers were men; but the need for more teachers at lower wages and the increase in other types of jobs for men brought women into the field in such force that by 1860 women teachers outnumbered men, as they have ever since. It is, however, difficult to obtain reliable knowledge regarding the effects of this change on the personality of growing boys.

The new psychology. Another type of education which has affected the relationship between the sexes can perhaps be designated sex education, if the term is understood very broadly. Specifically, we

[37] M. F. Nimkoff, *Marriage and the Family* (Boston: Houghton Mifflin Company, 1947), pp. 289–90.

[38] Edward A. Strecker, *Their Mothers' Sons* (Philadelphia: J. B. Lippincott Company, 1946); Philip Wylie, *A Generation of Vipers* (New York: Farrar and Rinehart, 1942).

would stress here the findings and teachings of psychoanalysis on the importance of sex in human personality. Exploration of the sexual basis of much unhappiness has led to the fuller knowledge of the sex nature and needs of women as well as men, repudiating the traditional idea that women are by nature sexually passive and that only men may enjoy sex. This has led to the concept of equal rights for women in the area of sex, an equality which is more consistent with a marriage based on companionship than one based on domination by the male, at least in the American culture.

The ideals of equality and companionship are reinforced by such findings as those by Maslow[39] that married couples that are psychiatrically superior do not emphasize differences in sex roles. Also a survey[40] of 2596 marriages in the educated part of the population showed that where the woman was thought to be the head of the household, 47 per cent of the marriages were rated happy; where the man was believed to be the head, the proportion of happy marriages was 61 per cent; but the highest proportion, 87 per cent, occurred where the control was judged to be equalitarian. It is to be noted that this report is about a well-educated group, including a great many college graduates, living in the United States in the twentieth century. The results for other groups might be different. But the better educated groups probably set a standard for the less well-educated, and there may be some effort at imitation.

The growth of the democratic idea. The reader may have wondered as he read this discussion of the causes of the rise in the status of women why there has been no mention of the idea of democracy. Improvement in the status of women is a step in the direction of equality, and is this not what democracy teaches? Is not the changing status of women just an extension of the democratic principle?

The democratic idea in governmental affairs is an old idea and was present in colonial times. If democracy is a constant factor, it would not contribute to the new status of women. Democracy, to

[39] A. H. Maslow, "Love in Healthy People," in Ashley Montagu, ed., *The Meaning of Love* (New York: The Julian Press, 1953), pp. 57–96.

[40] Paul Popenoe, "Can the Family Have Two Heads?" *Sociology and Social Research*, 18: 12–17, September–October, 1933.

be sure, is a progressive idea; and the idea of equality can be applied in new and different directions. If democracy is seen as a social invention, then like nearly all inventions, material or social, its diffusion will be gradual as obstacles are overcome. In colonial times political democracy was restricted to a small group of free-holders, and only slowly were other groups of men included; it took 150 years to reach the point where the franchise was extended to women. Democracy holds tremendous potentialities for growth like the acorn that becomes the mighty oak, given the proper setting and conditions. The democratic ideal was here in the United States 200 years ago. What has changed are the social soil and the social conditions, which are more hospitable to democracy than in earlier times.

The democratic ideal and the changed social conditions led to an increase in educational opportunities for women. At first the educational facilities were "equal but separate"; later, coeducational. The early crusaders for women's education were fierce advocates of equal rights, that is, advocates of democracy. The social forces at work here bore a reciprocal relationship. With the expanding economy bringing more economic opportunities for women as well as men, the times were favorable to the idea of more educational facilities for women. So the economic situation influenced the educational opportunities. In turn, the enlarged educational training for women meant that more and more of them were better prepared for jobs.

What of the feminist movement, which capitalized on the democratic tradition and sought to extend it to women? How important was feminism in achieving the emancipation of women? Feminism was propaganda making the trend articulate. But the idea of equality for women and men is not a new idea; it is, in fact, a very old one. If feminism became effective in the nineteenth and twentieth centuries in the United States, it was not because the idea was new but because the social situation was new and favorable. The growth of the feminist movement was more a result than a cause of the new opportunities for women. First came the increase in jobs and educational opportunities for women and the growing interest in sexual equality promoted by the new psychology. These led to more authority for women. The feminist movement was an outgrowth of the change which had as its goal opportunities for women equal to those of men.

The transfer of family functions. If we ask why more education for women is available in the twentieth than in the nineteenth century, the answer is the one we have already given. But if we ask why the more ample education is provided by the schools and not the homes, we see that an important part of the explanation is the transfer of functions out of the home. When with the advent of the Industrial Revolution, more and more fathers took jobs away from home, one parent who formerly might help a daughter with her education was no longer readily available for that purpose. When mothers also took jobs in larger numbers, the school became not only a necessity in the educational process but a shelter and source of chaperonage for children whose mothers were at work. Schools multiplied for this reason but even more because culture was growing apace; and the learning that children needed to fit them for the new society was too new and complicated for parents to handle alone. Their function in the educational process for children over six years of age was to become an auxiliary one, of rendering assistance, of providing encouragement, and of furnishing direction. In urban places and with smaller homes, there was also less work for daughters to do at home; so homework replaced housework.

The educational functions of the family were not the only ones to be shifted to outside agencies as we saw in an earlier chapter. Here we wish to show the relationship between the transfer of functions and the changes in the status of women. As the state and government added social services, the family relinquished many of those it had provided. The authority of the father diminished as policemen, firemen, judges, doctors, and social workers helped to relieve the family of responsibility for the care and protection of its members.

Likewise the loss of religious functions by males resulting from the secularization of Western society affected their authority patterns adversely. Traditionally religion in the Western world had given a larger role to males than females and had emphasized the authority of males. Adam was created first, and Eve was fashioned later to serve him. Eve was fashioned from Adam's rib, not from the bones of his head; woman must not presume to equality. In the long history of most churches, women have been barred from the ministry. More recently they have been admitted in a few instances. Among the effects of the spread of secularization is to be counted the decline of the authority of the male associated with traditional religion.

The decline of the reproductive function has meant smaller families. Modern contraception puts the protection of the female in her own hands and takes from the male the power to decide alone what the size of his family shall be. This lessens the dependence of the wife upon her husband and diminishes his authority.

The transfer of traditional functions from the family to other institutions has left marital stability dependent largely upon the quality of the personal relationship existing between husband and wife. The change in family patterns has been summarized as a change from "institution to companionship." [41] This is not strictly accurate, for the family remains an institution, although a greatly changed one. The characterization is useful in focusing on the shift from a type of family emphasizing formal functions, chiefly economic, to a type of family in which the informal personal factor is paramount. The change might also be aptly described as one from patriarchal authority to partnership.

Summary. Recent times, especially the first half of the twentieth century, have witnessed a marked elevation in the status of women in the United States, both inside and outside the home. Legally, and in the exercise of the franchise, woman is now man's equal. On the economic front, great gains have been made, especially within the marriage bonds. The effect of these changes has been to modify the old patriarchal pattern of masculine dominance in the direction of equalitarianism.

In searching for causes, we have found no inherited biological changes in either sex; and so we look to cultural factors for an explanation. Also, the direction of change in the sex ratio is such as to rule it out as a factor.

We find an immediate or proximate cause of the increased authority of women in the marked increase in paying jobs for women apart from the home. Stated differently, the trend away from masculine authority is a derivative effect of the increase in paid employment of women outside the home, which was documented in the preceding chapter. Jobs are a proximate cause of

---

[41] Ernest W. Burgess and Harvey Locke, *The Family: From Institution to Companionship* (New York: American Book Company, 1945).

the changed status of women. Back of this cause is the factory system which created jobs for women away from home and which broke up the system of economic production in the home where the man of the house was the manager and the boss of the joint economic enterprise. Now with outside employment, women were answerable to bosses other than their husbands or fathers. And back of the factory system is the Industrial Revolution; so the growth of factories is a once-removed cause of the greater authority of females; and the technological revolution is a twice-removed cause. The term factory is not used here in a precise and exclusive sense but rather in a symbolic sense to represent all the paying jobs, whether in factory, office, or shop, that urbanization brings. It is jobs suitable to women, making little demand on muscles, that mechanization has brought, highlighting the technological factor.

Other important proximate causes are increasing educational opportunities for women, especially coeducation, and the new psychology. More education for women is in turn the result of (a) an extension of the democratic principle made possible by the new circumstances; (b) the higher standard of living which provided the means for educating more daughters as well as sons; and (c) the need to equip women with the skills required by the new economic order.

The new psychology emphasized equality in the sexual function and therefore equality between the sexes.

9

Accent on the Child

Imagine a colonial family of, say, two hundred years ago returning to the United States today and dropping in on a modern middle-class family. The visitors would probably be very much surprised at what they see and hear, the parents shocked, the children envious. For it would appear that the younger members of the modern family enjoy very great privilege and attention. The children might be engaging in free and spontaneous conversation with their parents, asking frank and sometimes embarrassing questions, proffering suggestions of their own, and even disputing comments made by their elders. The children would not seem to have much work to do about the house, perhaps a few relatively unimtant chores like emptying wastebaskets, but instead occupy themselves almost completely with play. They have a profusion of playthings, toys and books. They have radio and television programs especially designed for them. Even before the children go to the public schools, where counselors are often employed to help frame a program of studies and activities suited to the interests and abilities of the individual child, they may attend nursery schools and kindergartens. Their mothers meet in groups to study the latest methods of child care; and there is great concern about whether this or that food, this or that program, this or that type of discipline is good for the child. The colonial family would indeed be astonished at so much emphasis on the child.

Things were different in colonial times. We know this even though our sources of information are deficient. When comparing colonial and modern conditions, we tend, in the absence of representative data, to contrast extreme variations because they are dramatic and command attention. If we were able to take at random 100 children today and 100 children in colonial times, what would their behavior show regarding, let us say, obedience? The distribution of scores on a scale of obedience would probably differ significantly for the two groups, but they would in all likelihood show considerable overlap. Hence caution needs to be exercised in interpreting the literature on the colonial child.

Even so, a good many inferences may be made regarding the role of children in colonial times from our knowledge of the social system, especially the economic, political, religious, and familial organization. The religious teachings on the proper role and behavior of children are revealing. The laws of the time are suggestive, even though we know that often there is a discrepancy between the legal codes and actual practice. Some light is also shed by diaries and letters that have come down to us, despite the fact that they are written by only a few selected individuals and we have no way of knowing whether the experiences they report are representative or not. The very absence in colonial times of a significant body of source material on the activities of children suggests that these activities were not considered important enough to document. By way of contrast, there was no dearth of religious literature in Puritan New England, reflecting the importance attached to theology. Today the body of literature on childhood, both popular and scientific, is vast, evidence of our accent on the child.

Goals for Children

To illuminate the changes that have taken place in the roles and status of children during the past two centuries, it is helpful to compare the goals toward which the nurture of children was directed in colonial times with those today. Prominent among the objectives in the education of children in the earlier period was conformity to tradition. This can be illustrated by reference to schooling. In the colonial period the curriculum was rather rigid, and the child was expected to adjust to it, whereas in modern times the curriculum is often adjusted to the child. Since elders in general, and parents in particular, are custodians of the existing culture, it is natural that subordination to them should have been stressed in colonial times. The ideal child of that period was more quiet, passive, and obedient than now, as expressed in the maxim that has come down to us that a child should be seen and not heard. The manners of children, we are told,[1] were formal; and parents were addressed as "esteemed parent" or "honored sir and madam." In a little book of etiquette which was circulated among the colonists, instruction as to the proper behavior of children at the table runs as follows.[2]

> Never sit down at the table till asked, and after the blessing. Ask for nothing; tarry till it be offered thee. Speak not. Bite not thy bread but break it. Take salt only with a clean knife. Dip not the meat in the same. Hold not thy knife upright but sloping, and lay it down at right hand of plate with blade on plate. Look not earnestly at any other that is eating. When moderately satisfied, leave the table. Sing not, hum not, wriggle not. . . .

While we are still concerned that the child shall show some deference to his elders and respect for tradition, the shift in emphasis has been away from obedience and conformity to a regard for the needs and interests of the child. A great deal is heard of the child's need for self-expression, and so-called progressive or permissive measures are espoused by many parents, yielding the child a good deal of freedom. Not so often as in the past is the question asked: Does society expect such and such conduct of the child? Heard more often is the query: Is it good for the child? Spontaneity and activity are in greater favor; formality and passivity are valued less highly. A phrase used with increasing frequency is "individual differences," with the implication that such differences should be respected. When the accent is on individual differences, the child becomes the main object of consideration, not the need of maintaining a particular social tradition.

In colonial times, children were in general more industrious than they are now. They began to work earlier, worked harder, and achieved earlier economic maturity and independence. The trend has been for children to devote more of their time to play, to remain economically dependent, resulting in what John Fiske called "the prolongation of infancy."

Colonial children were expected from very early childhood to

---

[1] Arthur W. Calhoun, *A Social History of the American Family* (Cleveland: The Arthur H. Clark Company, 1917), Vol. 1, pp. 110–2.

[2] Alice Morse Earle, *Child Life in Colonial Days* (New York: The Macmillan Company, 1904), p. 215.

do household chores commensurate with their age, strength, and intelligence. Little girls four years old knitted stockings and mittens, while those of about six spun wool on a spinning wheel so large that they had to stand on a footstool to reach their work. Small boys rose before breakfast to do their chores. Children of both sexes sowed seeds, weeded flax fields, and sometimes tended silkworms. Even those tending cattle and sheep were not considered to be sufficiently occupied, and the magistrates decreed that they should be "set to some other employment, withal, such as spinning upon the rock, knitting, weaving tape, . . ."[3]

Children were expected not only to accept considerable responsibility for the necessary household tasks but also to grow up very quickly in order to assume more important family duties. Small girls were sometimes called not Miss, but Mrs. "Miss was not exactly a term of reproach, but it was not one of respect. It denoted childishness, flippancy, lack of character. . . ."[4] It appears, then, that the child in the colonial family was not long permitted to remain a child and receive special care and attention but had his mind and body educated early to accept adult duties and responsibilities.

On the other hand, the dependency of the modern American child is often considerably prolonged. He is encouraged to be a child, to talk, play, and dress like one. His normal childish impulses are not stifled, but fostered; and he is usually introduced to adult tasks and responsibilities very gradually, over a rather extended period. "One of the most important discoveries of the past thirty years is that the child is not a small sized adult, but is a growing, developing, ever changing individual, whose treatment must differ not merely in degree but in kind from that received by the adult."[5]

One of the more important indications of the special concern with the child in the twentieth century has been the series of conferences on childhood called by the President of the United States and held in the White House. The first was convened by Theodore Roosevelt in 1909; the second by Herbert Hoover in 1930; and the

[3] *Ibid.*, pp. 339, 305–7, 307–10.
[4] *Ibid.*, pp. 22–3.
[5] Lawrence K. Frank, "Childhood and Youth," *Recent Social Trends* (New York: McGraw-Hill Book Company, 1933), p. 751.

third by Harry Truman in 1950. The second White House Conference formulated a Children's Charter, a portion of which is reproduced below, an impressive bit of evidence of our accent on the child.

This proposed Bill of Rights for children, while incorporating some new aims and safeguards, probably contains some rights which would have been recognized in colonial times. But, partic-

THE CHILDREN'S CHARTER,[6] President Hoover's White House Conference on Child Health and Protection, recognizing the rights of the child as the first rights of citizenship, pledges itself to these aims for the Children of America

   II. For every child understanding and the guarding of his personality as his most precious rights.

   IV. For every child full preparation for his birth, his mother receiving prenatal, natal, and postnatal care; and the establishment of such protective measures as will make child-bearing safer.

  VII. For every child a dwelling place safe, sanitary, and wholesome, with reasonable provisions for privacy, free from conditions which tend to thwart his development; and a home environment harmonious and enriching.

 VIII. For every child a school which is safe from hazards, sanitary, properly equipped, lighted, and ventilated. For younger children nursery schools and kindergartens to supplement home care.

  XI. For every child such teaching and training as will prepare him for successful parenthood, homemaking, and the rights of citizenship; and, for parents, supplementary training to fit them to deal wisely with the problems of parenthood.

XIII. For every child who is blind, deaf, crippled, or otherwise physically handicapped, and for the child who is mentally handicapped, such measures as will early discover and diagnose his handicap, provide care and treatment, and so train him that he may become an asset to society rather than a liability. Expenses of these services should be borne publicly where they cannot be privately met.

XVI. For every child protection against labor that stunts growth, either physical or mental, that limits education, that deprives children of the right of comradeship, of play, and of joy.

[6] Copyright, 1931, by the White House Conference on Child Health and Protection, Ray Lyman Wilbur, M.D., Chairman.

ulars aside, the significant fact is that in 1909 there was a White House Conference on Childhood, while in 1809, or any time before, there was no such White House Conference.

The change in the rights of children parallels the growth of the state, since authority has been shifted in part from the family to the state, which exercises its power in the interests of the children. The state now imposes restraints on the parent from the time of the birth of the child, which must be registered with the state. Guardianship is assigned to both parents equally, and not just to the father as in earlier times. If the parents separate, the child is not automatically awarded to the father, but custody is determined by the courts in the light of what is considered to be in the best interests of the child; and the mother is generally favored as usually being in a better position to serve the child. The accent, it will be noted, is on the child and his needs, not on the authority of the parents. The parents are, under the law, responsible for the support of their minor children; and support includes not only necessities of life like food and clothing, but medical expenses and the costs of an education commensurate with the family income. In the United States schooling is generally compulsory until the age of sixteen. Parents are responsible also for the protection of their children and may be punished if they fail to provide the requisite protection.

Although the shift is from the rights of parents to the rights of children, the change has been a relative, not an absolute one; and parents still have rights in their minor children, to wit: the right to their time and labor, at home or away, exclusive of the time required by schooling; the right to refuse consent to marriage; and the right to determine the child's religion. But these rights are fewer in number than in earlier times and are less effective in practice than in theory.

Governmental services for the child. The growth of the state represents in part a transfer of functions formerly exercised by parents and in part an expansion of functions inherent in the state itself. In a sense the state has taken power away from the parents and bestowed it on the child. The state has shown increasing interest in children by special services in their behalf, as exemplified by the establishment of a separate agency of the federal government devoted to children and named the Children's Bureau. This agency, working with state and local officials, has been instrumental in establishing hundreds of prenatal and child health centers in the United States, as well as promoting various child welfare services, especially aid to dependent children under the Social Security Act, and services for crippled children. In most of the principal nations today, the special interest of the state in children is evident in the subsidies granted for children. In the United States, while no bonuses for babies are provided, deductions are permitted for dependents under the income tax law.

In addition to health and economic support, the government renders help with regard to the education of the child. Although there is education for adults, the schools are mainly a service for minor children; and the expenditures for education are generally the biggest item in the budgets of cities and second only to those for highways in the budgets of state governments. Federal, state, and local governments combine to spend tremendous sums for this purpose. In 1900 the ratio of high school graduates to all seventeen-year-olds in the population of the United States was six per 100, whereas in 1950 it had risen to fifty-seven per 100.

So extensive are the special services and facilities for the child that are provided by government and other organizations that one author, in anticipation, termed the twentieth century "the century of the child." [7]

Causes

The new psychology. When we turn to the search for causes, with which this chapter is mainly concerned, we are impressed by the part that the new psychology has played in the trend toward the greater emphasis on the child.

To understand the new psychology fully, we must first understand the old, which laid great stress on biological or hereditary factors in the development of personality. The old psychology itself was an outgrowth of theology, in the sense that it was influenced by the latter, especially in its emphasis on innate factors, as exemplified by the tenets of Puritanism. A conviction of the

[7] Ellen Key, *The Century of the Child* (New York: G. P. Putnam's Sons, 1900).

early religious teaching in New England was that the child was born with a sinful nature and that nothing was more important than to save one's soul by repentance, prayer, and the faithful observance of the teachings of the church. The methods of achieving salvation were fear and strict discipline. "Hell, Satan, eternal damnation, everlasting torments were ever held up before these Puritan children. We could truthfully paraphrase Wordsworth's beautiful line 'Heaven lies about us in our infancy' and say of these Boston children, 'Hell lay about them in their infancy.'" [8]

It may be observed that although the religious teaching stressed the original nature of the child, it did not adhere to a position of biological determinism, that the original nature of man must prevail. Rather there was the conviction that environment, in the form of stern discipline, could turn the child from the evil ways to which his nature disposed him. The old psychology, then, emphasized learning, but a negative learning, aimed at stamping out inherent evil. It did not, so much as the new psychology, emphasize positive learning.

Later, when psychology began to divest itself of theological connections, it retained in modified form the emphasis on innate factors. In the theory of instincts it accentuated the belief in the deterministic nature of inherited behavior.

The new psychology, represented by the psychoanalysts and the behaviorists, constituted a marked departure from the old. Personality came to be regarded as more largely a social product, as a function of social situations. Freud drove home the crucial importance of the early years of life. "Conditioning" became the key concept in the learning process. John Watson boasted that given any dozen normal healthy children and an environment of his own choosing, he could make them at will into any kind of citizen.[9] If the early years of life are crucial for personality, and if personality is mainly the result of learning, then it is easy to see why so much attention should be paid the young child.

Another important contribution of modern psychological science has to do with the child's mental health. In earlier times there was concern over mental health, too, but less knowledge of how to

---

[8] Earle, *op. cit.*, pp. 238–9.
[9] *Psychology from the Standpoint of a Behaviorist* (Philadelphia: J. B. Lippincott Company, 1919).

achieve it, while in still earlier times, as in colonial New England, interest seems to have centered mainly on transmitting certain doctrines without much regard for their psychological consequences. Today the question is asked of any proposed behavior: Is it good for the child? There is on this account a changed attitude toward the use of fear as a disciplinary measure. Fear, widely used as a means of control in the past, is now regarded as frustrating and inhibiting, not liberating. Instead of fear of the devil, there is more disposition to stress the love of God. The fear of sex tends to be replaced by understanding of sex and its natural role in life. Authoritarian techniques of social control, "ordering and forbidding" the child, are replaced by reasoning with the child, answering his questions, and allowing him to make his own decisions. Punishment takes the form of group displeasure and isolation from the group rather than whipping as in earlier times. There is now a Society for the Prevention of Cruelty to Children, a far cry from the day when people believed that to spare the rod was to spoil the child.

Few changes are more revealing of our new focus on the child than those occurring in our attitude toward disciplining the child. Corporal punishment, especially if it is the principal method of control, emphasizes the authority of the one administering the punishment rather than the responsibility of the child for his own conduct. On this account corporal punishment is thought to be inconsistent with an emphasis on democracy in human relations. In addition, corporal punishment is regarded by psychologists as inimical to mental health, encouraging as it does the expression of parental frustration and aggression, and the development of hostility on the part of the child toward the parent. It is difficult for us to realize how revolutionary has been the change in this regard and how in the past corporal punishment was the established method of correcting the young, used extensively not just by parents but by teachers in the schools, whose primary focus was on maintaining order and authority. Alice Morse Earle [10] documents the situation in her account of child life in colonial days.

"Birch rods," she writes, "were tauntingly sold on London streets with a cry of 'Buy my fine Jemmies: Buy my London Tartars.' Even

[10] Earle, *op. cit.*, pp. 196–200.

that Miserable DYVES PRAGMATICUS enumerated 'Fyne Rod for Children of Wyllow and Burche' among his wares. A crowning insult was charging the cost of birch rod on schoolboys' bills; and in some cases making the boy pay for the birch out of his scant spending money.

"Birch trees were plentiful in America — and whippings too. Scholars in New England were not permitted to forget the methods of discipline of 'the good old days.' Massachusetts schools resounded with strokes of the rod. Varied instruments of chastisement were known, from

'A besomme of byrche for babes verye fit
To a long lasting lybbet for lubbers as meet.'

"A lybbet was a billet of wood, and the heavy walnut stick of one Boston master well deserved the name. A cruel inquisitor invented an instrument of torture which he termed a flapper. It was a heavy piece of leather six inches in diameter, with a hole in the middle. This was fastened by an edge to a pliable handle. Every stroke on the bare flesh raised a blister the size of the hole in the leather. Equally brutal was the tattling stick, a cat-o'nine-tails with heavy leather straps. . . . "

Apart from whippings, "many ingenious punishments were invented. A specially insulting one was to send the pupil out to cut a small branch of a tree. A split was made by the teacher at the severed end of the branch, and the culprit's nose was placed in the cleft end. Then he was forced to stand, painfully pinched, an object of ridicule. A familiar punishment of the dame school, which lingered till our own day, was the smart tapping of the child's head with a heavy thimble; this was known as 'thimmell-pie.' Another was to yoke two delinquents together in a yoke made with two bows like an ox yoke. Sometimes a boy and girl were yoked together — a terrible disgrace. 'Whispering sticks' were used to preserve quiet in the school room . . . wooden gags to be tied in the mouth with strings, somewhat as a bit is placed in a horse's mouth. Children were punished by being seated on a unipod, a stool with but a single leg, upon which it was most tiring to try to balance; they were made to stand on dunce stools and wear dunce caps and heavy leather spectacles; they were labelled with large placards marked with degrading or ridiculous names such as 'Tell-Tale,' 'Bite-Finger-Baby,' 'Lying Ananias,' 'Idle-Boy,' and 'Pert-Miss Prat-a-Face.' "

When parents systematically resort to corporal punishment and ridicule of their children, does this mean that they love their children less than do modern parents who do not use these methods of correction? It may be observed that when a method of social control like corporal punishment is in the folkways, its use by parents is usually routine and is taken for granted by the children as well as the parents. No animosity may be felt. Corporal punishment is, however, likely to be an immediate response to what is considered evil, whereas the new psychology would have the parent ask: "Why did my child do it?" Such a query allows for a fuller appreciation of the child and his behavior.

In England, in 1950, a panel of observers, a predominantly middle-class group, generally above average in education, was asked to tell what they thought of the maxim of "spare the rod and spoil the child." Only about one in three believed that some form of corporal punishment is generally necessary. "The Victorian 'heavy' father," the report [11] concludes, "is now a shadowy replica of his former robust self; the quiet, biddable child almost an historical survival." "Seventy-five years ago," asks Dorothy Canfield Fisher,[12] "did a parent confronted with a troublesome child, make any effort to find out what made him troublesome? No, his elder generation would have scorned him if he had made any such sissy effort. Like an unruly horse, a troublesome child was to be disciplined ('discipline' meant physically hurt) by the parent till he did what the parent wanted."

Still another contribution of the new psychology is the emphasis on individual differences, which has had the effect of centering attention on the child. If we stress the fact that A differs from B, B from C, C from D, et cetera, we are more likely to feel that for maximum effectiveness we ought to adjust programs to the individual than if we thought they did not differ or if we paid little or no attention to their differences. When individual differences in intelligence, interests, and aptitudes are stressed, the result is more testing, more counseling, more individual attention. When the emphasis on the special importance of the early years of life is combined with an emphasis on individual differences, the result is a concentration of interest and attention on *the individual child* rather than on (a) the individual adult or (b) children in general.

The growth of the sciences of man which have led to greater

[11] *Mass-Observation Bulletin*, New Series, No. 36, London, July/August, 1950.
[12] In the Introduction, pp. xvii-xviii, to *Our Children Today* (New York: The Viking Press, 1952).

concern with childhood does not seem to have much direct dependence on technology. The technological factor in intelligence tests is slight, consisting of paper and pencil, form board, and the like, which represent little or no new cultural innovation. In psychoanalysis the technological element is non-existent, and in learning theory it is negligible, except for laboratory apparatus used in experiments. Indirectly, technology plays a part in the growth of the social and psychological sciences, since it underlies our economic organization which has produced the wealth and the leisure which permit the development of the social sciences.

Progress in public health. In the quest for causes of the growing concern for the child, we pursue further the contribution of scientific discoveries. Developments in the biological sciences, in medicine, and in public health have favored young children more than any other age group and may therefore also be considered factors in the accentuation of youth in our time. Most of the remarkable increase in longevity in the last century or so has resulted from the saving of life in childhood, which in turn has resulted from (a) better feeding and (b) conquest of infectious diseases of childhood, like diphtheria and smallpox. These medical achievements are not the result of a special interest in children. Rather they are the outcome of the progressive process of medical discovery, which happened to have particular applicability to the period of childhood. Developments in medicine, public health, and the applied sciences are usually coupled with technological advances, hence the role of the latter in the accentuation of childhood via health programs has been great.

The increase in the knowledge of the causes of disease has meant that children have been the principal beneficiaries. As the diseases of childhood have been conquered one by one,[13] and more children survive into old age, more attention is being devoted to

---

[13] "The virtual elimination of the principal communicable diseases of childhood as causes of death constitutes one of the most remarkable chapters in the history of American medicine and public health. Measles, scarlet fever, whooping cough, and diphtheria together registered a death rate of only 0.5 per 100,000 policy-holders in 1951. In 1911 the rate for this group of diseases was 58.9 per 100,000." *Statistical Bulletin*, Metropolitan Life Insurance Company, January, 1952, p. 5. Accidents, not disease, are now the leading cause of death of children one to nineteen years old. Rheumatic fever and poliomyelitis remain the principal unconquered diseases of childhood.

the infirmities of old age. The shift in the focus of medical interest over the years seems to have been from adulthood to childhood to old age. While more attention will doubtless be paid to old age in the future, it is doubtful that less attention will be devoted to the health of children, except perhaps relatively, since the roots of many of the infirmities of old age may be traced back to the early years of life; and the knowledge of how to take preventive measures early may help to lessen degenerative disorders in old age.

The humanitarian movement. Tied in with the new psychology and with progress in public health as factors in the increased public concern over the welfare of children is the humanitarian movement, which has its roots also in religious and democratic ideologies. There were certain implications regarding the undesirable effects of severe punishment which were drawn from the teachings of the new psychology. In colonial times, and for a long period thereafter, children adjudged guilty of certain offenses were sometimes dealt with by the law as harshly as were adult offenders. There was for instance an old Connecticut law, derived from Old Testament and Roman tradition, which decreed capital punishment for a son who was found by the courts to have flagrantly and consistently disobeyed his parents.

> If a man have a stubborn and rebellious son of sufficient years and understanding, viz; sixteen years of age, which will not obey the voice of his father and the voice of his mother, and that when they have chastized him will not hearken unto them, then may his father and mother, being his natural parents, lay hold on him and bring him to the magistrates assembled in court, and testified unto them that their son is stubborn and rebellious. . . . such a son shall be put to death.[14]

Legal justice for children was before the twentieth century not as distinct and separate from criminal justice for adults as it is now. The trend in the law has been to develop separate procedures for juveniles, as in the juvenile court, the greater use of probation, and separate detention homes.

The special hazards of the city also led to efforts to protect the

---

[14] Trumbull, *Blue Laws True and False*, 1876, 69–70; cited by W. Goodsell, *A History of Marriage and the Family* (New York: The Macmillan Company, 1934), p. 367.

children. The dangers of city traffic, the lack of adequate play space and facilities, and the temptations of the street prompted the establishment of boys' clubs and settlement houses by private philanthropy, in addition to public playgrounds. Among the hazards of the city may be mentioned also the factories where in the early stages of the Industrial Revolution children sometimes worked long hours under unsanitary conditions and for very low wages. Child labor laws regulating the employment of minors were an expression of the humanitarian movement in behalf of children.

Transfer of functions from the family. Still another factor in the changed evaluation of childhood is the shift of the functions of the family to outside agencies. In earlier times the family was the central social unit; and the individual members, especially the children, were regarded as subordinate to the family. This is the case where the individual depends upon his family for the satisfaction of most of his needs. What was done for the child in earlier times was largely done by the family. The story is familiar and has often been told. The home was the schoolhouse, the church, the playground, the courthouse, the factory, and the hospital. The family was a half dozen or more institutions rolled into one; and it is easy to see why it was such a powerful organization, especially in determining the status of the individual. Children were known as members of a given family and not so much as individuals in their own right. Wealth, mainly in land, was transmitted through the family line, and the opportunities for acquiring wealth independently were not so good in the rural stable community as they are now in our rapidly changing urban industrial society. It is recorded that in colonial times boys in college had their names placed in the catalog, not by classes, years, scholarship, or alphabetical order, but by the status and wealth of their family. A college boy at Harvard had to give the baluster side of the staircase to anyone who was his social superior. The careful "seating of the meeting" was an evidence of this regard for rank and station.[15]

The transfer of functions from the home: productive functions to the factory; educational functions to the school; protective functions to the court and the clinic, et cetera, has meant considerable loss of control by parents over their children. Especially in the

[15] Earle, *op. cit.*, pp. 222–6.

city the child functions more as an individual in his own right, less
as a representative of his family. Family reputation counts for less
than it used to in securing employment; the competence of the
individual matters more. In school the child may be called by his
first name; and while his teacher knows his family name, she may
not know his family. Individualization of behavior means more
emphasis on the child.

The transfer of functions from the family to outside agencies was
discussed in detail in an earlier chapter,[16] where the role of steam
and steel in the development of the factory was shown, as well as
the importance of developments in communication and transportation for the growth of cities. The sequence of causes, then, appears
to be technology as a crucial factor in the growth of factories and
cities, leading to the transfer of productive and other functions
from the home, resulting in the reduction in the status and influence of the family, and the consequent increase in the recognition
of the individual in his own right.

The transfer of functions, especially the functions of production
which require a head, lessens the authority of the father over his
family. This in turn admits of a democratic relationship between
family members, all the more so because of the encouragement
given by the new psychology with its emphasis on evidence rather
than authority.

In the literature of child development, there are reports of attempts to define the democratic process as it operates in the family and to relate it to child behavior. In a study by Baldwin [17]
and others at the Fels Institute, using parent behavior rating scales
which were factor-analyzed, it was found that the democratic factor is characterized by (1) consultation about policy decisions,
explanations of the reasons for rules, and explanation in response
to the child's curiosity, entailing a higher level of verbal contact
between parent and child; (2) lack of arbitrariness about decisions; (3) general permissiveness or freedom for the child; and
(4) restraint on emotionality by parents.

The school. Among the causes of the greater recognition accorded
the child in recent times, mention should be made of the increase

---

[16] Chapter 6.

[17] Alfred L. Baldwin, "Socialization and the Parent-Child Relationship,"
Child Development, 19: 127–36, 1948.

in schooling. As stated earlier, schools are mainly a service for minor children; and it is a service that has been provided for increasing numbers. Nearly all children of elementary school age are now enrolled in school in the United States.

Is more interest in children a cause of the growth of schools or is the growth of schools a cause of the greater interest in children? While there is, of course, a reciprocal influence, the following may be noted. The schools are the result mainly of (a) the transfer of functions from the home and (b) the growth of culture. Skills formerly taught in the home are now taught in schools because parents who work outside the home are not at home to teach their children. But even if there had been no transfer of productive functions from the home, so vast has been the growth of knowledge in the last century that few if any parents would be equipped to give their children the schooling they require.

Rapid social change and the educational advantage of the young. Rapid social change favors the young by widening the cultural gap between the generations. In a relatively stationary society, where changes are infrequent, the elders are favored because they are the repositories of knowledge and wisdom. The young people depend upon them for training and advice. Where conditions remain much the same for long periods of time, experience is an important teacher; and to live long is to have more experience. But in a rapidly changing society like ours, where the accumulation of knowledge is vast and growing, and where schools are established to help transmit the vast accumulation, the most recent students — the young — are the ones in a position to learn the latest and the most effective ways of doing things. Many children in the urban public schools have more knowledge about certain subjects than their parents. Some of the fields of knowledge that the children learn, like sociology, may be entirely new to the parents, since the subject was not taught when the parents went to school. In other fields, like chemistry, physics, and mathematics, there have been extensive developments over short periods of time, with which the parents may be less familiar than their children. This was scarcely possible in earlier times, since nearly everything that a child learned he learned from his parents. Today, and increasingly in the future, we can say, with more confidence than before, that a little child shall lead them.

This increasing advantage which the young have in learning the new is only partly the result of changing technology. It is the result of the total accumulation of culture, material and non-material, and the exponential rate of cultural growth, with certain limitations. If culture accumulates at an increasing rate of speed, like compound interest, then the young who are privileged to give all or most of their time to their studies are in a better position to become familiar with the new developments than the adults who must work to support the young. The growth of culture is only partly technological; but the rise in the standard of living, which provides the young with the leisure to attend school, is in large part a result of improved technology which makes more production possible. The role of technology in the educational advantage of youth is largely indirect.

Social mobility. There is another way in which rapid change favors the young, and that is through increased social mobility. The child always begins life by sharing the social status of his family, and in a relatively stationary society there are fewer chances than in a changing society that he will change his status. Status depends mainly on wealth, and wealth in an agrarian society is mainly in land. Families remain on the land, become identified with it, and come to occupy a social position which is well known in a community of familiars. So family connections become important for status, and the important question is: Who are his family? But in an urban community of strangers with frequent change of residence, family connections are not so evident; and the individual is appraised in his own right. The opportunities for improved economic and social status through schooling, the acquisition of skills, the cultivation of talent, and the making of inventions and discoveries seem greater than before.

In Western society, and especially in the United States, success is highly esteemed. This fact, plus the additional one of greater social mobility, puts a premium on the child, for the parent whose own opportunities are limited may see the opportunity of improving his status through his offspring. This means sacrificing for his child, giving the child as much training as possible to cultivate whatever skills and talents he possesses. It often means having fewer children. Whether the motivation is interest in the child for his own sake, or for the sake of the parent's ambition vicariously satisfied, or both, is often a difficult psychological question; but whatever the parental motive, the accent is on the child. In a recent study,[18] evidence is presented to show that industrial workers in the United States, realizing that they themselves will never "get ahead," still cling verbally to the traditional ambition and cherish it for their children.

Fewer children. Parents have fewer children than formerly, it is commonly said, because they want to give them more of the good things of life. The reduction in size of the family is, then, a cause of the child's receiving more attention. It is, simply stated, a matter of supply and demand. Given a certain quantity of goods and services, the fewer the children, the greater the share of each child. In the case of the only child, the portion is commonly thought to be excessive and to be responsible for spoiling the child. Recent studies have tended to minimize the differences in emotional and social adjustment of only children and other children.[19] Such findings, however, do not necessarily mean that only children receive no more attention than other children. The findings may mean that in the case of only children precautions are taken to avoid spoiling, preventions which are not needed in the case of children who have brothers and sisters. The extra precautions in the case of the only children would represent extra attention from their parents.

The law of supply and demand operates in two ways. As regards the supply of goods, the fewer the children, the greater the number of goods per child. With reference to the supply of children, the fewer the children, the greater the value attached to each child. If demand remains the same and the supply diminishes, the value goes up. If a woman bears a child every two or three years, as she often does in simple agricultural societies, what if one or more dies? Another will come along in due course. But if she has only one or two children, the loss of a child is more keenly felt. The smaller family means, all things being equal, that the children are appreciated more.

It might be argued by some that the reduction in the number of

---

[18] Ely Chinoy, "The Tradition of Opportunity and the Aspirations of Automobile Workers," *American Journal of Sociology*, 57: 453–9, March, 1952.

[19] W. Paul Carter, *The Only Child and Other Birth Orders* (Doctoral dissertation, University of Chicago Libraries, 1937).

children is an indication of less regard for the child, not more. According to this view, increased indifference or hostility toward children would be evident if it could be shown that there has been an increase in married couples with no children. The incidence of childlessness in the United States does appear to have increased in recent times. In 1940 the percentage of native-white women who were married and living with their husbands, and who had reached the age of forty-five without having borne a child was 15.6, whereas in 1910 it was 9.3.[20] Women forty-five years of age and over have usually completed their families and passed beyond the fecund period. A number of religious groups hold the view that a basic concern for children is primarily manifested in having as many as health and circumstances will permit. We need to know why there has been an increase in childlessness, but the evidence is not clear. Various studies indicate that where women reach the age of forty-five without ever having borne a child, the childlessness is involuntary.[21] Contraception, it seems, is used mainly to space and postpone pregnancies rather than to avoid pregnancy altogether.

To return to the original question under discussion in this section: Does the decline in family size in the last century and especially the increase in childlessness mean that children are valued less highly than they used to be? This is a psychological and moral question which it is difficult to answer because of the conflicting ideas as to what is meant by "valuing the child." There are those who believe that affection for children is best expressed by having as many of them as possible, on the theory that souls are waiting to be born; and wilful failure to bear a child deprives a soul of the potentialities and opportunities of life, essential to immortality. On the other hand, there are those who believe that regard for children is best expressed by having only as many children as can be given a secure, happy childhood and adequate preparation for the responsibilities of adulthood. This discussion is, then, not very satisfactory because of the differing conceptions of "regard for the child."

[20] Bureau of the Census, *Population-Differential Fertility, 1940 and 1910: Women by Number of Children Ever Born* (Washington: U.S. Government Printing Office, 1945). Computed from Tables 13 and 15.

[21] *Social and Psychological Factors Affecting Fertility.* A study of 41,498 native-white couples in Indianapolis, sponsored by the Milbank Memorial Fund.

If, however, we take a more objective criterion of concern for the child, namely, what is done for the child, that is, the amount of attention, goods, and services he receives from adults, there seems to be little doubt that the trend has been toward a greater concern for the child. Fewer children, and more goods and services mean more goods and services per child, assuming that the increased productivity of our economic system and the increased services of government and other organizations are equally shared with our children. We need here a study of the shares of children and adults in the increased industrial and governmental output. Perhaps children today receive a relatively smaller share than the adults do, but in absolute terms there is no question that children in modern times receive more attention and more goods and services than did the children of yesteryear. Also, preliminary studies of children in the United States, from the standpoint of family size, indicate that the small family with its limitation of family size and emphasis on the proper training and education of children results in children's receiving considerable attention. They are constantly compared with other children and encouraged to reach certain goals. Cooperation with parents is sought, indicating that responsibility devolves upon the child, who is recognized as a person in his own right. In the large family, the group is emphasized, especially in economic matters, and the greater organization that is required leads more often to authoritarian patterns.[22]

Summary. This chapter has been concerned with the trend toward the greater emphasis on childhood in Western society in modern times. Recently societal interest has been shifting to the aged, but whether this will mean relatively less interest in children in the future is not clear. Both ends of the life span may gain in the relative amount of popular attention they command, at the expense of the middle years of life. In absolute terms, there may be gains for all three age categories because of the spectacular increase in productivity and leisure, making it possible for society to do more for all age groups. Relatively more may be done for the aged because of the increase in the proportion of old people and the increase in their power as voters; and more may be done

[22] James H. S. Bossard and Winogene Pratt Sanger, "The Large Family System — A Research Report," *American Sociological Review,* 17: 3–9, February, 1952.

for the children because of the advantage in getting off to a good start in matters of health and education. Whatever the future, in the recent past in the United States there has been a growing societal regard for the needs of children. This has expressed itself in more health and medical services, more education, more recreation, and more protection.

When we turn to the search for causes of this accentuation of childhood, we observe that they relate mainly to advances in the sciences of man, both psychological and biological. Discoveries as to (a) the special importance of the early years of life for personality development and mental health, inspired principally by the pioneer work of Sigmund Freud, and (b) the nature and importance of individual differences in intelligence, skills, and capacities have served to focus attention on the child. These developments are mainly of an ideological nature, with little or no basis in technology.

At the same time, the medical sciences have made great strides in nutrition, and in coping with the infectious and contagious diseases. These advances have greatest relevance to childhood. In them the technological factor is evident but subordinate.

A third set of factors relates to the changing institutional order. The transfer of functions from the home to industry and the state has resulted in the loss of status and power by the family and the concomitant increase in emphasis upon the individual. The transfer of functions was a factor in the growth of the school, although an even more important factor has been the phenomenal growth of culture. The school system, in which our society has a heavy investment, emphasizes the child inasmuch as the school is mainly an institution for children. Rapid social change, resulting from the multiplicity of inventions and discoveries, favors the young, since in the educational process they are the principal beneficiaries of the new knowledge. Rapid social change also favors the young because of the increased social mobility which it affords.

Of the changed functions of the family, another that has particular significance for this discussion is the reduction in family size. Family limitation means that children are more likely to be the result of choice, and wanted children are more likely to be the recipients of parental affection and attention. In earlier times children were valued more as workers, whereas today when the need for their labor is much less, they are valued more as persons. With the supply reduced, children are generally valued more highly, and they are also the beneficiaries of larger shares of available goods and services. The causes of the reduction in family size were considered in an earlier chapter,[23] where the role of the technological factor was delineated both in (a) creating the new economic order in which the need for the labor of children is lessened, and the cost of rearing them increased, resulting in a desire for smaller families; and (b) providing more effective means by which this desire may be satisfied and the size of family limited.

[23] Chapter 5.

10

More Disruption

Our principal charge in this chapter is to account for the increase in the divorce rate in the United States in the last century.
That it has increased is common knowledge. Many aspects of the
change in the divorce rate, however, are not so familiar as is the
fact of an increasing yearly rate. So our first task will be to describe in some detail the changes that have occurred, with special
attention to those aspects that are less familiar.

At the outset a word of caution is in order as to the meaning of
an increase in the divorce rate. It does not necessarily mean an
increase in marital unhappiness. Divorce reflects marital unhappiness, but not all marital unhappiness results in divorce. If divorce
is taboo, as in a Catholic community, unhappily married couples
will either remain together or they will separate. A well-known
Catholic prelate has offered advice on "How to Stay Married
Though Unhappy." [1] Separation is a better index of marital discord than divorce, but we do not have statistics on separation over
an extended period of time. Even separation rates would not fully
reflect the prevalence of marital unhappiness, because many
couples, although dissatisfied with their marriages, remain together
for the sake of their children or because of a sense of duty or
other similar reason. Annulments may sometimes be had in lieu
of divorces. An increase in the divorce rate may mean only that it
is easier to get a divorce, or to put it differently, that there are
fewer restraints upon discordant couples who wish to sever their
marital ties. These considerations will be further explored, after
we have examined some significant changes in the divorce rate itself.

[1] Fulton J. Sheen, *Good Housekeeping*, February, 1953, pp. 59 ff.

The Increasing Divorce Rate

It would be helpful to know the proportion of all marriages that end in divorce and the chances of divorce for a marital group of a given age, even as we know the life expectancy of the various age groups, but such knowledge is not available. Crude divorce rates are often expressed in terms of total population (number of divorces per 1,000 population); but plainly the whole population, which includes young children, does not contribute to the divorce rate. Hence this is an unrealistic basis for computing the divorce rate. Another method is to compare the number of divorces in a given year with the number of marriages in that same year. The marriage-divorce ratio gives the relative magnitude of marriages and divorces for a given year, not the number of marriages of a given year ending in divorce, for the divorces in any year represent marriages that were entered into at varying times in the past. A more realistic approach is to consider the segment of the total population which is exposed to the risk of divorce, namely, the married population. Data on this basis are shown in the extreme right-hand column of Table 21. But whether divorces are related to the total population, or to the number of marriages of that same year, or to the average number of marriages of the preceding ten years, the pattern turns out to be much the same.

Figure 2 shows an almost uninterrupted increase in the divorce rate for the period for which we have statistics. Shortly after the Civil War (1867) the rate was perhaps less than two per 1,000 married females. At the turn of the century, it was four; a few years after the close of World War I, in 1920, it was eight; and after World War II, in 1946, it was 17.8. The rate has been accelerating in every generation in the period under review.

Inspection of Figure 2 shows that there have been three major deviations from the long-time trend: a rise in 1920 (after World War I), a decline during the depression of the early 1930's, and a sharp upturn during and after World War II. The all-time high in the divorce rate was achieved in 1946: 4.3 per 1,000 population, 26.8 per 100 marriages in that same year, 18.5 per 1,000 married couples. Rates have dropped since 1946 but are still higher (1950) than at any time prior to 1942. These fluctuations around the trend

TABLE 21

Divorce Rate in the United States, 1887–1950*

(Number of divorces per 1000 total population; number per 100 marriages of the same years; number per 100 marriages, average for preceding 10 years, including the year in question; and number per 1000 married females 15 years of age and over)

Year	Number	Per 1000 Population	Per 100 Marriages in the Same Year	Per 100 Marriages Average for Preceding 10 Years	Per 1000 Married Females 15 yrs. of Age and Over
1867	9,937	0.3	2.8	...	...
1887	27,919	0.47	5.5	...	...
1900	55,751	0.73	7.9	9.27	4.0
1910	83,045	0.90	8.8	9.97	4.7
1915	104,298	1.05	10.4	...	...
1916	114,000	1.13	10.6	11.7	...
1917	121,564	1.20	10.6	12.3	...
1918	116,254	1.12	11.6	11.5	...
1919	141,527	1.35	12.3	13.7	...
1920	170,505	1.60	13.4	16.0	8.0
1921	159,580	1.47	13.7	14.7	...
1922	148,815	1.35	13.1	13.5	...
1923	165,096	1.48	13.4	14.7	...
1924	170,952	1.51	14.4	15.0	...
1925	175,449	1.53	14.8	15.2	...
1926	180,853	1.55	15.0	15.5	...
1927	192,037	1.62	16.0	16.4	...
1928	195,939	1.63	16.6	16.5	...
1929	201,468	1.66	16.3	16.8	...
1930	191,591	1.56	17.0	16.2	7.5
1931	183,664	1.48	17.3	15.6	7.1
1932	160,338	1.28	16.3	14.1	6.1
1933	165,000	1.3	15.0	14.3	6.1
1934	204,000	1.6	15.7	17.6	7.5
1935	218,000	1.7	16.4	18.6	7.8
1936	236,000	1.8	17.2	19.8	8.3
1937	249,000	1.9	17.5	20.6	8.7
1938	244,000	1.9	18.5	19.9	8.4
1939	251,000	1.9	18.3	20.3	8.5

Year	Number	Per 1000 Population	Per 100 Marriages in the Same Year	Per 100 Marriages Average for Preceding 10 Years	Per 1000 Married Females 15 yrs. of Age and Over
1940	264,000	2.0	16.9	20.6	8.7
1941	293,000	2.2	17.27	21.5	9.4
1942	321,000	2.4	18.11	22.4	10.1
1943	359,000	2.6	22.76	24.2	11.0
1944	400,000	2.9	27.54	26.7	12.1
1945	485,000	3.5	30.06	31.8	14.5
1946	610,000	4.3	26.62	37.7	17.8
1947	483,000	3.4	24.24	28.9	13.7
1948	408,000	2.8	22.48	23.7	11.3
1949	397,000	2.7	25.12	22.8	10.8
1950	385,000	2.6	23.05	22.1	10.3

* Bureau of the Census, *Marriage and Divorce, 1931* (Washington, D.C., 1932); *Marriage and Divorce, 1932* (1934); *Marriage and Divorce Statistics — United States, 1887–1937* (1940); *Estimated Number of Divorces by State: United States, 1937–1940* (1942). Office of Vital Statistics, *Vital Statistics, Special Reports, State Summaries*, Vol. 30, No. 1, 1947, Table 2, p. 13; *Statistical Abstract of the United States, 1952*, p. 80; Office of Vital Statistics, *Vital Statistics, Special Reports, National Summaries*, Vol. 36, No. 2, 1949, Table A, p. 13. Estimates for 1933 to 1937 made by Samuel A. Stouffer and Lyle M. Spencer, "Recent Increases in Marriage and Divorce," *American Journal of Sociology*, 44: 551–4. More recent estimates made by National Office of Vital Statistics, *Summary of Marriage and Divorce Statistics: United States, 1950* (Vital Statistics — Special Reports, Vol. 37, No. 3, October 29, 1952).

are thought to be associated with changes in the business cycle and with the effects of war. Divorces tend to increase during times of prosperity and to decrease during economic depressions. The influence of war is reflected in the increase in hasty and ill-advised marriages, in the strain and changed perspectives that are associated with long separation. The two World Wars of the United States have also affected the divorce rate indirectly because of the war-induced prosperity. War ordinarily brings a temporary decline in divorces, followed by a large postwar increase.

The divorce rate, it may be noted, has been increasing at a low exponential rate during the past half century in the United States.

The increase in the divorce rate during the past half century has not been limited to the United States but has been world-wide,

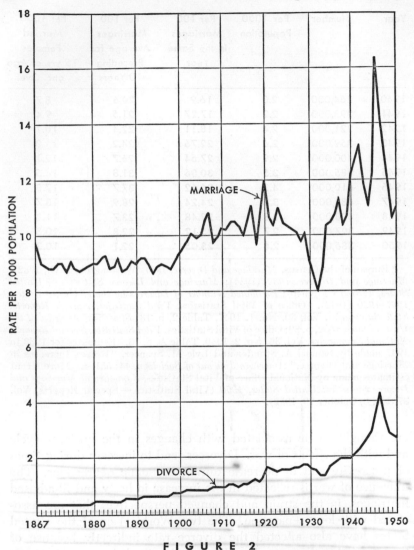

FIGURE 2

Marriage and Divorce Rates, United States, 1867–1950

and the situation in eight countries is shown in Figure 3. In most Western nations permitting divorce, the trend has been much like our own: a steady increase since the turn of the century, with a marked increase during World War II and immediately thereafter, and a downturn since then. Norway and Sweden have experienced

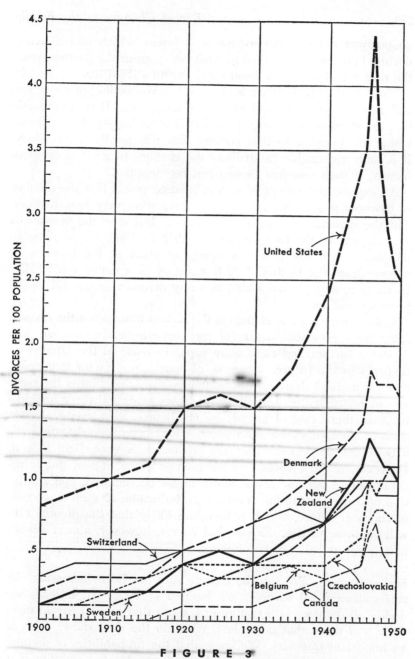

FIGURE 3

The Worldwide Increase in Divorce
(Annual Divorce Rates in Different Countries of the World, 1900–1950)

no postwar decline. An exception is Japan, which had a steady decline in divorce from 1900 to 1940, although in the postwar years the rate has risen to the level obtaining in 1915–1919.

The world-wide increase in divorce is a compelling phenomenon and raises at once the question as to its causes. It is conceivable that the increase in divorce in each country is largely due to causes which are peculiar to that country, but this hardly seems likely. It is more reasonable to attribute the changes to a set of common factors, if such common factors can be identified.

An exponential rate of growth of divorce means that the number of divorces is accelerating. At first there were very few divorces, and the increase proceeded very slowly. But now the increase is very rapid. In the four years from 1942 to 1946, the increase in the number of divorces was nearly as great as the increase in divorce from the beginning of our history as a nation until 1942.[2] In these four years we added as many divorces as we did in the previous 166 years.

Unless there is some change in the factors influencing the divorce rate, the exponential nature of the curve indicates that we may expect a further and even more rapid increase in the number of divorces in the future. There is, of course, one factor that could cause a marked decrease in the divorce rate; and that is the passage of restrictive legislation. If the laws against divorce are prohibitive, there can, of course, be no divorce. The probability of such prohibitive legislation in a country like the United States with a two-hundred-year-old tradition of divorce is very slight indeed. However, if the divorce rate should rise much higher, public reaction might become acute, alarm might be sounded, and restrictive measures instituted. There is no indication of such a reaction in the near future, and it is therefore likely that the divorce rate will continue to rise. Exponential curves, however, almost always flatten out and do not rise forever.

Earlier divorce. We say the divorce rate has been increasing. In this statement all divorces are lumped together. If, instead, we divide all divorces into two groups, those that occur early in marriage and those that occur late, what do the data show? This is an important question. We know that the probabilities of divorce are greater in the early years of marriage. Marital stability is a function of time, there is selection for happiness, and the unhappily wedded are sifted out. It is easier to remarry, especially in the case of women, at the younger ages. It is also easier to get a divorce at the younger ages because there are fewer children or no children. So we expect the divorce rate to be relatively high among those who have been married a short time, and we expect the rate to decrease among those who have been married a longer time. An exception is the middle years of married life when the children have grown up and left home, removing an obstacle to divorce; and when marital adjustment may be complicated by the menopause. The percentage of all divorces granted in the United States in 1950 decreased by single years of married life until the nineteenth year when it increased somewhat.[3]

T A B L E 22

Divorces by Duration of Marriage *

Number of years married	Per cent of all divorces		
	1887–1906	1932	1950
Less than 1 year	2.1	3.9	6.3
1 year	3.1	7.0	10.1
2 years	6.8	8.3	10.1
3 years	8.1	8.5	9.8
4 years	8.2	8.0	9.2
5 years	7.6	7.2	5.8
6 years	7.0	6.5	4.4
7 years	6.3	5.6	4.2
8 years	5.6	5.2	4.2
9 years	4.9	4.5	3.5
10–14 years	18.0	16.6	11.9
15–19 years	10.2	8.5	7.3
20 years and over	12.1	10.1	11.1

* Adapted from the Bureau of the Census, *Marriage and Divorce, 1931*, p. 27; 1932, p. 5. Figures for 1950 from Public Health Service, *Vital Statistics of the United States 1950*, p. 30. The 1950 data include annulments which were 1.9 per cent of the total dissolutions by divorce and annulments. In 1950, 2.1 per cent of divorces and annulments were not reported by duration of marriage. The data for 1950 are for 16 reporting states.

[3] Public Health Service, *Vital Statistics of the United States 1950* (Washington, D.C., 1953), p. 30.

These data tell us that divorce is more likely to occur in the early years of marriage than in the later ones, but they do not tell us whether there has been an *increase* in early divorces. When we examine the trend of divorce by duration of marriage, we note an increase in the rate for all durations but the sharpest increase among those married only a few years. Those married less than seven years accounted for 42.9 per cent of all divorces from 1887–1906, 49.4 per cent in 1932, and 55.7 per cent in 1950, as shown in Table 22. Another way to observe the change is to note that in the earliest period for which we have records, 1867–86, more divorces occurred in the seventh year of marriage than in any other year. From 1887–1906 the modal year for divorces was the fifth year, while from 1922 to 1932 it fluctuated between the third and the fourth year.[4] In 1950, divorces were at a maximum in the first and second years of marriage. Usually a period of separation precedes divorce. There is some evidence that the time interval between separation and legal divorce has been reduced, which means that the divorce process has been expedited.

If the increase in divorce were largely confined to marriages of short duration, we could conclude that the trend has been for marriages to stabilize in the later years. But the increase in divorce, while greater for those married a relatively short time, has been appreciable for all durations of marriage as shown in Figure 4. Consider also the per cent of males of given ages who are divorced. In 1950, of males twenty to twenty-four years old, 0.9 per cent were divorced; in 1920, the figure was 0.2 per cent. The later figure is four and one-half times the earlier. For those thirty-five to forty-four years old, the corresponding percentages are 2.5 and 0.9, or less than a threefold increase.[5] So the increase in divorce was appreciable at both age levels, but greater at the earlier years.

When we think of a normal marriage, we picture a husband and wife living together. Data on the percentage of married males, with wife present, give us a better idea of changes in family stability than do divorce statistics, which are more subject to error. In

[4] Kingsley Davis, "Children of Divorced Parents: A Sociological and Statistical Analysis," *Law and Contemporary Problems* (Duke Law School), Summer, 1944, p. 712.

[5] Bureau of the Census, *1950 United States Census of Population, U.S. Summary: Detailed Characteristics* (Washington, D.C., 1953), Table 102, p. 180.

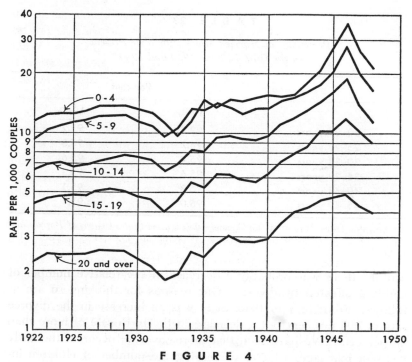

FIGURE 4

Divorce Rate, By Duration of Marriage, 1922–1950

(Source: Paul H. Jacobsen, "Differentials in Divorce by Duration of Marriage and Size of Family," *American Sociological Review*, 15: 241, April, 1950.)

Table 23 we have such data on unbroken marriages by certain age groups of husbands. These data show that in 1950 smaller percentages of husbands under thirty-five years of age had their wives living with them than in 1940, whereas for husbands aged thirty-five to forty-four, the percentage with wife present was somewhat higher in 1950. These data show that the change in the decade has been in the direction of less stability in the marriages of the younger husbands and somewhat more stability in the marriages of the older husbands.

Trend of number of children in divorce. It is obvious that since the number of divorces has increased over the years, an increasing number of children have been affected by divorce. What we want to know, though, is whether the proportion of children involved in divorce has changed. Until the third decade of the twentieth

T A B L E   23

Percentage of Married Males with Wife Present
*in the United States, 1950 and 1940 ***

Age	Per cent	
	1950	1940
20–24 years	92.7	93.2
25–29 years	94.7	95.3
30–34 years	95.4	95.6
35–39 years	95.6	95.3
40–44 years	95.3	95.1
45–49 years	95.0	95.1

* Adapted from Bureau of the Census, *1950 United States Census of Population*, *U.S. Summary: Detailed Characteristics* (Washington, D.C., 1953), Table 106, p. 191.

century there was probably a decrease in the relative number of children affected by divorce. Our reasons for thinking so are as follows. From 1871 to 1940, there was an increase in the divorce rate of 600 per cent but a decrease in the birth rate of more than 50 per cent. We have seen that more divorces occur in the early years of marriage, a factor decreasing the number of children involved. The divorce rate has risen more rapidly in the city than on the farm, where the birth rate is higher. During the last two decades, however, a change has occurred. If we compare the average for the period 1922–32 with the year 1948, we find that, whether children are involved or not, the number of children per divorce increased from 0.68 to 0.74.[6] In this period during which the birth rate increased, the total number of children affected by divorce increased more rapidly than the number of divorces. If this change continues, in the future children may not be so great an obstacle to divorce as they have been in the past.

More remarriage. The significance of divorce lies mainly in what it does to those affected. We are greatly concerned about the effects of divorce on children, especially in our small-family system which often leaves the child of divorce without the association, love, protection, and socializing influence of one of his parents.

[6] Paul H. Jacobson, "Differentials in Divorce by Duration of Marriage and Size of Family," *American Sociological Review*, 15: 241, April, 1950.

This contrasts sharply with the situation in the large-family system of many societies where the kinship group serves to shield the child from many of the traumatic effects of divorce. This is what makes it significant to consider, as we have in preceding paragraphs, whether we have had an increase in the proportion of children affected by divorce.

What happens to the adults is also important. If divorce means loneliness, emotional deprivation, and economic dependency, it is one thing; it is quite another thing if it leads to remarriage with the possibility of happiness and adjustment. It is therefore highly significant that the data show an increase in remarriage following divorce.

In 1940 in the United States the Bureau of the Census showed that the total number of divorced persons who had not remarried was 1.5 million. From 1940 to 1947 the total number of divorces granted was 2.7 million. If we make allowance for those who died during this period, probably not more than 100,000, we have a total pool of divorced persons, 1940–47, of about 6.8 million. In April, 1947, a nation-wide sample survey revealed that there were about two million divorced persons who had not remarried.[7] This means that in the seven year period a great majority of the divorced persons had remarried.

The next year (April, 1948) for the first time the Bureau of the Census collected nation-wide data on the number of times men and women had married and the duration of the present marital status.[8] A comparison of the survey data with vital statistics data on divorce showed that about three-fourths of the persons getting a divorce from 1943–48 had remarried. For those divorced in the period 1934–43, about six-sevenths had remarried by April, 1948.[9]

Another study [10] shows that the percentage of remarried women

[7] Bureau of the Census, *Current Population Reports — Population Characteristics: Characteristics of Single, Widowed, and Divorced Persons in 1947.* Series P–20, No. 10, February 6, 1948.

[8] Bureau of the Census, *Current Population Reports — Population Characteristics: Marital Status, Number of Times Married, and Duration of Present Marital Status: April, 1948.* Series P–20, No. 23, March 4, 1949.

[9] Paul Glick, "First Marriages and Remarriages," *American Sociological Review,* 14: 730, December, 1949.

[10] Metropolitan Life Insurance Company, "The Frequency of Remarriage," *Statistical Bulletin,* January, 1949, p. 8.

among those previously widowed or divorced was about one-sixth greater in 1940 than in 1910. The gains occurred at all ages but especially at the younger ages. For those between the ages of twenty-five and thirty-four years, somewhat more than three-fifths had remarried in 1940, whereas in 1910 the proportion was about one-half. So there is more remarriage after divorce.

We turn now to the consideration of a group of selected individuals, a group of gifted children (I.Q. over 140) that Lewis Terman met and studied in early childhood and has followed through the years as they have grown up. In 1945, when the average age of the group was thirty-five years, 14.4 per cent of the men and 16.3 per cent of the women had been divorced or separated, and 73 per cent and 64 per cent respectively had already remarried.[11] This study does not throw light on divorce trends; but it does furnish us with data on the high rate of remarriage in our time, for a selected group.

An interesting question is whether remarriages are taking place sooner than they used to. Is the interval between divorce and remarriage shorter? In an earlier chapter [12] we saw that first marriages are occurring sooner, and in this chapter we have shown that first divorces are occurring sooner. Perhaps remarriages are happening sooner, too; and divorced persons do not wait so long as they once did after the interlocutory decree to get remarried. We do not have any data on this question, but it is widely thought by students of the family that in many cases of divorce the candle to the new love has been lighted before the candle to the old love has been snuffed out. Reno has the highest marriage rate of any American city, mainly because many couples remarry immediately after being divorced.

On the question of the remarriage of divorced persons, it is interesting to know that the marriage rate for the divorced is higher than that for the single or the widowed of the same age.[13] Widowed persons may be handicapped by having more children. It

11 Lewis M. Terman and Melita H. Oden, *The Gifted Child Grows Up* (Stanford, California: Stanford University Press, 1947).

12 Chapter 4.

13 Metropolitan Life Insurance Company, *Statistical Bulletin*, "Chances of Eventual Marriage for the Single, Widowed, and Divorced Persons, New England, 1940," May, 1945, p. 2.

is thought that the divorced are more marriageable than the single of the same age.

If a person gets a divorce and is remarried, are his chances of being divorced a second time greater than the chances of divorce for married persons generally? If so, this would mean that divorced persons as a group do not make as desirable mates as, say, widowed persons who remarry. A sample survey in the United States in April, 1948,[14] showed that divorced persons included relatively larger proportions of persons who had been married more than once than did non-divorced persons. It is possible that for some of these persons the earlier marriages terminated in bereavement and they are not persons who have been twice-divorced. On the other hand, as stated above, the chances of remarriage are, age for age, greater for the divorced than for the widowed; and the probabilities are, therefore, that most of these divorced persons who have been twice-married were previously divorced.

The high divorce rate in the United States is publicized but not so the increasingly high rates of remarriage. Yet the latter is very significant. In the public mind a high divorce rate is associated with societal instability and is generally regarded as an evil. But a high divorce rate in itself does not mean that the society is unstable. There are many societies not considered unstable that have divorce rates higher than ours. Murdock [15] undertook to assess the relative stability of the American family by comparing it with a sample of forty societies, eight each from Asia, Oceania, Africa, and native North and South America. Among twenty-four of these societies, divorce rates exceeded those in the United States, yet these societies are not considered unstable. Perhaps one factor in their stability is the high remarriage rate that usually obtains.

There is evidence that a good many divorced persons who remarry make good adjustments in their new marriages. Terman [16]

[14] Bureau of the Census, *op. cit.*
[15] George P. Murdock, "Family Stability in Non-European Cultures," *The Annals of the American Academy of Political and Social Science*, 272: 195–201, November, 1950.
[16] Lewis M. Terman, *Psychological Factors in Marital Happiness* (New York: McGraw-Hill Book Company, 1948), p. 174. In this sample, fifty-four husbands and thirty-three wives had been previously married and divorced. It may be noted that Terman's subjects were volunteers and therefore probably selected for happiness.

in his study of 792 California couples concluded that a majority of the divorced couples remarry and are on the average about as happy in their new marriages as those who have not been divorced. In another study[17] the marital adjustment scores of forty-seven remarried divorced persons were compared with the scores of a group of sixty-four persons married only once. Divorced-remarried women, it is reported, are as good risks in their subsequent marriages as women who marry only once; but this is not true of men. There is probably a selective process at work in marriage. In general those who are most stable emotionally get married and stay married. But even those who are stable and who are temperamentally disposed to happiness may make bad choices of a mate or may be affected adversely by trying circumstances. Divorces presumably are contributed by the latter group as well as by those who are emotionally unsuited for matrimony. Selection continues among the divorced; most of them, as we have seen, remarry, but some do not. It is quite likely that there is a selection on the basis of aptitude for happiness. Of those who marry a second time, some will get a second divorce. Among these, there are more frequent repeaters to whom divorce becomes a chronic experience. A comparison[18] of the profiles on the Johnson Temperament Analysis of twice-divorced persons and maritally maladjusted men and women in their first marriages showed that the outstanding difference between the "two-time losers" and the other group lay in the greater tendency of the former to nag and find fault.

Appraisal of the data on divorce rates. Before turning to the consideration of the causes of the increase of divorce, which is our principal interest in this chapter, some observations are in order on the shortcomings of the data on divorce rates. Divorces do not tell the whole story of domestic discord. In addition to an undetermined number of unhappily married couples who continue to live together, a large number are not living together. The 1950

[17] Harvey J. Locke and William J. Klausner, "Prediction of Marital Adjustment of Divorced Persons in Subsequent Marriages," *Research Studies of the State College of Washington,* Vol. 16, pp. 30–33, 1948.

[18] Shirley Raines, *Personality Traits of Persons Who Divorced and Remarried* (Unpublished Master's Thesis in the Library of the University of Southern California, January, 1949).

Census reported that there were 2.4 million divorced persons in the United States that year, and in addition there were a little over two million married persons who were separated from their spouses as a result of marital discord. Separations were relatively more numerous among non-whites and in cities.[19] An earlier study, based on 1940 data, showed that separations were more prevalent in the young and old-age groups, in service occupations, and in low-income groups of laborers.[20]

There is perhaps a tendency for the relative number of separated persons to decline and the number of divorced persons to increase, as divorce comes to be more acceptable. There is evidence in some of our northern cities, for instance, of the greater use of divorce by Negroes, who are persuaded that divorce is a sign of respectability, as desertion is not. Divorce is more common in the middle class, desertion in the lower class; and the up-grading of the population in recent decades has probably resulted in an increased preference for divorce as compared with desertion.

Where statistics are limited to divorce, annulments are also ignored. In 1946, the peak year of marital dissolutions to date, 22,000 or 3.5 per cent of all legal dissolutions were annulments. In some jurisdictions annulments loom large in the total picture of family disorganization. In the state of New York in 1946 annulments constituted about one-third of all dissolutions. The reason is that in New York divorce is for adultery only, while annulment may be had on any one of eight grounds, some ill-defined. The Catholic Church permits annulments but not divorces.

The limitations of the divorce statistics may be briefly stated as follows. The raw data are available at the county level as records of the divorce proceedings. Abstracts of the divorces are filed with a central state agency in a limited number of states. The items reported vary greatly. Tables are supplied to the National Office of Vital Statistics in Washington by about one-half of the states. Some information on divorce is obtained by the decennial census; and also at the national level, there are periodic sample surveys, the results of which are published as *Current Population*

[19] Bureau of the Census, *1950 United States Census of Population, U.S. Summary: Detailed Characteristics* (Washington, D.C., 1953), Table 104.

[20] William F. Ogburn, "Marital Separations," *American Journal of Sociology,* 49: 316–23, January, 1944.

Reports. There is under-enumeration of divorced persons who report themselves as single or widowed because of the onus and penalties attaching to divorce. Insofar as these limitations of the data vary from year to year, they introduce an error into comparative studies of divorce rates; but it is hardly likely that they invalidate the general observation of an increasing divorce rate.

Causes of the Increasing Divorce Rate

What is the increasing divorce rate due to? It may mean that men and women are less happy in marriage than they used to be, or that it is easier to get a divorce, or both. In terms of divorce, the two variables are *desire* and *opportunity.* There may be more desire for divorce because there is more marital unhappiness, or there may be more opportunity for divorce because there are fewer obstacles in the path of those who wish to terminate their marriages. These two factors may combine in four possible ways: (1) more desire and more opportunity, which would provide the most favorable conditions for an increase in the divorce rates; (2) more desire and less opportunity. This could lead to more divorce if the weight of the first factor was greater than that of the second; (3) less desire and more opportunity, which could result in more divorce if the weight of the second factor exceeded that of the first; (4) less desire and less opportunity. This would lead to a reduction in the divorce rate and may therefore be ruled out of consideration. The evidence favors the view that there is now more opportunity for divorce than there used to be, and so the question to be answered is whether this is accompanied by an increase or decrease or a constant amount of marital happiness.

The trend of marital happiness. The evidence on this question of the trend of marital happiness in the United States is very scanty and almost non-existent. The Institute of Family Relations in Los Angeles accumulated information on 394 marriages which took place toward the end of the last century. The marriages were from various parts of the United States, middle class, white, with one child each. Ratings of these marriages by people who knew them showed 60 per cent as "definitely happy," 24 per cent as "doubtful," and 16 per cent as "definitely unhappy." [21] These figures may be compared with those for another group of 4,256 marriages, also representing a generation around the turn of the century, which rated 62 per cent happy, 17 per cent doubtful, and 21 per cent unhappy. These families likewise included only those with children.[22] How do these findings that at least 60 per cent of the marriages that produced at least one child back in the horse and buggy days were definitely happy compare with the findings of today? The well-known surveys of L. M. Terman [23] and E. W. Burgess [24] indicate that up to World War II from 60 to 70 per cent of the marriages in the educated part of the population were rated as happy. These studies show no marked differences between the proportion of happy marriages in the decade before World War II and in the period half a century earlier; but in these studies duration of marriage is not controlled, nor are the studies based on representative, random samples. The studies therefore do not permit us to make valid generalizations about the married population of the United States.[25]

In the spring of 1947, married students at the State College of Washington were asked in an anonymous questionnaire [26] to rate their marriages as happy or unhappy; and the same question was put to their mothers. The results were about the same: 49 per cent happy for the mothers and 51 per cent for the daughters. The report is not, however, based on a representative sample, nor is the age factor kept constant.

[21] "Marital Happiness — Then and Now," *Family Life* (Los Angeles: American Institute of Family Relations), Vol. 7, No. 8, August, 1947, pp. 1–3.

[22] Paul Popenoe and Donna Wicks, "Marital Happiness in Two Generations," *Mental Hygiene*, 21(2): 218–223, April, 1937.

[23] *Op. cit.*

[24] *Predicting Success or Failure in Marriage* (with Leonard Cottrell, Jr.) (New York: Prentice-Hall, Inc., 1939).

[25] Terman also compared the happiness scores of his younger and older subjects (*op. cit.*, p. 178). Those married zero to five years, both sexes, were somewhat more happy than those married fifteen years or more. This is a comparison of two different age groups at the same time, whereas what we need for present purposes are data for the same age group at two different historical periods.

[26] Paul H. Landis, *Two Generations of Rural and Urban Women Appraise Marital Happiness*. Bulletin No. 524. Washington Agricultural Experiment Station, Institute of Agricultural Sciences, The State College of Washington, March, 1951.

There is another approach to the problem of the nature of the
trend of marital happiness, and that is via the analysis of changes
in the factors affecting marital happiness. A number of these factors have been isolated by research, and the question is whether
changes may be noted in these factors over a period of time. Terman concluded from his data that two factors in marital happiness
are a happy temperament and about equal mental ability in husband and wife. The causes of happy temperament, whether
genetic or situational or both, are not clear, nor is there any evidence that the temperament of Americans has changed in the last
century or so. On the relative mental ability of husbands and
wives, then and now, there is also no knowledge. Another highly
significant item in marital happiness is the happiness of one's
parents; but this is not helpful to us here, because it is precisely
what we are trying to discover, namely, how much happiness there
was in earlier generations. Another finding is that children who
had no conflict with their mothers tend to make happier marriages.
Do children today have less conflict with their mothers than in
earlier times? Still another factor associated with marital happiness
is "firm but not harsh discipline." It is probably quite generally
believed that discipline for children is not so harsh as it once was;
but in this permissive age, many believe that it is not so firm either,

There are a number of factors which are more easily measured
or on which we have some data, and these have been investigated
as to their bearing on marital happiness but without decisive result.
The relationship of the length of acquaintanceship before marriage
to marital adjustment has been investigated, with the Burgess-
Cottrell study finding that a long acquaintance is more favorable
and the Terman study reporting that this factor has only slight
significance. It may be assumed that in our heterogeneous and
mobile modern society, young people have shorter periods of acquaintance before marriage than was the case when boy and girl
lived on adjoining farms. Age at marriage has also been investigated in its relationship to marital adjustment but with inconclusive
results. There is a little suggestion that marriage at an early age
(under twenty) is less favorable than marriage at a later age. That
marriage has been occurring at an earlier age in the United States
was reported in an earlier chapter. Indeed the prospects of early
marriage are better in the United States than in any other Western

country for which we have data. About 17 per cent of our girls at ages fifteen to nineteen are married (1951), compared with 6 per cent in France and 4 per cent in England.[27]

Other factors that have been studied in relation to marital happiness are occupation, education, and income. It is known that the marriages of farmers are more stable than those of other groups, the farmers having only about one-half their proportionate share of divorces. Does this mean they are more happily married? A survey [28] of 3,528 marriages that had lasted five years or more indicated that this is so. Of the farm marriages, 68 per cent were rated happy. The rating of other occupational groups was as follows: professional, 61 per cent; higher semi-professional and business, 59 per cent; lower semi-professional and business, 54.7 per cent; skilled labor, 54.5 per cent; semi-skilled labor, 47.2 per cent; unskilled labor, 41.9 per cent. The percentage of happiness in each of these groups was compared with that of the farmers and the Critical Ratio calculated. This showed significant differences between the scores of the farmers and those of all the groups except the professional. It is thought that farmers and their wives make better adjustments in marriage than other occupational groups because they are more likely to perform many functions together and to have common interests in home, work, and children. The relationship between marital happiness and the interests of married couples has been investigated, with the finding that interests of an individualistic, pleasure-seeking nature are on the average inimical to marital happiness, while interests in home, children, and religion are favorable.[29] Individualistic values are associated with modern urban life, whereas familistic values are linked to the traditional rural society.[30] Also in a rural society, conflict in marital roles is less likely because these roles are traditional, well-established, expected. In urban society, possible roles are more numerous, and the possi-

[27] Metropolitan Life Insurance Company, *Statistical Bulletin*, May, 1953, p. 8.

[28] "Farm Marriages are the Happiest," *Family Life* (Los Angeles: American Institute of Family Relations), Vol. 7, No. 5, May, 1947, pp. 1–2.

[29] Purnell Benson, "Interests of Happily Married Couples," *Marriage and Family Living*, 14: 276, November, 1952.

[30] Frederic LePlay, *Les Ouvriers Européens* (Paris, 1878), 2nd ed., 6 vols., translated, abridged, and summarized in Carle C. Zimmerman and Merle Frampton, *Family and Society* (New York: D. Van Nostrand Company, Inc., 1935), pp. 402–467.

bilities for conflict are greater. There is a greater disparity in attitudes toward marital roles among divorced persons than married persons.[31] There is, it would seem, greater freedom of choice of a mate in the city, but this need not mean that mates are chosen with compatible ideas as to marital roles.

There are other studies showing divorce rate inversely correlated with occupational status,[32] while a survey of opinion polls [33] indicates that farmers are more satisfied with their lot in life than the general public. From 1910 to 1950, the number of farmers declined by eight million and the number of farms by 15 per cent. Since the farmers now constitute a smaller proportion of the total population than they did in earlier times, does this mean a decrease also in marital happiness?

The inferences from the data on income and education point the other way. The farmers have dwindled, but there has been a relative increase in number of white collar workers and higher occupational groups which make comparatively good marital adjustment scores. On the basis of his evidence, Terman [34] concluded that there is no correlation between divorce and childhood I.Q., but the divorce rate is less than half as high among our college graduates as among our non-graduates. Another study [35] of the same problem reports that between the ages of twenty-two and thirty-five a smaller proportion of better educated women than those with less education reported broken marriages. The trend, of course, has been for the proportion of persons with a college education to increase, but relatively small numbers are involved.

As to the role of economic factors in marital adjustment, the earlier studies were not altogether clear. Terman reported that there was no correlation between income and marital happiness in his sample. It is indeed surprising to learn that income is not correlated with marital adjustment when it is associated with so

[31] Alver Hilding Jacobson, "Conflict of Attitudes Toward the Roles of the Husband and Wife in Marriage," *American Sociological Review,* 17: 146–150, April, 1952.

[32] H. Ashley Weeks, "Differential Divorce Rates by Occupation," *Social Forces,* 21: 336, 1943.

[33] Howard W. Beers, "Rural-Urban Differences," *Rural Sociology,* 18: 1–11, March, 1953.

[34] Lewis M. Terman and Melita H. Oden, *The Gifted Child Grows Up* (Stanford, California: Stanford University Press, 1947), p. 238.

[35] Edmund DeS. Brunner, *Teachers College Record,* 49: 7–9, 1948.

many other family phenomena like size of family, infant mortality, et cetera. More recent findings are to the effect that white collar workers, professional men, and executives obtain higher adjustment scores in marriage than unskilled, semi-skilled, and skilled workers. Also that other economic variables are associated with marital happiness, such as income, home ownership, savings, and employment, although the correlations are not high.[36] Census data for a nation-wide sample [37] show that median money income in 1950 of persons fourteen years old and over with income varied by marital status, with married males who were living with their wives having the highest average income, $2,959. Widowed males had the lowest median income, $1,045 (the age factor is probably important here), while married males separated from their spouses averaged $1,750 for the year and divorced men $2,242. Separated males may more often belong to lower income groups.

What do the foregoing observations add up to? We have considered (a) a number of factors involved in marital happiness and (b) the changes that have occurred in these factors during the past 100 years or so. The object was to see whether by this indirect approach we might be able to tell whether marital happiness had increased or decreased. The result is, however, contradictory and inconclusive, with some of the changes tending to increase and others to decrease the incidence of marital adjustment. On the basis of these observations, no conclusion is possible with regard to the trend of marital happiness in the United States during the last century, although there may be value in identifying the favorable and unfavorable factors as we have done.[38]

[36] Robert C. Williamson, "Economic Factors in Marital Adjustment," *Marriage and Family Living*, 14: 298, November, 1952.

[37] *Current Population Reports: Population Characteristics — Marital Status and Household Characteristics,* April, 1951. Series P–20, No. 38, April 29, 1952.

[38] There are at least two further sets of limitations to the indirect approach that has been utilized above. The first is the assumption that if a factor is found to be associated with marital happiness at the present time, it was also associated with marital happiness in earlier historical periods. This is an assumption and must be proved. Second, the level of aspiration may have changed. Many observers think that is higher now than in earlier times. Let us say, as an illustration, that those with "Z" amount of money or status or achievement are now happier than those with "X" or "Y" amount; and that it can be shown that 100 years ago there were fewer individuals on level "Z" than there are today. This would be meaningful for estimating changes

Factors in the changing divorce rate: the law. We have concluded that the knowledge is not available for determining whether the need for divorce, as reflected in marital unhappiness, has changed in the last century or two. We turn next to a consideration of possible changes in the opportunities for divorce. When we think of the ease or difficulty of divorce, we think of certain conditions that must be met, conditions imposed by the law, church policy, economic considerations, and considerations of public opinion. These factors may be regarded as obstacles to be overcome. Have there been any changes in the number and force of these obstacles that stand in the way of divorce?

When we consider divorce policy in the United States, we turn at once to the roles of the state and the church in determining that policy and in affecting the number of divorces. Both the state and the church have a considerable stake in family stability, the state making its influence felt through the law and the church through moral pressure. We know that the divorce rate can be regulated by law; it can occasionally be turned on or off like a faucet. Russia provides an instructive example. When the Bolsheviks took over, they revolutionized the relationship between the sexes as well as the economic order. Divorce became a casual affair and could be had at the request of either party, without stated cause. The divorce was registered, and notification of the action sent to the other spouse by ordinary government postcard. The divorce rate zoomed. In Leningrad, in 1926, the divorce rate was 3.43 per 1000 population. The next year, after the introduction of the new liberal Russian code, the rate jumped to 9.83 or nearly three times what it had been the year before.[39] At the time it was felt that loyalty to family was an obstacle to loyalty to the state. In due course, the Soviet authorities had a change of heart and decided that more family stability was desirable. The slogan was changed to read that a good communist had to be a good family man. A new family law went into effect in 1944 requiring advance publicity for the

in marital happiness if size of income and occupational status were absolute factors in adjustment. If, however, they are relative factors and happiness depends on a comparative view, then a general upgrading of the population in social status might have no effect on differentials in happiness. The real income and occupational level have risen in the United States in the last 100 years, but the level of aspiration may have risen also.

[39] Frank H. Hankins, "Divorce," *Encyclopaedia of the Social Sciences* (New York: The Macmillan Company, 1933), 5: 177–84.

divorce action in a local newspaper at considerable expense, compulsory entry of divorce on home passports, and a series of lower and higher court actions, all at high fees. The result was to make divorce prohibitive for most Russians; and in August, 1944, the Russian press reported that in the month following the promulgation of the new law not a single petition for divorce had been filed in all Russia.[40] The Russian experience is not an isolated case. England liberalized her divorce law in 1938, adding additional grounds to the traditional ground of adultery; and a decade later, the number of divorces had increased sevenfold.[41] In the United States we have had similar demonstrations of the effectiveness of legal changes in throttling or stimulating divorces. When at the close of 1938 investigations were initiated into the possibility of perjury [42] in divorce cases in New York County, the number of divorce cases in New York City declined by one-third in a single year.

What then has been the history of divorce legislation in the United States in the last century? Have the laws tended to become more liberal or more conservative? The popular opinion probably is that the divorce laws have become more lenient. But the situation is not easy to assess, and the experts are not certain. A difficulty is that the divorce laws present a complex of several factors, and the situation or trend may not be the same for all aspects. There is, first, the theory of the law, which has shown little or no change in most jurisdictions. This is the theory of the guilty party, the idea that one of the spouses in a divorce action must be the offender and the other spouse an innocent party. This introduces plaintiff and defendant in every action for divorce and gives us "adversary proceedings." Hence there can be no recognized divorce by mutual consent; and if it is known that the married couple has collaborated in seeking and planning the divorce, they are guilty of an offense called collusion.

[40] Lewis A. Coser, "Some Aspects of Soviet Family Policy," *American Journal of Sociology*, 56: 430, March, 1951.

[41] *Marriage Guidance* (National Marriage Guidance Council, London), Vol. 4, No. 1, July, 1950, p. 6. It is interesting to note that the increase in the remarriages of the divorced was also sevenfold, from 8,179 in 1938 to 58,728 in 1948.

[42] Metropolitan Life Insurance Company, *Statistical Bulletin*, November, 1950, p. 7.

A second aspect of the divorce law has to do with the nature of the allowable grounds, with New York having only one allowable ground for divorce and Kentucky fifteen. Here there is considerable variation from state to state. In many jurisdictions, like New York and Illinois, there have been no changes in the last two or three generations. Only three jurisdictions, New Mexico (1933), Alaska (1935), and Oklahoma (1953) have laws which recognize incompatibility as a ground for divorce, while eleven states have added "living separate and apart" for a period of years, varying from two to ten, as a valid ground, which has the effect of removing the stigma which attaches to the complaint of "desertion." A close student [43] of divorce trends concluded that:

> When we come to consider the legislation in regard to causes we find it somewhat difficult to discover any clearcut trend. We should classify all those cases in which new causes were added or in which there is relaxation of restrictions already in existence as tendencies toward leniency. But some states added new causes while at the same time they omitted existing causes in code revisions or repealed others. In some instances the causes for absolute divorce which were deleted were, in reality, causes for annulment and merely were transferred to that category of statutes. In still other cases the repeal of statutory grounds indicates restrictive tendencies. On the whole there seems to be . . . a wider possibility for the selection of grounds upon which divorces may be secured although, it should be observed, many of the revisions in the direction of leniency are of minor importance.

Another writer [44] reports that the process of divorce legislation has been one of backing and filling. From 1800 to 1870, there was a period of liberalization, with some "omnibus laws" similar to those of Nevada today. After 1870, reaction set in. The writer concludes:

> A detailed analysis and summary of divorce legislation from the Civil War to the present time shows that the number of changes has been many, but their importance slight, because the divorce laws of today (sic) are not substantially different from those of 63 years ago.

In respect to residence requirements there has been some change, especially in Nevada and Idaho, which reduced the required period

---

[43] J. P. Lichtenberger, *Divorce: A Social Interpretation* (New York: McGraw-Hill Book Company, 1931), pp. 167–8.

[44] A. Cahen, *A Statistical Analysis of Divorce* (New York: Columbia University Press, 1932), p. 92.

to six weeks, and in Florida, where it was lowered to three months. On the other hand, the residence requirement in Massachusetts is five years.

Laws affecting the remarriage of divorced persons need to be considered as well as laws pertaining to divorce itself, for if there are obstacles to remarriage after divorce they may deter some individuals from getting a divorce. On this account, it is significant that the remarriage of divorced persons was prohibited or in some way limited by eighteen states and the District of Columbia between 1887 and 1906.[45] Since that time, the tendency has been to relax such restrictions.

We conclude that the trend of changes in the divorce law in the United States in the last century is not strong, but the indications are that the law has been somewhat moderated. The changes in the law do not seem to be sufficiently great, however, to account for the considerable rise which has occurred in the divorce rate.

Why has there been little change in divorce legislation? A number of reasons may be indicated. First, the law is a conservative institution designed to maintain social control and stability, hence old laws change slowly. This conservatism of the law has been reinforced in the United States by the balance existing between religious and secular forces. The secular forces are preponderant, but the religious forces are better organized. If the religious forces were to prevail, we would have stricter divorce laws, since, with the exception of the Methodists, not a single church body in its official code recognizes cruelty as a ground for divorce, although it is actually the most frequent alleged ground in divorce actions. A third factor limiting changes in the divorce law is the lack of effective organization in behalf of easier divorce. Potentially the strongest advocates of reform should be those who have received divorces; but they are sensitive about their experience, prefer to remain anonymous, are not organized, and do not constitute a pressure group for divorce reform. Finally, the status quo in divorce legislation is maintained because of the existence of "sub rosa" institutions which make it possible to circumvent the law and to achieve the purpose of obtaining divorces. If there is strong opposition to changing the law, and there are ways of getting around the law, why bother to change it? In New York state, for instance,

[45] J. P. Lichtenberger, *op. cit.*, Chapter 7, "Civil Divorce Legislation," pp. 154–86.

the law permits divorce for adultery only. New Yorkers get around the law by (1) going to Reno; (2) resorting to annulments; and (3) using so-called "hotel evidence" in divorce suits alleging adultery. More Reno divorces are granted to New Yorkers than to any other group.[46] More annulments are granted in New York than divorces.

While the law of divorce has remained fairly static, court procedure has greatly changed. Formerly divorce actions were carefully considered by the court and perjury and collusion were serious offenses. Now these violations of the letter of the law are routine and are ignored. Lawyers, detectives, and clients create false evidence. The way to get a divorce is to select some legal "cause" and then have an uncontested case. Not a judgment entered after agreement (that would be collusion) but an "uncontested" case. Nearly all divorces today are uncontested. Divorce hearings are short, and the cases move rapidly. In Chattanooga, which has had the highest divorce rate of any city in the United States, the records reveal that in one court session twelve divorces were granted in seventeen minutes.[47]

Obstacles to divorce: church policy. The churches, with their special interest in ethical values, are much concerned with family life, where the growing child gets his first lessons in moral behavior. The churches in Western society have taken the view that marriage is holy or sacred, which makes divorce a very serious matter. The teachings of the churches are deterrents to divorce. It is therefore instructive to inquire what changes, if any, have occurred in church policy respecting divorce in the United States in recent decades.

The authors addressed inquiries along this line to the leading churches, and the replies indicate that few churches have made any significant changes in divorce policy in the last fifty years.

The official position of most of the Protestant churches has remained that divorce may be granted for adultery only, in keeping

[46] On the basis of data on place of marriage of those divorced in 1922, Cahen estimated that about 30 per cent of all divorces granted to New Yorkers were obtained outside the state, *op. cit.,* p. 68.

[47] *Journal of the American Judicators Society,* April, 1947, reported in Reginald Heber Smith, "Dishonest Divorce," *The Atlantic Monthly,* 180: 42–5, December, 1947.

with the teaching of the New Testament in Matthew 5:31–32, and that remarriage is to be sanctioned only for "the innocent party." The United Lutheran Church and the Presbyterian Churches admit the additional ground of malicious or willful desertion. The Central Conference of American Rabbis reports that the attitude of the Synagogue is that divorce is a matter regulated by the State and that the Synagogue is governed by the Talmudic regulation: "The Law of the Land is the Law." The Roman Catholic Church has kept to its teaching that marriage is a sacrament and therefore indissoluble.

As to changes in church polity, the Protestant Episcopal Church for many years permitted remarriage of the innocent party to a divorce for the cause of adultery. But this was allowed only with the consent of the bishop of the diocese; and he could not give his consent until he had shown the divorce papers to the chancellor of the diocese, who is always a lawyer. One year had to elapse before the remarriage. On January 1, 1947, a revision of the canon went into effect, permitting a member of the Church in good standing who desires to marry a person whose marriage has been dissolved by a civil court of competent jurisdiction to apply to the bishop of the diocese for permission to be married by a minister of the Church, provided one year shall have elapsed since the entry of the judgment of the court. Such application is to be made at least thirty days before the contemplated marriage.[48] The Methodist Episcopal Church added physical and mental cruelty as grounds in 1932; and when the several divisions of Methodism were united in the Methodist Church in 1944, this provision was adopted.

Church polity regarding divorce has changed very little over a long period of time but not so the behavior of church members. According to a Reno judge,[49] fifty years ago adultery as a ground for divorce was cited more than twice as often as it is today. The significance of adultery is that it is the Biblical ground for divorce and the one that has the official support of the churches permitting divorce. Church members and others now resort more frequently

---

[48] *Marriage Laws of the Episcopal Church* (New York: Morehouse-Gorham Co., 1946), p. 7.

[49] George A. Bartlett, *Is Marriage Necessary?* (New York: Penguin Books, Inc., 1947), Rev. Ed., p. 24.

to other grounds, but the church almost never takes any punitive
action. The secretary of one leading denomination writes in a
letter to the authors, "A person who obtains a divorce on other
grounds is theoretically liable to dismissal from the Communion,
but as a matter of practical fact one seldom hears of this happening." Another writes: "As to the action taken against those who
get divorces on other grounds, there is nowadays practically none.
A hundred years ago such a divorced person might well have been
summoned before his local church session and severely disciplined.
This seldom if ever happens any more." The foregoing are typical
responses to the question put by the authors: "What action, if
any, is taken by your church against a member who obtains a
divorce on other grounds (than those recognized by the church)?"
The church is more stringent when it comes to the marriage of
ministers of the church to divorced persons.

We conclude that changes in church policy respecting divorce
have been minor or non-existent, hence are not responsible for
the increase in the divorce rate.

Obstacles to divorce: cost. Some discussion is in order with regard to costs, for it costs money to get a divorce; and the number
of divorces can be controlled in part by regulating the price, as we
saw had been done in a sharply upward direction in Russia. The
reverse situation is reported for England,[50] where the sevenfold
increase in divorces from 1938 to 1948 is ascribed to the new law
of 1938 and to "a decrease in legal costs and a corresponding increase in living standards (that) has brought divorce within the
reach of multitudes for whom it would previously have been an
unattainable luxury." Unfortunately there are no figures available
on comparative average costs in the United States 100 years ago
and now. The cost of divorce has, of course, increased, and so has
income; but what relation these two factors bear to each other, we
do not know. The cost of divorce varies by community, income of
the client, difficulty of the case, et cetera. For the poor in many
places, legal aid clinics exist to provide free services, a condition
that did not exist in earlier times.

The expenses of the court action for divorce may be only a

---

[50] *Marriage Guidance* (Monthly Bulletin of the National Marriage Guidance
Council), Vol. 2, No. 4, October, 1948, p. 1.

part of the cost of divorce. A larger part is alimony, maintenance or support orders, when granted. While no comparative data are available on a national basis, we do know that there has been a decline in alimony awards with the greater employment of women. It is probably safe to conclude that this economic item has declined in relative importance as a limiting factor in divorce.

We conclude from our analysis that the divorce laws of the states and the divorce laws of the churches in the United States have been relatively constant during the past century and cannot therefore be responsible for the marked increase in the divorce rate. The courts, however, have made divorce easier in response to a more liberal public opinion, and the increasingly favorable economic situation has probably made the cost of divorce less of an obstacle.

Public opinion and divorce. It is usual to explain the rise in divorces by saying that public opinion has changed, as indeed it has. There has been a gradual change in American opinion on divorce from sharp to rather mild disapproval.[51] The view that marriage is an end in itself, divinely ordained, has largely yielded to the idea that marriage is a means to individual happiness, dissoluble if happiness is not achieved. The idea that divorce is a moral evil has been largely replaced by the idea that it is a social problem and a personal tragedy. An analysis of fifty novels [52] published from 1858 to 1937 in which divorce is the central theme shows that they reflect the changing attitude toward divorce from "concern over the fact of divorce, to the effects of divorce on children, to the question of alimony, and later to the problem of post-divorce adjustment." The increasing public tolerance of easy divorce has been measured as reflected in magazine articles between 1905 and 1931 [53] and in various polls of public opinion.[54] Of a representative sample of adults in the state of Washington in

[51] Kingsley Davis, "Children of Divorced Parents: A Sociological and Statistical Analysis," *Law and Contemporary Problems,* Summer, 1944, p. 707.

[52] James Harwood Barnett, *Divorce and the American Divorce Novel, 1858–1937* (Philadelphia: privately printed doctoral dissertation, University of Pennsylvania, 1939).

[53] Hornell Hart, "Changing Social Attitudes and Interests," *Recent Social Trends* (New York: McGraw-Hill Book Company, 1933), Vol. II, pp. 382, 414–17.

[54] *Fortune Magazine,* April, 1937, and *The Ladies Home Journal,* February, 1938.

December, 1949, 62 per cent checked the statement that divorce should be granted only under certain circumstances, 31 per cent the statement that it should be granted whenever the married couple decide they no longer wish to remain married, and only 6 per cent the statement that divorce should never be granted.[55]

To explain the rise in divorce by saying that public opinion has changed is not satisfying to the sociologist, who wants to know why it has changed and who looks to changes in social situations for an answer. The changed public opinion is the result of changes in the society, after which the changed opinion itself becomes the cause of further change. There are some [56] who think that the effect of the more tolerant attitude toward divorce is to create in the minds of young people the idea of marriage as a "trial run." Young people are said to approach marriage with the idea that it is impermanent. "Let's try it and if it doesn't work, there's a way out." There is no evidence that this is actually what young people think. Most competent observers believe that young people expect their marriages to last and give no thought to divorce until or unless their marriage falters.

The loss of family functions. When we ask what social changes have occurred in American society in the last 100 years which account for the changed attitude toward divorce, we note at once the loss of functions by the American family which has been described in preceding chapters. The functions are numerous: economic, educational, protective, reproductive, recreational, religious. When our nation consisted mainly of farms, production was in and about the home; and the family had the added cohesive influence that flowed from the fact that the family was in business together. Divorce meant serious disruption of economic activities as well as of personal relationships. It is not surprising that even today, despite the considerable urbanization of rural life and the availability of urban institutions to the rural population, the divorce rate of farmers is appreciably less than that of city dwellers. In-

[55] Washington Public Opinion Laboratory, Poll No. 13: Marital Adjustment Poll, December, 1949. State College of Washington, Pullman.

[56] Margaret Mead, "What is Happening to the American Family?" *Journal of Social Casework*, 28: 5–6, November, 1947.

vestigation [57] in Iowa showed that the rural-urban differential is probably the greatest single factor affecting divorce rates. In general the more rural the county the lower the divorce rate; and the more urban the county, the higher the divorce rate.

More jobs for women deserves to be singled out for special mention as a factor in the increasing divorce rate. When there were few jobs for women outside the home and women were dependent upon marriage or their parents for support, divorce entailed great economic hazards. Now women have in jobs a great liberating force; and it is a new force, for never before have women had such opportunities for economic independence as are made available to them by modern industrial civilization. The relation of jobs to divorce is suggested by data like the following: of every ten divorced women (1948), five are heads of households. [58] Seventy per cent have jobs compared with 51 per cent of the single women and 22 per cent of the married women who are living with their husbands.

Educational and protective functions, once centered in the home, have been transferred to the state and elaborated, encouraging the welfare state. It is easier for a divorced couple to manage, now that the state helps with education and protection of the children, and with financial aid, if needed, for dependent children.

The transfer of economic functions from the home to the factory and the rationalization of the industrial process have led to greater economic security. This, plus greater dependence on the state in times of economic crisis, has reduced the feeling of insecurity and therefore the dependence on religion is less. The impact of science is generally thought to be responsible for increasing secularization which is reflected in changed concepts of marriage. Discoveries in the psychological and social sciences of the role of unconscious factors in personality, the importance of the learning process and of social situations, and the influence of the culture have led to less acceptance of the view that marriages are (sacred) made in heaven and less adherence in practice to traditional church doctrines re-

[57] Kenneth L. Cannon, "Marriage and Divorce in Iowa 1940–47," *Marriage and Family Living*, 9: 98, Autumn, 1947.

[58] Bureau of the Census, *Current Population Reports — Population Characteristics: Marital Status, Number of Times Married, and Duration of Present Status: April, 1948.* Series P–20, No. 23, March 4, 1949, p. 4.

garding divorce. Most persons still have religious weddings, so
that the form is retained even when the meaning has changed.
Divorce itself becomes a secularizing force, as shown by the report [59] that the proportion of brides who had a civil ceremony in
New York state in 1949 was least among those who were contracting their first marriage and highest among those who had been previously divorced.

The decrease in the reproductive function is manifest in smaller
families, although the movement has been reversed during the 1940's
and the early 1950's. Whether this reversal is a fluctuation around
the trend or a change in the long-time down trend in the birth
rate remains to be seen. We know that children are associated
with marital stability; the divorce rate decreases as the number of
children per family increases, and the chances of divorce are several times as great for childless couples as for those with children.
The increase in the divorce rate during the 1940's when the birth
rate was also high suggests that while children are an important
factor in marital stability, they are not the only factor; and with
less stigma attaching to divorce, with better means of economic
support available to divorced women, and with more services
furnished by government, children in the future may not be such
an important factor in marital stability as in the past.

While losing traditional functions, the family has been gaining
new ones, especially those having to do with affection between
mates. There is now more emphasis on love, congeniality, companionship, and the sharing of common intellectual and recreational
interests. There is more freedom in the choice of a mate, less dictation by family, social class, ethnic group, and community. If
the several functions of the family are viewed as bonds, then six
bonds are more binding than one, especially when the new bond
is affection, which is volatile. Love may be a sufficient tie while it
lasts, but when a husband looks across the breakfast table and says
to his wife, "I don't love you any longer. I want a divorce," there
is less to hold them together than there used to be. Actually, of
course, there are many bonds now besides affection; some of the
old ties are there, but they are weaker.

[59] J. V. DePorte, "Civil Marriage in New York State, apart from New York
City," *American Sociological Review*, 17: 232–35, April, 1952.

Factors once removed. There are the immediate factors underlying the increase in the divorce rate which we have detailed, the increase in jobs for women, smaller families, more social services, and the like. Then there are the factors once removed that brought about these social changes. They are the factors which collectively we call the Industrial Revolution, which took production out of the home and put it in factories and so created in due course the need for all the other social services to families which governments are providing. The revolution was not alone in industry but in the other social institutions as well with which industry is linked. The Industrial Revolution, based initially on steam and steel and methods of mass production, created our urban civilization with its anonymity [60] and impersonalization of social interaction, removing much of the control over behavior exercised by the group in earlier times in more simple, personal societies. When individuals are not identified and their background is unknown, the stigma of divorce is weakened. Since the census enumerator is a stranger, the divorced person can report himself as single or widowed. The city becomes a haven for the divorced, and it is a place to which divorced persons migrate.

The changes in the divorce rate can then be traced to momentous technological changes, changes in the means of production. The influence is indirect, via the growth of factories and the rise of cities, affecting the functions of the family. There is little direct influence of technology on the divorce rate. To the extent that labor-saving devices in office equipment and record-keeping, like the typewriter, the telephone, filing cabinets, and microfilm, expedite the divorce process and speed up divorces, technology may be said to have had some direct effect on the divorce rate; but these factors are probably negligible. Technology is also immediately present in the improved transportation and communication facilities which are particularly helpful in migratory divorce. There is a special New York-Reno chartered plane service available to

[60] A recent news item reports the exceptional case of a woman whose husband kidnapped their new-born son while she was hospitalized. She did not see her son again until thirty-eight years later, when she learned that she had been a resident of Cleveland twenty-two years without knowing that her former husband and son were also living in the community. Associated Press dispatch, *Tallahassee Democrat*, June 15, 1953.

New Yorkers. The automobile makes it possible for Californians wishing to be married to avoid the waiting period required by their state and to cross over into Nevada, which has no waiting period before marriage. There is some evidence [61] that migratory marriages are more unstable than those that take place within the state, and the number of migratory marriages has increased, but this factor is probably of minor significance in the total divorce picture. The influence of technology on divorce in this instance is indirect, via hasty marriage. The same technological traits, however, operate to affect divorces directly, as when, thanks to the automobile, Georgians cross the line to secure easier divorces in Tennessee. Whether there is relatively more migratory divorce than formerly is not known, and in any case the percentage is probably very small.[62]

Conclusion. To sum up, the increase in the divorce rate may be the result of an increase in (a) marital unhappiness, (b) opportunities for divorce, or (c) both. The evidence regarding the trend of marital happiness is not good, and we do not know whether marital happiness has increased or decreased or remained constant in the United States during the past century.

Opportunities for divorce are affected by church and legal policies regarding divorce, since divorce is an ideological matter; and if there is an ideological barrier to divorce, there will be little or no divorce, although there will be marital separations. There have, however, been no significant changes in the formal ideology regarding divorce on the part of the church or the law during the last 100 years.

Yet there has been a considerable increase in divorce. The proximate reason is that divorce is easier to get because of court procedures which reflect more favorable public opinion. The latter is in turn a reflection of complex social changes including the cumulative effect of the increase in the number of divorced persons, and the secularization which has resulted from scientific discoveries.

[61] Arthur Hopson, "The Relationship of Migratory Marriages to Divorces in Tennessee," *Social Forces*, 30: 449–55, May, 1952. Couples married and divorced in Tennessee were divorced after a longer period of marriage than those married outside Tennessee.

[62] It is estimated to have been about 3 per cent in the early 1930's. A. Cahen, *op. cit.*

Among the proximate causes of the increase in divorce are also to be counted (a) the increase in jobs for women, (b) the increase in social services, (c) the decrease in number of children, (d) the decrease in family functions, and (e) the spread of the urban environment, which provides a refuge for the divorced. These social changes may be viewed as having removed or reduced certain obstacles to divorce. Back of these immediate causes are the changes in production associated with the Industrial Revolution.

11

How and Why the Family has Changed

The subject of this inquiry has been the family, a social institution. It has been changing greatly over the past century and a half in the United States. We have sought to know what has caused these changes. However we did not proceed to treat the family as a single unit and seek out the causes of change in this unit. Rather we broke the family down into eight parts and proceeded to search for the causes of changes in each part. These eight parts were not all of our choosing, but were mainly the parts of the family which the family experts in the United States voted as having experienced the most significant changes. So far then we do not have the causes of the changes of the family as a whole but the causes of the changes of each of these eight parts.

The family as a unit. It seems desirable in this summary to look at the family as a whole. But first we note that since there are eight parts or aspects of the family and the family is a single social institution, the presumption is that all these eight aspects of the family are interrelated. It is of course theoretically possible for eight parts of a whole to be very little related, like eight pebbles in a pile. A pile of pebbles is not a highly integrated whole, as is for instance a watch. Nor are the interrelationships of the several parts necessarily of equal magnitude. Some parts may be much more closely related than others. For instance the color of the face of a watch has only slight relationship to the other parts, but the size of the mainspring is closely related to many parts.

The eight parts of the family. If we look at these eight aspects, which the experts have chosen, we observe that three of them have to do with the formation and disruption of the family. Marrying for love is a way of getting the family formed; and marrying early forms the family soon. Divorce breaks up the family.

Three other aspects of the family which have been chosen for analysis have to do with the relationship of each of the family's three types of members to the family and to each other. These are the husband-father, the wife-mother, and the children. The chapters that deal with these relationships are called "More Working Wives," "Away from Authority," and "Accent on the Child."

There remain two other aspects. These deal with attributes of the family as a whole. One is the size of the family and the other is what the family does.

It is obvious that all these parts are interrelated either closely or slightly. If we were to attempt to describe all these interrelationships, we would have at least forty-nine descriptions, a rather extended summary.

Interrelationships of parts. Still, as an illustration we may consider the relations of one aspect, namely marrying younger, to the seven other aspects. Marrying younger probably means more emphasis on love in the choice of the bride or groom if the choice is not decided by the parents. Early marriage, other things being equal, increases the size of the family. Marrying early has some relation to how adequately the functions of the family are performed, since the very young have less skill and less wisdom than older persons. Early marriage increases the chances of the wife working outside the home, since young couples are likely to have less ample financial resources than older couples. A young husband may be less disposed to exercise authority. Very early marriages are said to be a bit more brittle than later ones. There are many other relationships. Only a few have been mentioned and these most briefly.

Some of these relationships are important and significant. Others are rather slight. A summary should be concerned with only the more important. It hardly seems necessary to chart out all these possible relationships, both significant and slight.

Another suggested procedure is to view these interrelations from the standpoint of their basic nature and of their priority in historical development.

Viewed from these two angles, it appears that a change in the family functions, that is, in what the family does, is very important because the change is basic and because it occurred early in the evolution of the family. Thus at one time the family was a small factory of production. Now it is not. The loss of this function alone profoundly affects the attitude toward the choice of a mate, toward the working of wives outside the home, toward the authority of the husband and toward the rearing of children. Other effects have been to weaken the desire for a large family and to lessen resistance toward its disruption by separation and divorce.

We have just shown that a loss of many of the functions of the family affected profoundly the other parts of the family. The reduction in size must also have had a very great effect upon all aspects of the family. A family of two persons, or even, for a few years, of three persons must be quite different from a large family for the wife and her duties and for the children, and somewhat for the husband who must provide most of the income for the family. A family consisting only of husband and wife is more readily separated than a larger one. Perhaps the prospects of a small family may cause young people to view marriage as an earlier possibility and to see it more in terms of love than of duties and obligations.

We think therefore that causes affecting the functions and the size of the family are basic and came early in the process of family change over the years. Once these changes are under way, the formation and disruption of the family are affected. Perhaps last of all come the changes in the status of the wife, husband and children.

Outside influences on the family. We have just shown some of the important changes that have taken place within the family because of some change in a part or parts of the family reacting on the other parts of the family. But the changes in the family do not all come from within the family. Many changes are caused by factors wholly without the family, changes coming from other social institutions and different parts of culture. The most important of these we should expect to modify the size and functions of the family, but others would bear directly on the members, husband, wife and children, and still others of the forces coming from the outside would bear upon the formation and disruption of the family. But upon whatever part of the family these outside forces impinge, they will affect the whole family since the different parts of the family are closely interrelated. So in the preceding chapters which dealt with separate parts of the family, any cause of a change in any part would cause a change in the family as a whole.

We wish now to summarize our findings on these outside forces that cause changes in the parts of the family and hence in the family as a unit. But first a brief comment on how causes operate to bring about changes.

How causes of change operate. These forces are quite complex. Some are immediate and others are remote. Causes therefore occur in a sequence. Thus cruelty is the most commonly alleged immediate or proximate cause of divorce. But cruelty does not always lead to divorce and we do not know that cruelty is any greater in this age of humanitarianism than formerly. But if a wife, experiencing cruelty, can now be supported by work outside the home better than when a livelihood was obtainable only in the family household, she is more likely to have cruelty drive her to a divorce. So a cause of the increase in divorces lies in more opportunities for a livelihood outside the home. In turn, the increased opportunities for a livelihood have their causes too. In such a chain of causes we have tried to emphasize the more basic or important cause. To give the full account of the causes is to cite the whole chain of them. This has frequently been done in the preceding chapters. But in a summary, it is desirable to concentrate on the more important or fundamental causes rather than on the superficial or slight causes.

The causes of family changes are also made more complex because a change is seldom the result of just one changing factor. Often there are several factors operating to produce a change. Thus there are fewer children in the family today because of the increased expense in rearing them, because of competing outside activities, and because of desires to give children advantages in endowments. Therefore several causes can verge to produce a change. Some are less important than others. The fact that it is often desirable to mention only the most important leads one to think there is only one cause. It is however often better to think of such converging causes as a cluster rather than as just a single cause. Thus the increase in cities is the result of an increase in a cluster of causes.

Another source of complexity in the battery of causes of family changes is the fact that one cause has a multitude of effects dispersing outward onto many other objectives. Thus the increase in the use of contraceptives affects the size of the family, the standard of living, the market for the purchase of goods, international relations and religious sanctions.

This dispersal of influences coupled with the convergence of influences means, sometimes, that a single cause becomes an extraordinarily powerful one. Thus the increased use of mechanical power developed by the steam engine dispersed its effects upon innumerable activities. Its influence, among others, was felt, for instance, on (1) home production, (2) jobs for men outside the home, (3) jobs for women for pay, (4) the growth of cities, (5) the increase of governmental functions, (6) the development of commercial recreation, and on many other activities. Thus the dispersed effects of the steam engine were varied and many. Now these same effects resulting from dispersion converged in turn as causes of changes in the family. Thus the authority of the husband in the family is less because of (1) the loss of production from the home of which he was the boss, (2) the creation of jobs for men away from home where for many hours of the day they are not in a position to exercise authority over their families, (3) the trend of women to work not for their husbands but for others for pay which brought them independence from their husbands' authority, and rights not allowed them in the authoritarian family, (4) the increase of governmental functions which provided protection and services to women and children which husbands formerly provided, and (5) the development of recreation in commercial places that took the members of the family away from the home.

Thus an invention, which has many dispersed effects on various activities which later converge to produce a single change in the family, becomes a very important cause of a family change.

One final factor we have found in the complexity of causes of changes in the family is the removal of obstacles to change. For instance in the household economy a wise commentary was that woman's place was in the home. This was useful advice because there was work to be done and children to be cared for, which would not be well done if women were gadding about away from home. This idea became widely prevalent in the days of the household economy and was a popular idea.

Obviously this conception of woman's place would be an obstacle to her working away from home. Because of this conception, many men thought it bad for their wives to have paid work. So the causes that were operating to increase the number of married women working would be less effective because of this ideological obstacle. Hence its removal would, in a way, encourage changes in the family.

From the foregoing summary of the causation process which we have found operating in the changes occurring in the family, it is apparent that the most important causes of family changes are likely to be clusters of converging influences; and such clusters if fundamental are likely to be somewhat removed from the many and varied proximate causes which are often either superficial or unsatisfactory because they need further explaining.

Before turning to the discussion of the basic causative factors in recent family changes, it is desirable first to indicate briefly the general nature of the factors which were found not to be causes.

Constant factors, not causes, generally biological. In accounting for a change, we seek other changes as causes. A factor that does not change cannot be responsible for change. We rule out of consideration, therefore, as factors in family change any factor that is constant. And in reviewing the constant factors observed in connection with the eight family changes, we note that they are nearly always biological and not social or cultural factors. For instance, in explaining the decrease in the authority of the male, biological factors were not useful, since the relative physical advantage of the male over the female is a constant factor. Biological factors, however, need not be constant. The sex ratio, for example, may change and a change in the sex ratio is due to changes in social and economic conditions. It has in fact changed in recent decades in the United States, and there are now more women than men. This information was not useful in accounting for the tendency to marry earlier, because the change in the sex ratio is not in the desired direction; a surplus of men, not women, is favorable to a high marriage rate.

Biological factors are more likely than cultural factors to be constant, because biological factors, and especially genetic factors, are less subject to change.

Increased urbanism as a cause. We shall now proceed to list some of the fundamental causes which we have found in preceding chapters operating to bring about the most significant changes in the family. As we have pointed out, these fundamental causes will generally be clusters of converging influences, for several influences will usually be more important than one.

One such cluster of causes is cities. It is in cities that we find the greatest departure from the family of the household economy. It is in cities that families are the smallest, that there are the most divorces and that there are the fewest functions. It is not, however, the place where there are the earliest marriages. In cities the husband we think has less authority, for he more often works away from home. Also it is in cities that more married women are employed. We also think that in cities there are more organized efforts to care for the child.

The city is a place of residence, and it does not seem that a geographical situation could cause these changes. It is therefore the nature of this place of residence, that brings about these changes. There are of course many aspects of city life. Which are the ones that have caused the changes? Certainly one such urban characteristic is the separation of place of work from the family dwelling for men and for women. Another is that in the city production is not centered in the home, and the family buys what it consumes.

On the farms both men and women work on the homestead, neither receiving pay from an outside employer. But on some commercial one-crop farms such as orange groves, the family must buy what it consumes. Also some farmers, who keep no animals, may live away from the farm. Again, a farmer and his wife may occasionally work part of the year in a nearby town, if there is a shortage of labor. The automobile makes this possible. But in the main the conditions of employment which affect family life so much are different in cities and on the farms.

Thus cities affect family functions, especially the economic function of production. They also increase the family's role in the economic function of consumption, because of the large quantity of goods that must be purchased.

Cities seem to affect the size of the family as well as the functions. The birth rate is lower in cities than on the farms, partly because birth control techniques are more easily spread in cities than in the open country. Though the birth rate may in the future decrease greatly in the rural areas, it is unlikely to drop as low as in the cities, for the conditions are said to be more favorable for rearing children outside the cities.

The occupational situation in cities, that is, the separation of residence from place of work, causes a decrease in the effective authority of the male and the provision of opportunities for the wife to work makes separation and divorce less prohibitive for her.

These urban influences flow from the separation of occupations from residence. There are other aspects of urban life that affect the family. One is the density of population, which sometimes reaches 15,000 to 25,000 per square mile. There arise in such congested cities problems of fire and police protection, sewage and garbage disposal, health regulation, and measures for the protection of children. ʿThe density of population then causes a transfer of certain protective functions from the family to the government, and also a diminution of the authority in the family.

Another aspect of city life that affects the family is the relative hospitality of the cities to most new ideas as compared to more isolated rural areas. The city is at the junction of highways of travel, and is a place for the diffusion of existing ideas and the creation of new ones due to a cross-fertilization of ideas coming from heterogeneous sources. Thus the city tends to have fewer of the traditional ideologies and resistances to change that often exist in more isolated areas.

In brief, the city represents a cluster of factors, concerned with occupation, density, and ideologies that affect changes in the family.

If we wish to look further in the chain of causes, we may ask what causes cities? Before answering this question we must ask what are the essential characteristics of a city. A city has a large population living close together which is not able to produce in the city the food they need but must have the food imported. The residents pay for the food by exchange of manufactured products or from the profits of trade. Cities therefore are trading or manufacturing centers and are dependent on trade routes.

The great growth of cities during the past one or two centuries has been due to the application of mechanical power to the tools of production and to the vehicles of transportation. Steam was this mechanical power and steel made its application feasible. This use of steam and steel is the Industrial Revolution, though it has been speeded by electrical and gas power and by the use of other metals than steel. The cause of the rise of cities of the nineteenth and twentieth centuries then was the steam and steel of the Industrial Revolution.

There were a few large cities before steam and steel even in ancient times. They were much the same as modern cities and their origin was due to transportation, trade and manufacture. They were not so dense and occupations were less proliferated. Manufacture was more often around the urban household. In other words the forces of urban life were perhaps less accentuated and it is thought that the influence of urban life upon families before the Industrial Revolution was less strong but in the same direction as in modern cities.

While the technology of steam and steel created modern cities and its influence operates generally through cities, still this mechanical revolution also expressed itself directly upon rural families without flowing through the medium of cities. Thus farm machinery and transportation have led to more commercial farming and diminished the number of self-sustaining farms, characteristic of the household economy, which was the main economy for so many centuries. Even though the influence of machine power was direct and immediate on farm families, there was an indirect influence of cities, since products of commercial farms went in large part to urban markets.

We have asked what caused the rise of cities and have found the answer in the Industrial Revolution based upon the technology of steam and steel plus a lot of other inventions and discoveries in applied science. If we try to pursue the chain of causes one link further and ask what caused the Industrial Revolution with its mechanical inventions and scientific discoveries, we find no brief, clear-cut answer. It was the concatenation of several important inventions which occurred at that time because of the accumulation of technical and scientific knowledge to the point where these important inventions were possible. So we rest our search at the Industrial Revolution.

The welfare state and subsidiary organizations. The functions of city governments in behalf of the family, which we have just considered, are only a part of the services which government renders the family. The state and national governments also serve the family in many ways. In respect to some services, like education, the local and state governments co-operate, with some federal assistance for special purposes; certain other services, like old age insurance, the federal government provides alone.

The political ideology that the state should provide services for all the people, when put into practice, produces the "welfare state," which in its extreme form is said to provide services "from the cradle to the grave."

If we inquire into the causes of the growth of the welfare state, we note that states with differing economic ideologies, such as private capitalism, socialism, co-operatives, fascism, and communism, provide extensive social services. Examples are the United States, Australia, England, Sweden, Bismarckian Germany, Italy under Mussolini, and Russia. So it appears that economic organization in these nations is not a major cause of social services, although it may be a factor affecting the types and degrees of services rendered.

In all these states, a prominent cause of the welfare state is the decline in family functions associated with the Industrial Revolution. If the family loses certain essential functions, like education and protection, then some other agency must provide these functions, just as industry provides the jobs which the family cannot provide. The government is able to provide certain functions that the family relinquished, because it has the taxing power and because it represents all the people. Also the rapid growth of the federal government has meant improved social services. So the welfare state develops because (a) the family cannot continue to render the social services it once provided, and (b) the government can render these services and additional services, and render them better.

What we have said is that the welfare state is in part the result of family changes. But the welfare state is also an important cause of family change. We recall here the observation made in an earlier chapter[1] that social effects may also become social causes;

[1] Chapter 2.

that is, we have a circular chain of causes and effects. Thus the welfare state by providing more protection for family members lessens the authority and prestige of the family head. The teacher, the policeman, the judge, the playground director, and the soldier take authority away from the father. A social security program relieves children in part of economic responsibility for their aged parents. So the welfare state is a cause as well as a result of the reduction in family functions.

Protection and other services are provided for family members by insurance companies, by fraternal orders, and by other special purpose organizations, as well as by government. The growth of special purpose organizations, which has been phenomenal in the United States, is due to the growth of population as well as to the growth of culture. In a very small community, the population cannot support many special purpose organizations; and in earlier times, the culture was not sufficiently complex to warrant them.

An important cause of recent family changes, especially in the protective and recreational functions, is the growth of the welfare state and the increase in voluntary associations.

Birth control. Another influence that has affected the family is the cluster of birth control practices which has been the medium through which the size of the family has been limited. These birth control practices are of two kinds. One consists of earlier folk methods not using appliances; the other in the main has been the use of various kinds of contraceptives. It is the use of this latter kind that has been largely the cause of the decrease in the size of the family, which, however, was found to be not so great as is popularly supposed. But the decrease in size has together with the loss of family functions brought about the small family system with its effects on the earlier formation of families and their earlier dissolution. The small family has made it possible for more women to work outside the home, and has led to an appreciation of the child by the development of practical measures for his welfare. So the decrease in the size of the family has been important, and this decrease has been largely due to the invention and use of contraceptives.

Scientific discoveries. Another converging set of influences affecting the family may be called scientific discoveries of a basic nature, in contrast to applied science which relates to technology. One of these has been discoveries relating to the influence of the social environment as contrasted to heredity upon the personality and character of the young. The behavior of a chicken is different from the behavior of a duck, and that of a cat is different from that of a dog because of heredity, and no amount of training or similarity of environment can make their behavior alike. But human beings are not different animals; they are one species, and with a tremendous capacity for learning and developing different habits. These discoveries in psychology and sociology emphasize the importance of learning and social environment on the personality and character of a young individual. These discoveries in fundamental science have been practical influences on family life, especially placing the accent upon the child and emphasizing the importance of training. These discoveries also have great potentiality for the adjustment of mates and hence for the possible lessening of maladjustment and family disruption.

Other scientific discoveries that have affected the family are those that operate through the influence of religion. These are discoveries regarding the origin and evolution of man, the nature of the universe, the operation of disease, et cetera. These discoveries affect some religious beliefs. Religious beliefs affect family behavior because religion, whatever its nature, establishes controls over behavior. Thus religions tell us what to eat and what not to eat. But discoveries in the science of nutrition affect these religious sanctions. The fear of hell and the promise of heaven in a life everlasting are not without influence on conduct. Hence scientific discoveries about the nature of man affect certain specific religious beliefs and controls. Certain scientific discoveries in astronomy, biology, anthropology, and psychology have affected the operation of religious sanctions in various walks of life, causing a withdrawal of specific religious practices. Thus the ill resort more to scientific medicine than to prayer for recovery. The practice of medicine has become secularized. So also family life has become more secularized, and the religious functions of the family have been reduced. There are fewer family prayers and religious differences are less a barrier to marriage. Changes in religious beliefs or practices (if not in the nature of religion) have then affected family life, especially in its moral behavior, since religion has had a great influence over morals.

We may, of course, stop at this point of religious change in our search for causes. But if we ask what is the cause of this secularization, of this change in religious practices, we find a major cause to be discoveries in science.

Ideologies. Religious beliefs are a great cluster of what is currently called ideologies, and ideologies are a converging set of influences that are changing the family as are technological influences. Ideologies are important ideas that are widely accepted and integrated into guiding forces of social life. They thus become a sort of system. Thus democracy is an ideology. We have found, for instance, that the accent on the child is due in large part to (1) scientific discoveries regarding human nature and child training and (2) the evolving ideology of humanitarianism. We know that children are less limited by heredity than was formerly thought and more affected by the result of group influences. Hence we put great emphasis on the care and rearing of children. Also we have become more humane, as the rigors of natural selection have lessened. Compared to the past, punishment at the present time is less a factor in penology than rehabilitation. There are fewer crimes punishable by death. Physical punishment of the child or wife is less frequently resorted to. Hence the ideology of humanitarianism has affected the status of the wife and the child, as has also the ideology of democracy.

Ideologies are not all-powerful, however. Humanitarianism has not wholly abolished capital punishment or war. Nor has democracy affected the production in factories, which are not run by committees of workmen but by bosses who are managers and foremen. Nor has democracy given little children an equal voice in running the family.

Also the importance of ideas is not the same as the importance of ideologies. Much of human behavior, except for the purely impulsive or automatic acts, is a result of ideas, or occurs through the medium of ideas. We have ideas as to what we shall eat, where we shall eat, what occupation we shall follow. Inventions and discoveries and technological developments are preceded by ideas.

So ideas are said to be all-important. But if we look further as to causes, we want to know what causes the ideas, and under what conditions they are effective.

We have the same concern about what causes these systems of ideas we call ideologies. Some arise from supernatural origins, such as beliefs as to abodes of the soul after the body dies. Others arise from material conditions, such as the ideologies of hospitality found generally among all isolated peoples and families. Of some ideologies it is difficult to trace the origins; such are democracy and humanitarianism.

Ideologies are sometimes positive forces for change in the family, as for instance democracy. In other cases, ideologies are obstacles to change and change occurs more rapidly after the modification or removal of the ideology. Thus among many peoples there are ideologies regarding family fecundity, especially among pastoral and agricultural peoples who need labor and among hunters whose hazardous occupation makes survival difficult. There are also ideologies regarding moral aspects of sex. In some religions there are ideologies about birth and sex which favor large families. Where such ideologies are strong, there is a resistance to birth control which reduces the size of the family. Hence the effect of birth control on the size of the family will be greater where this ideological obstacle is less.

It is possible to see a very large number of changes in the family as being due to changes in ideas, especially if we do not ask what caused the changes in the ideas. Thus young men now seek a bride for love rather than, as in the past, for capability as a housekeeper. There is the idea of affection and companionship instead of the idea of obedience and efficiency. So this change in the basis of choosing a bride is due to a change in ideas. But if we ask whence comes this change in ideas, we find it is due in large part to the decrease in the economic function of family production.

Summary. This chapter is a summary chapter, hence a summary of this chapter is a summary of a summary and must be brief, with many omissions. We have seen that the family has changed largely because of forces outside the family impinging on some part of the family, such as the size of the family structure and the functions of this structure. But once a part of the family has been changed, then other parts of the family change also, because the different parts of the family are closely interrelated.

As to the forces that impinge on the family from the outside, we observe that the nature of their operation is complex, involving a chain of causes, with many different causes converging to produce a change. These converging factors may be called a cluster. We have found that some causes are more effective than others in producing family changes. In noting the more important causes, we observe that a cluster is more important generally than a single cause. But in a chain of causes, how shall the more important ones be noted? Often they are not the immediate causes which are of the nature of motives, desires, or ideas. Back of these are more fundamental causes, sometimes twice or thrice or further removed.

Basic clusters of causes are cities where place of occupation is separated from place of residence. But the growth of cities is due to non-human power applied to manufacture and transportation. The latter have in the main centered about the inventions of steam and steel. Another important cause of a change in family size and hence in various family activities has been the invention of contraceptives. Discoveries in science affecting religion and education have been important causes of family change. Also, changing ideologies regarding democracy, the welfare state, humanitarianism, and education, not readily traceable to technology, have been important factors in family changes.

What of the Future?

PART THREE

What of the Future?

12

Technology and the Future of the Family

Among the many causes, summarized in the preceding chapter, that have revolutionized the modern family, technological developments were outstanding. This finding is not a surprise because once before in its long history the family was transformed by inventions and discoveries. At the beginning of historical times, a great change occurred in the family with the discovery of agriculture, especially the use of the plow and the use of domesticated animals for work and for food. Small bands of wandering hunters and food gatherers gave way to larger settled communities with the family as the great center of production. This long era of the family as a great institution of power and prestige, based on production, continued in the Western world until two centuries ago.

In view of the demonstrated significance of technological influences on the family in the past, we are naturally curious as to what implications can be drawn for the family of the future from new and impending inventions and scientific discoveries. We propose to undertake such an inquiry. Since the inquiry is long we divide it into two parts. The first part, found in this chapter, concerns the influence of mechanical inventions. The following and last chapter is devoted to the influence of scientific discoveries.

It should be said at the outset, however, that this inquiry is not an attempt to describe the family of the future. For the family of the future will be the product of various forces in addition to technology. Other forces such as moral, religious, and ideological influences not primarily affected by science and machines are difficult to project into the future in detail. On the other hand we do have a good deal of knowledge about the new inventions and scientific discoveries. Though these do not tell the whole story of family changes, persons who are interested in the family will profit by a careful consideration of them. It is a mistake to overlook these technological influences, be they aids or obstacles to change.

Even though we know a good deal about these new material changes, looking into the future is somewhat hazardous as regards accuracy. Usually careful scholars do not try to look ahead. Yet the leaders of many other occupations do. Business men and executives in general are forced to look ahead, and frequently with success, as in planning their construction, in locating plants, and in estimating markets. The founding fathers who wrote the Constitution for the government of the young United States were looking ahead. If exact prediction of the future is not possible, then practical planners think in terms of probabilities. There are indeed many conditions of the future that appear highly probable. Thus we think it very probable that the people of the United States in the foreseeable future will be speaking the English language and not Russian.

Yet looking ahead, outlining the future influences of new inventions, is not haphazard, not wholly a matter of guesswork. Indeed there is a rather highly developed set of procedures for doing so.[1] To describe this methodology satisfactorily would require much space and would be of no particular interest to readers who are primarily interested in the family.[2]

---

[1] William F. Ogburn, *The Social Effects of Aviation* (Boston: Houghton Mifflin Company, 1946), Chapters II and III.

[2] A few methodological observations may be listed merely as illustrations:
The first observation is that the effects of an invention occur many years after the invention is made, and usually it takes more than one decade for an invention to be made after it is conceived. Hence there is some basis for a forecast. Not all inventions are put to use however.

To predict the dates and extent of uses of an invention is more difficult than to forecast a use at an unstated time in the future.

Inventions once made are more likely to be perfected and practical for extensive use if there is great demand and no adequate substitute.

The future looks rather dim in many cases if we try to see more than twenty to fifty years ahead.

For the next twenty to fifty years, probably most of the inventional influences that will change the family will come from inventions already in existence.

Inventions of the future and their influence cannot be forecast in terms of numerical probability; but it is useful to think of them in some such categories as the following: certain, probable, possible, fanciful, and unknown. It is

Though new technological innovations do have great and even revolutionary effects, there are limits to these influences. An illustration is the limit to the influence of the tractor, which increased the productivity of a farm worker and which led to an excess of farmers who remained partly employed or who migrated to cities. The tractor, which was at first very large and suited to huge farms, did not lead to the abolition of the small family farm. Rather the family farm was so robust an institution that it caused a modification in this invention. The tractor was made smaller. The family is likewise so strong an institution that modern inventions have not destroyed it, though these inventions can provide — in the city and outside the family — all the goods and physical services that spinsters and bachelors need, so that there is no need to marry in order to obtain them. However, young people do form families and there are relatively few spinsters and bachelors. Technology changes the family but there are limits to these changes. These limits are largely of a biological nature.

What then are these technological and scientific developments which are likely to affect the family of the future? In the past they consisted of several clusters. One was the cluster of inventions affecting production, taking it out of the home and augmenting it in outside economic organizations. Another cluster comprised those inventions that led to densely populated urban areas. Still another group was the electrical inventions affecting the home. Finally there were the inventions affecting the size of the family. We naturally look to the new inventions in these clusters as sources of future influences on the family. However the discussion will not

---

from the latter two categories that a forecaster is especially likely to err by omissions.

As a safeguard, it is well to note whether any new invention will impinge upon a trend. Thus new electrical appliances for the home will bear upon the trend of the transfer of economic functions away from the home. In such a case, there is little likelihood that the effect of the invention will modify greatly this trend in a short time. For trends seldom change their direction quickly and radically. Inventions do affect trends, more often gradually, but occasionally violently.

Hence a good basis for forecasting is to project trends into the future, as for instance, the divorce rate. The further the projection, the greater the error; and a projection of a trend line is not a projection of a fluctuation around a trend line. Future technological influences should be appraised in terms of some knowledge of projected trends.

be classified by inventions. Rather the classification will be the social effects on the family, and the new inventions will be related to these family functions and structures that will be modified. Thus, first we shall have a look at the function of household production by the members of the family.

Home production. The family lost most of its productive economic functions when mechanical energy, largely steam, was applied to the tools of production. Later, gas was introduced, which made cooking and heating of homes easier. Electricity has been increasingly used as a source of power, as has also oil and its derivatives. Chemical transformations have also taken the place of transformations by mechanical power. Thus, instead of plows and weed choppers, chemicals kill weeds on the farms. Then, recently, an entirely new type of energy has appeared, atomic energy, of such a revolutionary nature as to forecast an atomic age.

These types of energy when applied to tools and appliances affect home production by developing it away from the home, by lessening the transfer of production from the home, and by placing new types of production in the home.

The preparation of meals has been an important family function. Man must eat several times a day, and the gathering of food and its preparation takes time. It is almost the sole occupation of the lower animals, and required much of the time of the primitive hunter. When food is eaten in a restaurant, the preparation of food is wholly away from the home. The transfer has been greatest for the mid-day meal on work days where the place of work is some distance from the residence; though for workers with low incomes the lunch is prepared at home and eaten at the place of work. So, too, many school children do not eat lunch at home. The growth of transportation and the increase in family income increase this trend, as perhaps will a dispersal of urban population or a loosening up of congestion in cities. There are planners who are designing communities where work and residence will be close together. These plans are more likely to prosper if present transportation is costly relative to income.

Occupations which take men and women away from home for days, weeks, or months increase the eating of meals away from home. So, too, does the short working week which provides opportunities for vacations away from home.

The eating of meals is of course not production as is the preparation of food for eating. The projection of present trends indicates that, in the future, the preparation of food is expected to be done increasingly away from the home, despite the fact that there are many new inventions that make processing of foods in the home quick and easy. The tin can is still being diffused. There are many new inventions that process food at some stage in the fairly extended operation of processing. Notable is the freezing of foods in the last stage of preparation. Foods are now packaged against dirt only after cleansing and selection. There are cans which will heat the contents from a chemical in the lining of the can. Since there is an easy substitute for heating, this device may never come into wide use. It is cited as an evidence of ingenuity in this field. Various foods now come pre-cooked to the extent they only require heat for a very few minutes before being ready to serve. There is also the promise that radiation will preserve meats and other foods for very long periods of time. As more and more processing of food occurs outside the home, the preparation of a meal becomes as simple as applying a few minutes of heat or merely placing food upon the table, though gourmets may be little affected.

A new type of food for which there is no processing at home is being increasingly consumed. Examples are vitamins, amino acids, and minerals, which are purchased in the form of pellets from drug stores, but which might more appropriately be sold at food stores, since they are foods and not drugs. They are taken as supplementary foods, not for gastronomic appeal but for their chemical value, which is of course the real value of all foods.

Another type of productive service that is leaving the home or developing outside is the cleaning and pressing of garments that are not readily washable in water.

The departure of economic services from the home is being retarded or lessened by various inventions, especially those using electricity. Laundering is made very simple by the electric washing machines using the proper cleansing chemicals. The process is aided by the drier, and an electrically heated ironer. Then there are some new fabrics made of chemical fibers that need no ironing and dry quickly without the aid of any special heat.

Cooking is being made easier and quicker by thermostats, pressures, and timing devices, and in the future it will probably be made still easier by electronic radiation. Eating away from home, especially for a large family or group, is discouraged somewhat by the electric dishwashing machines. These may have some effect in increasing the eating at home, as, of course, do the refrigerators of low and very low temperatures.

The departure of sewing from the home may possibly be retarded somewhat by the use of electric sewing machinery.

There are some inventions that create products in the home never produced there before. Thus the refrigerator manufactures ice. It is possible that homes may have radiation units that sterilize food at home, though this service may be more economically rendered outside. Hydroponics enables much food to be grown in very small areas, which may be included in a dwelling. Though plants with roots in pans of liquid fertilizer become prodigious producers, it is still easy to let the rain and the farmer grow food for us, and at present relatively cheap. The disposal of garbage automatically at home may come to replace some collection of garbage from outside. In rural homes the piping of water into the dwelling will be done by pumps at the homestead, instead of by an outside agency. Some homes have workshops, which serve as an opportunity for a hobby or for education of the young. It is possible that in the future these workshops may come to render more useful services, if not in making new objects then in repairing the many appliances that the homes of the future will have.

Most of these delayed departures from homes and the addition of new types of production make use of electricity. We may wonder whether electricity may not bring back even more production into the home. This query arises quite naturally when we recall that it was a type of mechanical energy, steam, which took production away from the home, apparently because a steam engine was too big to be adapted to a dwelling. But since electricity can be run in on a small wire, why will it not bring back spinning, weaving, furniture making and other manufacture into the home? The answer is an economic one. It would cost more in the home partly because the home would be without the advantages of mass production. Economy of production depends upon a larger market than the members of a single family. Then, too, the cost of equipment would be great for some machines which would have infrequent use, as for instance a power loom. The electric bench saw, with the jointer-planer combination and other rotary accessories, will not restore furniture making to the home, except in rare cases as an expensive hobby. Electricity keeps production in the home or returns it there only where there is frequent use of the appliance, where its cost is not great, and where little labor is needed to run the machine.

Atomic energy is too recent a discovery for us to tell very much about its effect upon home production. Its possibilities lie in the tremendous amount of energy that a small amount of uranium releases. One way in which this energy manifests itself is heat. So far the reactors which produce this heat have had to be quite large though recently one has been made small enough for a submarine. This heat can be piped in the form of water or steam to heat homes but its greatest use is to produce steam which makes electricity in the usual way by turning a dynamo. The use of this electricity requires the same appliances as electricity produced by heat from burning coal. From this analysis not much of a radical influence is expected on the home. What influence this source may have on the home in the future would come from some possible saving in cost, which would be slight, if any, during the near future.

Another way of getting electricity from the atom has recently been announced. The electricity is derived directly from the electrons radiated from a waste product of a reactor called strontium, which radiates only a few harmful rays but many electrons. These can be routed outward and stepped up through a transistor into an electric wire. So far the current is minute (one millionth of a watt) but detectable. Should more current be channelled, such a battery might run a radio; and if still more then it might be used in an automobile or to run household appliances. The life of such a battery is about twenty years. But as yet it has not been developed enough to say much definitely about its possibilities.

The sun, wind and waves as sources of energy seem to present no new prospects for the home not now in use. There is some possibility that the sun in some areas may be used to heat homes or the water therein. This may be done directly by the sun's rays through a glass side of a house facing toward the south, or through the storing up of heat in water or some chemical on the roof.

In discussing the future of the economic aspects of the home we have dealt with specific effects. Some general consequences may also be noted.

These influences come through a number of appliances using electricity. These will need repair and servicing, some of which may be done at home by members of the family, if they have the skill. It is not necessary to know very much about electricity, so that the necessary knowledge can be acquired without a great deal of difficulty. Still repair men from outside are likely to be needed. Indeed it might be said that the electrician will replace the servant in the home of the future. Certainly the home of the future can get along better without labor (and hence the labor of the servant) than the homes of the past.

The function of consumption. Production is not the only economic function of the family. Purchasing is also an economic activity. The family of the future will buy even more of what it consumes than does the family today. This marketing function has increased greatly since, and because of, the Industrial Revolution. It is important for the finances of the family and for the activities of its members, particularly of the wife. The economic status of the family is affected by the skill and judgment in buying, as in any business. Records of divorce courts show that monetary difficulties, allowances to the wife, et cetera, are sources of discord.

Marketing is affected somewhat by the family automobile. The delivery service of the merchants is curtailed or transferred to the family in part. Goods that are bought are of several kinds. One is the kind that is needed day by day, such as groceries. The stores for these are never far away. For other goods, such as shoes, a member of a village family may travel many miles. For still other purchases, as of luxury goods, bought only rarely, the travel may be a long distance, for those not living in large cities. The purchasing function tends therefore to take the buyer away from home for shorter or longer periods. There are more purchases, obviously, the larger the family income. Whether discord over the spending of money is greater or less according to size of income, we do not know.

The increasing attractiveness of homes. New inventions using electricity and new chemicals are making the modern home a very pleasant place in which to spend one's time, in so far as physical surroundings contribute to making life pleasant. The significance of the physical attractiveness of a home for family living is related to its influence on the harmony of interaction between members of the family and on keeping the members of the family together at home. The modern American home has been characterized as merely a parking place for the night for the members of the family who spend their day time elsewhere. As to whether time spent at home or elsewhere is more profitable, we do not judge. It depends on how the time is spent. However, whether the members of a family are together or separate has a good deal to do with family living, and with the influence they have upon one another.

Modern inventions make it possible to create in the home any climate desired, provided the costs can be paid. The cost is not high for most of the varieties of climate desired. Heating the inside of the dwelling to some extent has been practiced for centuries in cold climates. More recently the control of quantity of heat has been greatly improved by automatic controls in each room which keep the temperature at any degree desired. New materials for insulation make the system more efficient. In addition to the circulation of warmed air, radiation is also used in homes in the heating of the human body. This is done presently by pipes in the walls and floors. It is possible that the body may be warmed by electronic radiation as is done for parts of the body by diathermal therapy. This development has not reached the stage to be appraised practically.

Cooling the inside of a home in hot weather is already practicable at reasonable costs. In northern climates where the heat is uncomfortable only for short periods, the capital invested in equipment is idle nearly all the year. This lowering of the temperature is coming to private dwellings only after it has been applied to restaurants, theaters, hotels and offices. Its use in homes is then countering an outside attraction.

The quality of the air as regards moisture, dust, mold, pollen and the ultraviolet rays that bring sun tan, Vitamin D, and some sterilization can be assured in the homes of the future for those that desire it.

The homes of tomorrow should be free from all insects. Light should be adequate for whatever purpose, indoors and outdoors, and may well be used for artistic as well as practical purposes.

The comfort and appeal of homes will also be enhanced by the furnishings made of light metals, plastics (which take color beautifully) and glass. Of all these products there are many varieties suited to different purposes. Functionalism in construction will make chairs more comfortable. Early chairs were modeled after a throne, to make a person look important. Later they were overstuffed to appear comfortable. Now the structure is making them comfortable. The demand for cleanliness makes the future of the carpet or rug problematical in view of the invention of new types of floor covering.

Dwellings. What the structure of the house itself will be is difficult to say. Surely new types of structural material will be tried, and varieties other than wood, brick and stone will be used, with such developments as are occurring in glass, steel, aluminum, titanium, plywood, and plastics. These developments concern windows, doors, screens, roofs, awnings, garages, closets and built-in furniture.

An entirely new type of housing has appeared and is likely to be developed even more in the future. It is the house on wheels, but the wheels are seldom used. These trailer homes are prefabricated and sold furnished. Since they are small, there is very little housework. They are cheap, and unlike most household inventions, are fitted for families with low incomes. The consideration of their influence on the family brings out the observation that there are varieties of families. Thus these mobile homes are suited to families whose heads are in occupations that do not keep them long in one locality. Such are some construction workers, engineers, foresters, and contractors. Their jobs may last only a year or two in one place. The trailer home makes it possible for a worker more readily to have his wife and children with him. The mobile home may thus help to hold these families together.

The house trailer is also suited to older couples whose children are not living with them. This adaptation is true not only because of the size of the family but also because of the low cost of the trailer. It is also suited to young entries into the labor force whose income is small and who have few or no children. It is also a type of emergency housing for which there may be occasion if a war comes or if much crisis construction of plants is needed.

Trailer developments are in the direction of increasing size. In warmer climates, a sort of lean-to can be readily added, making an additional outdoor room. Walls may be let down for floors. Prefabricated structural parts can be added to give additional room.

The trailer affects only selected types of families which, however, number several hundred thousand in the United States. Trailers appear to enable the wives to be more with their husbands whose jobs are semimigratory. Whether they diminish the birth rate or not cannot be said. It appears that they are not likely to increase it.

The improvement of homes through prefabrication is a question that should be considered by anyone thinking of future housing. Up to the present time complete fabrication of the ordinary type of dwelling house has been most practical in mass construction, as in the case of laying out a new suburb. Obstacles to the increase of homes that are completely factory-built are the low rate of obsolescence and the high price for a dwelling. But we have not yet reached an end to ingenuity in prefabricating dwellings and there may be new developments not yet known which will extend further this type of construction. The most vigorous trend in prefabrication is in the construction of parts. Homes are now assembled on the location, using parts from mills or factories. These parts are not standardized, interchangeable, or mass-produced, though there is standardization of plumbing, bathroom and kitchen parts. There may also be standard measurements of screens, glass walls, roofs and panels.

Prefabrication makes it more difficult for a home to express the personality of its occupants, as is the case with the prefabricated automobile. Personality finds expression, however, in the furnishings and in the landscaping of a prefabricated home.

An interesting effect on the family of some prefabricated mass constructed houses and of mobile homes in trailer parks may be noted.[3] The effect is to increase cooperation, to lessen privacy and to check snobbishness and status differences. These characteristics seem to be due to the small range in incomes and to the transient nature of the families. Perhaps the same age class and also the

---

[3] Articles by William Whyte, in *Fortune,* May to August, 1953.

newness of the community lead to social intercourse and co-opera-tive activity. Rather inflexible status rankings are more readily seen in older permanent communities with great differences in income.

The greater attractiveness of homes and dwellings because of new inventions, it is argued, may lessen family discord and in-crease association of members at home. The home is thus not merely a couple of rooms over a garage. In reflecting on this pos-sible effect it should be noted that places outside the home have become more attractive, too, as may be observed in offices, stores, schools, some churches, and even in factories, where there is tem-perature control, light, and cleanliness. Travel has become rather pleasant in most systems of transportation, compared to a century or more ago. So the appeals of the family dwelling have competi-tion from outside attractions. The improvements in the comforts and conveniences of the residence began a long time ago. Piped-in hot and cold water, gas stoves, fixed bathtubs, electric lights, and inside toilets all of which appeared years ago bettered the home for daily living. Yet since these conveniences came, the divorce rate has increased and more time seems to be spent away from home. But perhaps the discords and the departures from home would have been even greater during the past century had it not been for the introduction of new conveniences.

The attractiveness of a home depends not so much on inanimate objects as on the relations of human beings, which may be affected one way or another by factors other than material ones. The mate-rial comforts of home may be overshadowed by personal relation-ships. Hence not a great deal of importance attaches to the in-crease in the comforts and conveniences of the home for changes in the family. One activity in the home affected by modern mate-rials that makes it attractive is recreation. We treat this family function separately.

Recreation. The electrical inventions are doing much to make a home a place for recreation. The radio programs of music, drama and comedy are well known. Now television is bringing a theater into the home. The union of television and the motion picture is inevitable and hence motion pictures of as good quality as seen in motion-picture theatres are expected to be shown over the tele-vision receiver in the home. Then there will be theatrical performances not on film. The nature of the programs will be such as to appeal to all members of the family, and to families of different incomes, religions, and varying degrees of education and sophistication. These requirements set artistic and other limitations.

The time spent on looking at television performances will reduce the time spent in other ways by the family, for it is difficult to talk, read, cook, or clean house and look at the TV screen at the same time. It will be interesting to see if knitting, crocheting and other semi-automatic skills are fostered. The television shows limit the activities, such as conversation or reading, of other members of the family not wishing to look at the screen, unless there is a separate recreation room. It is argued by some that television will take less of the family time after the novelty wears off. Others claim that improvements in the programs will increase its use and develop the habit. The competition of other home activities will curtail the use of television. The effect of television on children is to take their time away from other activities, especially physical activities which are important for growth and appetite. Some of the programs are, like fiction and fairy tales, a land of make-believe, which retards the child's learning to draw the line between fantasy and reality, but which stimulates the imagination, at least of one kind.

The tape recorder is well suited to providing music in the home because of its fidelity and because of a long uninterrupted performance. The selection is under the control of the listener. It is easy to build one's musical library from tape recordings of radio broadcasts of music. However, long playing records in high-fidelity record players are an excellent and possibly preferable substitute.

The taping of vision as well as of sound is expected, but not enough is known about it to appraise its use in the home. Recording sound is quite easy; recording vision may be more difficult.

Home moving pictures in color and with sound directly from film are likely to be used for showing personal or family experiences, particularly in travel or on vacations or at family reunions.

The projection of color transparencies of family visits and travels is also a home recreation. The photographic darkroom is a locale for a hobby which may be classed as recreation. In the same category is the workshop for woodcarving and the making of various objects of a variety of materials.

These home recreations imply little conversation. Visiting was in the days of the household economy a most common family recreation, especially on Sundays or evenings. One inducement to visiting and conversation is the ease and speed with which refreshments may be served in a home with refrigeration. The refrigerator and processed foods and drinks favor social gatherings.

This inventory of the newer recreations for the home shows that these electrical inventions are both keeping some established forms of recreation in the home and adding new forms thereto. Though the electric wire is not doing much to bring production from the factory back to the home, it is making an appreciable increase in home recreations. In this connection, we note that persons who like the same recreations often like each other. Certainly in marital separations, disagreement over recreation is commonly found, as for instance, when the wife wishes to go out in the evening and the husband wishes to stay at home. The need of play is fully appreciated for children, but for adults, who compete strenuously for success, the value of play for companionship has not been so fully recognized in our society.

There are, however, recreations away from home that compete with those at home. These are well known. Dancing, museums, public parks, participant athletics, automobiling, and other travel are not brought into the home by these new inventions as are motion pictures and the spectacle of athletic contests. Of the newer inventions, television, wire recording, radio and color photography do little in the way of offering recreation away from home, unlike the helicopter and the transport planes of great speed and long distances.

Recreation becomes important in view of the increase in leisure time. The weekly hours of leisure have trebled in the past century,[4] and a projection of the trend indicates still fewer hours of work. To be sure, not all of leisure time is spent in recreation; nevertheless man's appetite for recreation is enormous. The long weekend and the long annual vacation are inducements to travel. Another competitor for one's leisure is education, especially education outside the classroom.

---

[4] Simon Kuznets and Raymond Goldsmith, *Income and Wealth in the United States, Trends and Structure* (Cambridge, England: Bowes, 1952), p. 65.

Education. For children over six years old, the educational function has been transferred in large part from the home to the school. Furthermore, the amount of knowledge learned through formal education has accumulated so much and has become so highly specialized that it is beyond the capacity of the family to transmit. The function has been taken over largely by the government.

The inventions that assist in retaining some education in the family or bringing new kinds of education into the home are, again, those using the electric wire. These inventions are much the same as those that provide recreation. Thus television brings education about civic affairs, foreign relations, the government, home economics, social problems, local community matters and conditions, geography, and even the instruction of the classroom. Many of these types of education were brought into the home by the radio. But with the addition of vision to sound, television does it much better. Thus weather forecasting over the radio is as routine as reading a weather report in the corner of a newspaper. Over television it is a thrilling venture into science and an interesting lesson in probability. The proportions of the telecasts that are recreational and that are educational may afford some indication of the strength of the two appeals. Recreational programs far outnumber the educational.

The wire recorder makes talking books a technical possibility, though the technique of mass-producing them would seem to present obstacles; nor is the cost known as compared with that of the ordinary printed book. The earliest use appears to be for the blind and perhaps for schools. Competitors, in addition to the usual printed book, are the books on small cards which must be read through a magnifier. A book of 200 pages may be put on a card three by five inches. We may much prefer to read the usual book without a magnifying projector; but there is the lure of low price and space saving.

A viewer for microfilm is an educational invention that will surely find a place in many homes that have libraries. Microfilm has one great advantage of storing in very small space copies of letters, manuscripts, pictures, family documents, records of various kinds, and copies of rare books or books of small editions. Microfilm and its reader are products of chemistry and electricity.

A classroom type of education may be transferred to the home, though to a quite limited extent in the United States. In learning to speak a foreign language the phonograph and the tape recorder make an excellent combination. The classroom is, of course, not a good place in which to learn to speak a foreign language. Living in a family that speaks the desired language is a better way. So, after all, learning to speak another language has been a family function. The phonograph record furnishes the pronunciation and the vocabulary; while the tape in a recorder permits the student to hear his own efforts. Since sound on tape is readily erasable, only a small roll of tape is needed.

These inventions are merely a new addition to educational functions already exercised by the family, notably training in musical taste and the education from books, magazines and newspapers. These kinds of education are particularly suited to adults, as contrasted with the formal education of school children and the fundamental education of nursery children.

Personality modifications. These electrical inventions may, as a remote and slight possibility, not be without influence on the personalities or at least certain psychological activities of the members of the family. For instance, television may reduce the time spent in reading and in conversations. But then there are now many long silent moments between the members of the family when they are not reading. The invention of printing long ago and the recent spread of reading have had some limiting effect upon conversation, but it has been slight. Conversation with people who read a good deal often tends to be merely imparting and receiving information, whereas among the earlier non-reading peoples conversation was often a game, a recreation involving a variety of emotions, sometimes even gaiety.

Of the various new recreations being introduced into the home, many are of the passive type. A person sits and looks or listens. Games, singing, and talk require active participation.

A man's home is said to be his castle, but the radio, telephone, and television admit outside influences without opening the front door. These inventions bring a lot of the outside world, even from distant parts, into the home. The seeing of new customs and different values will have its educative effect, even on the formerly isolated homes and communities of the distant mountains and seldom visited islands. One observer[5] has remarked that these inventions are giving man the attributes traditionally assigned to the deities: omnipresence, omniscience, omnipotence.

There has been some concern about privacy, perhaps most invaded by the telephone, and even more so where television makes it possible to see the person to whom one is talking. The mechanical recording of telephone messages gives some protection. The lack of privacy may not, however, be a concern to many homes.

Personality expression in the family and in the home may be affected by the mass production and standardization of houses, of furniture, of radio and television programs, of many of the goods produced in factories for homes. The age of the handicrafts led to a good deal of variety. Yet in homes and in families today there are many different ways in which individuality may find expression. Indeed the social pressure of the Main Streets of the villages of the handicraft era ironed out eccentricities more than does the anonymity of the Broadways of modern cities.

Since the communication inventions bring the outside world to shut-ins, the question arises as to whether they may reduce the mobility of normal persons. The newspaper and the postman have not done so, perhaps because of increased transportation facilities and increased outside demands. For the same reasons the personality of the home dweller with these inventions is not likely to be of the sedentary type.

Rearing children. Few new inventions assist in rearing children and the trend in the departure of this function from the family is negligible. There are some nursery schools and kindergartens that keep the child part of the day which attend to some of his elementary needs as well as teaching play and manual dexterity. In cities there is a diaper service furnished by outside laundries; and where mothers do not nurse from the breast, they use food that is prepared outside the home. The problem of child care is acute in young families because of the high wages and short hours of nursemaids, and the scarcity of relatives and older children to help in the care of the younger children. Yet about one-seventh

[5] Erwin D. Canham, *Awakening: The World at Mid-Century* (New York: Longmans, Green & Company, 1950), p. 8.

of married women in cities with one or more children under six years of age are employed outside the home.[6] What is needed is a robot baby sitter that does not cost too much. The closed circuit television can be fitted to the nursery as can also a sound transmitter attached to a cradle. The problem may be met better by a social invention such as a common playroom or playground visible from the windows of a group of family dwellings, or a cooperative baby-sitter league.

The dispersal of urban populations. In previous chapters it was seen that technological influences which changed families operated through the medium of cities, and that urban families changed more and sooner than did rural families. Obviously we should inquire about cities in the near future, and how families may be affected by any urban changes in prospect. We note first, vis-à-vis the rural-urban axis, that a redistribution of population is occurring. The result of this redistribution is the diminution in the number of families living on farms and the exceptionally great increase in the populations that live in the nearby environs of cities. Cities are also growing but at a somewhat slower rate. Contrary to popular belief, cities increased in density during the decade from 1940 to 1950. So the more rapid growth of suburbs and satellite towns has not been depleting cities of their population, though many of their new inhabitants do come from cities. Others, however, move in from other villages, towns, and from the open country. In any case we shall certainly see in the next twenty to fifty years an increasingly large part of our population living in clusters of towns, villages, small cities, near large cities as well as in the suburbs and fringes of the cities.

This movement is ordinarily slower than described. Cities are not yet "ghost towns," nor is grass growing through the pavements of downtown business sections. It may be speeded by the prospect of war, not any war, but a war using airplanes and bombs, atomic, thermonuclear, and perhaps still other types.

What will be the effect on the family of this new type of urbanism, this life in satellite towns, villages and suburbs?

6 U.S. Bureau of the Census, *Current Population Reports: Marital and Family Characteristics of the Labor Force in the United States: April, 1952.* Series P–50, No. 44, June, 1953.

One effect will be further to accentuate different types of families. There are more children per unit of population living on the "fringes" of our large cities than within the cities.[7] With the population the same for the central cities and for the fringes in areas of over one million population forty-three out of 100 children under fourteen will be in the central cities and fifty-seven will be found in the fringes.[8] Fewer middle-aged families and more older families will live in the cities, where there also will be more persons who have never married, and a good many more divorced and separated persons.[9] In other words, the central cities are not quite as attractive for families as are the areas just outside these cities. The differences are, however, not great, not as great as is implied by the statement that a child cannot be reared satisfactorily in a city apartment house.

With regard to suburban family life, the husband and father is supposed to be away from home more than in cities, and there is talk of the coming rule of woman, the emergence of the matriarchate. The suburban husband is away from home because of the length of the journey to and from work more than was the city husband of a generation or two ago; but this does not necessarily mean that he is away from home longer, for the hours of the working day are shorter. The suggestion of the matriarchate is strengthened more by the decline in the authority of the male and the growth of purchasing, over which the wife exercises much control. But such a trend is not due to any dispersal of urban population.

Richer families. The new inventions mentioned in this chapter are more likely to affect now the well-to-do families than those with low incomes. For instance, meals prepared from food processed largely outside the home are said to cost roughly one third more than those that are processed and prepared at home. Private helicopters will be first owned by the rich. High fidelity musical instruments are not purchased first by the poor. The sewing machine will probably be used longer by families with low incomes. Television sets have, however, been bought early by urban families with low incomes.

[7] U.S. Census of Population, *Characteristics by Size of Place.* Special Report P.E. No. 5A. 1950. Table 1.
[8] *Ibid.*   [9] *Ibid.*

This pattern will be changed a good deal in the future because of the rise in the standard of living. The median family income in the United States in 1949 was $3000,[10] earned in some homes by more than one member of the family. A half century ago it was about $1500 in 1950 dollars.[11] A projection of this trend leads us to expect a family income of $6000 in 1950 dollars before the end of the twentieth century. A doubling of family incomes by then could, of course, be prevented by one or more destructive wars, and the amount of increase might be affected by various events.

We think that the main cause of this great increase in income is the developments in technology and applied science, for national income is the result of national productivity and per capita production which have doubled in the past half century,[12] as have also capital goods which are the manifestations of technological achievements. The way in which technology increases productivity is seen from the invention of the mechanical cotton picker, with which one man can pick as much cotton as twenty hand pickers. Increasing productivity is, of course, due to many factors such as changes in management, organization, labor unions, education. We are not concerned here, though, with the factors in productivity, nor the factors that explain why one factory is more productive than another. Our concern is to explain the *increase* in the average per capita production during past decades. No doubt improved organization and better education are factors in this increase in productivity; but much of this improvement in organization is, in turn, caused by the new machines used. Similarly, much of the education that is responsible for increased productivity is technological, rather than, say, that found in a liberal arts college.

We think therefore that the increase in family income is largely due to technological and scientific developments. The effect of this increased income will be to abolish poverty and to raise the incomes of working class families into those of the present middle class. In which case, the new inventions mentioned in preceding pages will affect the families of the working classes of the future, for nearly every one will then belong to the middle class, thinking

---

[10] U.S. *Summary of the 1950 Census of Population, General Characteristics*, P–B1, Table 57.

[11] Computed from data supplied in part by Kuznets and Goldsmith, *op. cit.*

[12] *Ibid.*

in terms of amounts of income today rather than of rank on a scale of future incomes.

There may also be a smaller percentage of very rich families in the future than now. If so, the reason will be the system of taxation necessary for the garrison state but also for the welfare state. These types of government are only indirectly affected by the technology and are not technological influences on the family of the future, which is the subject of this chapter.

The status of members in the family. No increase in the authority of the male head of the family over its members is indicated by the new inventions. Rather the growth of traveling occupations and possibly a greater separation of residence from place of work indicate otherwise. The authority of the wives over the children may be lessened somewhat if more wives work away from home and if children go to school earlier.

The position of the wife in the family may be affected by the inventions that process food and affect housekeeping. Pride in being known as a good housekeeper was once great; if wives lose the art of cooking, less value may attach to it. On the other hand, the wife's skill and power as a purchaser of consumer goods for the family may bring her appreciation and rewards. The decrease of the authority of the man reacts to increase the status of the woman in the home.

The status of woman both in the home and out of it has been affected by her working away from home and by her adding to the family income. A projected trend foreshadows even more employment of married women, unless the expected rise in the husbands' earning power during the latter half of the twentieth century changes the trend. Even though the husband earns more money, advertising and new goods increase family demands. Television brings as much knowledge of the world outside the family to the woman who stays at home as a husband who spends his time in the city acquires.

The size of the household. In the past the household has been as large as it has been for several reasons. One reason is that sons with their wives, and daughters with their husbands, have sometimes lived in their parents' homes for economy, or because of a shortage of houses, or in emergencies. The amount of this "doubling up" decreased greatly during the prosperous years of the 1940's. With still higher incomes in the latter half of the twentieth century we should expect fewer two-family households.

The presence of kin in households increases their size. When homes were factories, kin were often a needed labor force. The situation is different with production outside the home. These kin are often fragments of families, such as widows, separated or divorced persons, and orphans. With higher incomes and facilities for living alone, and with actually fewer relatives due to the lowered birth rate, there will be fewer kin found in the average household.

Servants living in the home are now vanishing. With more family wealth in the future, there may possibly be more servants such as gardeners but it is not expected that they will live in the home, but be brought in from outside. The number of children in the homes of the future will be discussed in the next chapter.

Diversification and family types. The two outstanding types of families have been the rural and the urban. The difference is quite great between the rural family of the household economy and the apartment family in a metropolis. The transportation and communication inventions are lessening this difference. Television, radio, motion picture, school busses and higher rural incomes will reduce still further this difference.

The suburban family or the family in the satellite community is somewhat like the town family outside the metropolitan orbit and somewhat like the city family. It is unlike the town family in that there are fewer old people and unlike the city family in that there are more children and fewer elders.[13] There are also fewer divorced and widowed persons in the suburbs. The suburban family wishes to have the advantages of town and village life with fresher air, more space and more neighborliness and at the same time to obtain the advantages of the city found in stores, recreations, and educational opportunities.

It is possible that the families in the great cities, at least in the highly congested areas, will consist more frequently of adults only and also of more fragmented families. Wars and atom bombs may

[13] *Characteristics by Size of Place, op. cit.*

change the density of cities, but otherwise a building has considerable permanence and there will be great resistance to lessening density.

The increasing proportion of elders in the population will result from scientific developments discussed in the next chapter; but insofar as life is prolonged there will be more older families. These are expected to live apart from their children more than now because of old age pensions and increasing incomes. Hence they will augment the number of small families.

The type of habitation is an indication of family types. The residential hotel is for families of elders with larger incomes. Families in elevator apartments have fewer children living at home. Single family dwellings with sizeable lots are more for families with children. Trailers are for the very young couples, those with migratory occupations, and for elders. Prefabricated housing developments are inhabited much by young married couples. Perhaps these types of dwellings, the result of technology, may sometimes be a cause of family differentiation as well as a result, though not to the same extent.

Conclusion. This chapter did not purport to describe the family of the future, but to report on the possible influences of new inventions upon the families of the next twenty to fifty years, more or less. The new inventions have been reviewed and their influences indicated as we saw them. Some inventions may have been omitted, but probably few, and some influences may be unforeseen. The important point is that there has been a review.

The inventions most significant for the family of the future lie in the fields of electricity, chemistry and possibly in atomic energy.

These have the effect of delaying the departure from the home of some few existing productive functions and of adding still fewer new ones. These effects are more than offset by the continued shift of the processing of food away from the family dwelling. The departure of the economic functions from the home, decreasing the authority of the male, has almost run its course, and no great changes of this nature are expected during the foreseeable future. However, the growing function of purchasing enhances an economic function of the family, largely affecting the position of women in the family. Nevertheless the family as a great social

institution of power and prestige, which it was in former times, has
gone with the winds of time, despite the present existence of the
du Ponts, the Fords and the Rockefellers; and the future family
cannot compare in this regard with the governmental and economic
institutions.

Electrical inventions are bringing many new recreations, notably
the theater, into the home and are adding many new home aids
to adult education, through the media of television, high fidelity
musical instruments, tape recorders, microfilm and microcard
viewers, photographic equipment, and workshop tools and other
materials. To these inventions are added scores of others which
directly affect the family dwelling and its furnishings. These will
make the home of the future a very comfortable place in which to
live, a place with artistic possibilities also, which offset somewhat
the competing attractions outside, and perhaps also have some influence in lessening discord and increasing the benefits accruing
from social intercourse among the members. The expected great
increase in family income during the next half century, a result
largely of continued technological advance, will make these afore-
mentioned attractions available to future families with low incomes, low by future standards but not by present ones.

Any possible redistribution of population into suburbs because
of the fear of atomic fusion and fission bombs and because of transportation inventions will hardly affect the family as much as did
the growth of cities, though increased differences are expected between the families of satellite communities and the families of the
great cities.

The agencies of communication and the distribution of income
are tending to make families more alike, yet differentiations will
persist especially because of changes in age and composition, as
seen in rural, urban, and suburban families, young married couples,
families with children, and married couples of older ages.

The remaining functions of the family with great vitality are the
personality functions dealing with companionship, affection, and
education. There are possibilities that these may be greatly influenced by scientific discoveries discussed in the next and final
chapter.

13

Scientific Discoveries and the Future of the Family

In the preceding chapter we saw how the technological developments leading to urbanism in the past century or two have reduced the power of the family as an institution while increasing the power of industry and government. In particular, the economic function of production has departed in large part from the family, as has also much of the protective function. The function of formal education is elsewhere than in the family, but recreation seems to be coming back somewhat to the family domicile through the electrical inventions.

Left to the family are two functions, aside from procreation. One is the provision of affection, happiness, and companionship between the mates, between parents and children, and between the children; and the other is the function of education, especially for little children before they go to school. This type of education for the very young children is essentially a development of personality and a training in character, and by character is meant the moral aspects of personality. It may be said therefore that the chief functions of the modern family are personality functions.

This concluding chapter on the future influences bearing on the family is concerned with the influence of new discoveries in science, as the preceding chapter dealt with the influence of new inventions. Scientific discoveries and mechanical inventions are operationally much the same. This division of the discussion of the impact of science on the family into two chapters was largely to reduce the length of presentation. However, it does happen that the new scientific discoveries have their influence largely on the personality functions, while the mechanical inventions affect in the main what may be called the institutional functions. Moreover, the impact of technology on the social psychological functions has been largely indirect or remote, via the changed institutional functions, whereas the impact of scientific discoveries on the personality functions is direct. All other factors being equal, a proximate cause is more important than a remote cause. Hence the impact of selected scientific discoveries on the personality functions of the family are potentially very significant.

It has proved somewhat difficult to date the possible influence of scientific discoveries affecting the family. In general we have tried to focus on the foreseeable future, which varies somewhat according to the particular scientific discovery that is being considered. Probably most of the anticipations have been over a stretch of time of not more than twenty to fifty years hence. In the case of scientific discoveries, we have dealt with some that may not influence the family much within the next half century but are likely to be of significance at some time further ahead. Indeed some of the biological discoveries may well have the effect of transforming some family behavior, even if the transformation does not occur quickly.

Biological Discoveries

The scientific discoveries which are likely to exert a substantial direct influence on the family in the near future will be derived from many fields of inquiry, including biology, chemistry, psychology, anthropology, and sociology. Not all of the relevant discoveries in these fields will be considered; indeed we may not now be mindful of all the important discoveries which may be imminent. The following discussion, which should be considered as suggestive rather than as comprehensive, will explore new and anticipated developments in four areas where control is sought: fertility, the sex of the child, the aging process, and human relationships. The scientific discoveries in these areas will be described only briefly, without much detail, since our concern is mainly with the social effects.

Conception control. Developments in the field of anti-conception have been mainly due to scientific discoveries, although technology has played a part as evidenced by mechanical contraceptives. Recent and prospective developments in mechanical appliances are of relatively minor significance, the more important advances occurring in chemical means like new spermicidal gels. One such gel when tested on rabbits, an easily fertilized animal, is reported to be the first preparation ever to succeed in preventing conception; and when tested on nearly 6,000 women of child-bearing years in some fifty different areas is said to have resulted in better than 99 per cent complete protection.[1] For large destitute populations of the world, such a gel is too complicated and expensive, hence the search has been for contraceptives utilizing cheap and widely available substances. All that is necessary in one such recipe, it is reported, is to boil a handful of rice flour in a pan of water for half an hour with enough salt to make a 10 per cent solution, and let it cool.[2] However, a limitation of gels is that they generally require applicators.

A newer and different type of approach to contraception is the physiological approach, utilizing knowledge of the several phases of the reproductive process.[3] It is known that the reproductive system is complex and that it maintains a fine balance. In normal life, a female alternates between periods of fertility and infertility. Specific changes must occur in the pituitary, ovary, oviducts, uterus, and vagina, in an ordered sequence, if fertility is to result. At each point in the process, there is a biochemical system of checks and balances; and a slight shift in the balance may break the reproductive chain. The shift may be induced by introducing more of some existing substance, like a hormone, or by using an inhibiting factor. Thus the synthetic hormone, stilbestrol, has been used to keep women from ovulating, and steroid hormones induce temporary sterility in the male. Experiments have been performed using anti-enzymes like phosphorated hesperdin, and an English physician has inhibited ovulatory changes in a female subject by using an extract of cultivated gromwell, a cousin of the forget-me-not.[4] Spermatoxins have also been employed in the effort to induce

[1] Albert Q. Maisel, "The World's Exploding Population," *Look Magazine*, 15: 38, October 23, 1951.

[2] *Time Magazine*, 62: 70, July 20, 1953.

[3] Paul S. Henshaw, *Science*, 117: 572–582, May 29, 1953.

[4] Dr. B. P. Wiesner and Professor John Yudkin, "Inhibition of Oestrus by Cultivated Gromwell," *Nature*, 170: 274, August 16, 1952.

temporary immunization against fertilization, with better success in lower animals than in women.[5]

There have been experiments with hormones, anti-hormones, anti-enzymes, immune bodies, modified media, symbiotic organisms, dietary factors, and special agents. What is impressive here is the variety of approaches utilized in the quest for better contraceptives, indicating the great demand that exists. With such strong demand, especially among leaders in a country like India with an immense population and limited resources, and with the advanced state of our knowledge of the reproductive function, improved contraceptives are inevitable. While progress is certain, it is not possible to tell in advance which particular research leads will materialize and which contraceptive will prove most effective. Research to develop birth control methods capable of relieving the world's population pressures was given first priority by program planners at the Fourth International Conference on Planned Parenthood recently held in Stockholm.[6] The experts in the field are quite sanguine as to the possibilities.[7] Ex-President Conant of Harvard, at the Diamond Jubilee Meeting of the American Chemical Society (1951), predicted that in ten years biochemists would make available cheap and harmless antifertility compounds that could be added to the diet. To be harmless, these compounds must not disturb digestion or nutrition; even more important, they must not upset the delicate endocrine balance of the body. Conant also thought that religious leaders would change their attitude toward birth control without any loss of religious feeling, although on this latter point he could not, of course, speak with equal confidence.

The developments in contraceptives are highly promising, but there are time-consuming stages through which these developments must pass: (1) experiments with animals to observe effectiveness and to check on possible harmful side-effects; (2) clinical use with a limited number of human subjects, and if results are encouraging, a follow-up with a pilot test; (3) large-scale field studies to provide sufficient cases to determine probabilities of effectiveness. If

[5] Dr. Stuart Mudd, University of Pennsylvania Medical School.
[6] *Planned Parenthood News*, No. 5, Fall, 1953.
[7] Abraham Stone, M.D., Editor of *Human Fertility*, writes: "Concerning your inquiry about the prospects for a long-term contraceptive, may I say that personally I am very much hopeful about such a development within the next decade or so." In letter to the authors dated October 24, 1947.

the new contraceptive passes all these tests, it must still meet the tests of cost and convenience. Even then many years may be required to spread the method and get it widely used. Since we are concerned in this chapter mainly with family life in the United States in the next twenty-five years, it is difficult to say whether any of the physiological means of contraception now being explored and developed will be an important influence in this country in the next quarter century. But there is no doubt that highly improved contraceptives will be a factor to be reckoned with in the future.

Even if new methods are not speedily developed, methods already in existence will continue to spread and influence family life. The further extension of contraceptive methods to the open country may be expected, as well as to the low-income groups and to certain religious groups where there is now some opposition. These groups comprise a large percentage of the total population. The birth rate will probably continue to fall; and within twenty-five years, the United States may have a declining population or a stationary population. If the age distribution in the cities were normal, which it is not, the cities would not at the present time have a sufficient birth rate to maintain their numbers; and if it were not for migrants, the cities would dwindle in size. The farms and villages are the seed bed of our nation; but in the future with more machines on farms to replace human labor, and with contraceptive knowledge more readily available, the birth rate on farms may be expected to fall, although perhaps not to the low point of the cities. The effect of the extension of birth control to low-income groups may be expected to lead to a reduction in the differential birth rate between high- and low-income groups. At the present time there is in general an inverse relation between income and size of family which seems to be in large measure a consequence of the uneven diffusion of contraceptive knowledge and practice. With simpler, more effective methods more widely disseminated, the poor may not continue to have more children than the rich.

Fertility promotion. In addition to an interest in methods of preventing births not wanted and spacing wanted births which birth control encompasses, there is also considerable interest in improved methods of dealing with infertility, for the sake of those who want children but have difficulty bearing them. Technological innovations are important here, as in the Rubin insufflation test, which is used to determine whether the fallopian tubes are open, and to open the tubes in certain cases, if they are closed. A relatively new electrical apparatus makes it possible for doctors to determine in advance whether labor is to be normal or abnormal, and also whether labor signs are real or false.[8] If Caesarean section is needed, the operation is now ten times safer for mothers than it was in 1920. Only one mother in 100 now dies after this operation, while thirty years ago the death rate was one in ten. Blood transfusions and new medicines help to make the difference.[9]

Perhaps the most revolutionary discovery affecting infertility was the finding that husbands contribute about half of all the factors accounting for childlessness. This may have, over time, a profound effect on the relationship between the sexes, since in earlier times the woman had to assume the entire blame for barrenness; and failure to bear a child was a sufficient ground for a husband to divorce his wife. This traditional viewpoint, always putting the blame on the wife, is interesting as an evidence of the power of men and the inferior status of women in the past.

Hormones to induce ovulation have been successful in the lower animals, not yet in human subjects.[10] Experimentation with the reproductive process in lower animals is providing us with much new knowledge which should prove useful in treating women who have difficulty bearing children. For instance, it has been found that in the case of rabbits spermatozoa deposited directly into the fallopian tubes do not fertilize as well as sperm that follow the normal channels in reaching tubes; apparently sperm need to increase their fertilizing capacity while in the female tract.[11] For the most part, though, the process of human reproduction is still a mystery. It has been only within the past decade that the fertilization and cleavage of human ovarian eggs through the three-cell stage have been achieved and observed *in vitro.*[12]

[8] *The American Journal of Obstetrics and Gynecology,* January, 1950.
[9] *The New York Times,* March 16, 1950.
[10] *The New York Times,* May 20, 1950.
[11] M. C. Chang, "Fertilizing Capacity of Spermatozoa Deposited into the Fallopian Tubes," *Nature,* 168: 697, October 20, 1951.
[12] "In Vitro Fertilization and Cleavage of Human Ovarian Eggs," *Science,* 100: 105–7, August 4, 1944.

The great strides forward that have been taken in the study of sterility mean that of every 100 involuntarily childless marriages at least one-third would prove fruitful if husband and wife co-operated in diagnosis and treatment. As our knowledge of the factors in infertility increases, the percentage of success will doubtless increase. If it is assumed that couples that do not have children and want them are made happier by becoming parents, then progress in reducing the incidence of involuntary childlessness means more happiness in family life. This benefit accrues to only a relatively small number of persons, since probably less than 10 per cent of all married couples are involuntarily childless.

Artificial insemination and preservation of germ cells. Interest in treating infertility has led to concern with artificial insemination. At first where the wife was fertile but had some structural impediment to fertilization by natural means, she was fertilized artificially with her husband's semen. Later came the practice where the wife was fertile but her husband sterile, of using donor semen. No exact knowledge exists as to the number of inseminations of the latter kind, but one source estimates that about 10,000 children in the United States have been produced in this way.[13]

Artificial insemination becomes a particularly significant process when coupled with another of the newer developments, namely, preserved semen. Recently a calf was born in the United States sired by bull semen that had been kept frozen at −110°F.[14] Unfrozen semen begins to lose its potency after two days and is of little use after seven days, whereas frozen semen will keep its viability for at least eight months, and perhaps indefinitely. Frozen semen can be stored, and a famous bull might via artificial insemination become the father of as many as 100,000 calves. This, of course, can start a revolution in the cattle-breeding business.

Human sperm have been frozen and stored for over a year, while still retaining their viability, although nothing has been said about their fertilizing capacity.[15] Three women inseminated (1953) with

---

[13] Watson Davis, "Babies for the Childless," *Science News Letter*, September 26, 1953, pp. 202–3.

[14] *Time*, 61: 102, June 15, 1953.

[15] Information supplied by R. G. Bunge, M.D., in letter to the authors, March 15, 1954.

semen that had been frozen became pregnant.[16] Ova are more difficult to collect and preserve.[17]

If there are no harmful effects from vitrified sperm, there would probably be no organized religious objection where the donor is the woman's husband. Radically new possibilities would be opened up. A woman who was married a short time before a war and who bore no children before her husband was separated from her, could, if he were killed in action, still bear his child if his semen was preserved and if economic circumstances permitted.

The transplantation of ova. In animal husbandry, the purpose of frozen semen and artificial insemination is to utilize the sperm capacity of genetically superior animals for livestock improvement. Can the tables be turned, and the egg capacity similarly utilized? Mention has already been made of the fact that it is much more difficult to get and preserve ova than sperm. But where ova are obtainable, a method has long been available for utilizing the ova to advantage by transplanting them in animals better able to bring them to term.[18] As early as 1890 rabbit eggs were successfully transplanted,[19] and considerable work has been done along this line with small animals. Rabbits from small breeds have been incubated in the bodies of hardy giants.[20] Rugged species serve as hosts for more delicate ones, and the expectation is that pure-bred animals of prize stock can be born of run-of-the-mill farm animals of the same species, since thoroughbreds are often poor breeders. Success has been achieved in the birth of a calf through the transfer of a fertilized egg from one cow to another, which promises well for experiments in egg-transfer with large animals.

[16] R. G. Bunge and J. K. Sherman, "Fertilizing Capacity of Frozen Human Spermatozoa," *Nature*, 172: 767, October 24, 1953.

[17] In experiments with rabbits, it was found that when slowed down by cooling, sperm last longer than eggs. This is thought to be partly because sperm are differentiated for "motility," ova for "future development." M. C. Chang, "Fertilizability of rabbit ova and the effects of temperature in vitro on their subsequent fertilization and activation in vivo," *Journal of Experimental Zoology*, 121: 351–82, November, 1952.

[18] "Revolution in Animal Breeding," *Science News Letter*, April 1, 1950, p. 202.

[19] M. C. Chang and G. Pincus, "Artificial Insemination of Rabbits and Transplantation of Rabbit Eggs (Motion Picture)" *Federation Proceedings*, Vol. 8, No. 1, March, 1949.

[20] "Proxy Mothers is Science's Aim," *Science News Letter*, April 21, 1951, p. 250.

These are reports of experiments with lower animals, not man. There would probably be objections by some organized groups to transplantations in human beings. But ignoring the question of opposition, what would be the demand for such transplantation? Donors of ova might be women who want babies of their own but who have serious constitutional handicaps as mothers. The foster mothers might be those women who derive a health benefit from maternity or an economic benefit. If the practice were instituted, it would doubtless require secrecy, as in the case of artificial insemination with donor semen at present; that is, the donor of the ova and the foster mothers would remain strangers to one another. The demand for such services would probably not be great and would involve relatively few families. The effect on the American family in general would be negligible. While real, the prospect of ova transplantation in human beings is rather remote, and is mentioned here only to indicate the revolutionary direction in which biological research is moving.

When a worn-out ovary from an old dog was transplanted to a young dog, the ovary was rejuvenated.[21] Another transplantation is planned; and, if it succeeds, a method may have been developed for preserving an ovary for a long time. In this way a pedigreed champion could have puppies after her death. There is at present no societal opposition to the transplantation of organs from one human being to another; and if the transfer indicated here for ovaries should be developed for human beings, no effective opposition is anticipated.

Controlling the sex of the child. Another line of development in biology has to do with determining the sex of the child before conception. This is not the same as predicting the child's sex before birth, which can now be done in certain cases on the basis of various tests, although with less than 100 per cent accuracy.[22]

It has been known for some time that the child's sex is determined by the type of sperm cell contributed by the father. There are male-producing Y-sperm and female-producing X-sperm,

___

[21] "Sex Organs Rejuvenate," *Science News Letter*, December 31, 1949, p. 419.

[22] *Science News Letter*, June 14, 1947, p. 377   Also Gustav W. Rapp and Garwood C. Richardson, "A Saliva Test for Prenatal Sex Determination," *Science*, 115: 265, March 7, 1952.

whereas in ova there is only one type, the X-type. Each parent contributes one sex chromosome to the child; and if two X's combine, the child is a female, whereas an X and a Y produce a male. Before we had this knowledge, the sole responsibility for the sex of the child was often attributed to the mother; and the new knowledge is still not very widespread. King Farouk of Egypt was reported by the press to have divorced his queen because she bore him no son, and other kings have done the same in the past. We see in this injustice to women an expression of their unequal rights and inferior status. This is not to say that the mother may not play a part in determining the sex of her child. More boy babies are born than girl babies; and we do not know why, but two of the three main theories that have been advanced as explanations emphasize selective factors in the female.[23]

The X-chromosome is slightly larger than the Y-chromosome and contains more chromosomal material, making it somewhat more dense. Harvey[24] has calculated that the Y-sperm should have a density of 1.07132 and the X-sperm a density of 1.1705. He believes it is possible to separate these two kinds of cells by means of a special centrifuge and the use of a proper medium for the density gradient. The technique required for success, he points out, is comparable to that which separated Uranium 235 and 238; and on this account he says that "we may designate any process of sorting the two kinds of sperm for control of sex as essentially a separation of biological isotopes."

Harvey thinks there is about a fifty-fifty chance for the separation of male-producing and female-producing sperm by the type of centrifuging which he describes.[25] There are other approaches to sex control having to do with the date of conception; or more specifically, with the stage in the fertile period of the female during which conception occurs.[26] The evidence indicates that sex con-

[23] These theories are (1) the environment of the female ducts may be somewhat more unfavorable to the survival of X sperm than of Y sperm and (2) the egg may react more readily to the approach of a Y sperm than of an X sperm. A third possibility is that the Y sperm may be intrinsically more capable of reaching the egg than X sperm. These possibilities are set forth in a letter to the authors from Laurence H. Snyder, September 21, 1953.

[24] E. Newton Harvey, "Can the Sex of Mammalian Offspring be Controlled?" *Journal of Heredity,* 37: 71–73, March, 1946.

[25] Letter to authors dated January 19, 1950.

[26] *Science News Letter,* June 18, 1949, p. 387.

trol is not a fantastic idea, not just a product of the imagination. It belongs in the category of achievements which are likely to be made in the future but probably not in the near future, the chief reason being that the demand for sex control is not great.

The problem of demand can be approached by asking: if we could control the sex of the child, how would the knowledge be used? Is there a preference for one sex rather than the other? In some cultures, especially oriental rural societies, sons are preferred because they bring economic, religious, and status advantages to parents. But the preference for sons is not universal. In urban United States in the middle of the twentieth century there is no evidence that parents generally prefer one sex to the other. The most common expression of preference is for at least one child of each sex.[27] When 1,309 couples in Indianapolis in 1941 were asked which sex they would prefer if they were to have only one child, 53 per cent of the wives and 42 per cent of the husbands said they had no preference. Of the wives remaining, slightly more preferred a boy to a girl; among the remaining husbands, there was a considerable preference for boys. So, where a preference is expressed, the preference is usually for boys. This is consistent with the observation that some girls in our society want to be boys, whereas the reverse is hardly ever the case.

If they could have only two children, about two-thirds of the wives and three-fourths of the husbands would prefer a boy and a girl. The responses also show that most couples are satisfied with the sex of the children they have. Sex preference was found to be an important determinant of fertility among only a relatively few couples.

The foregoing are reports of statistical averages. In a given instance, a couple may greatly desire a boy or a girl. The happiness of such a couple might be much affected if the sex of the child could be controlled.

These are, of course, responses to hypothetical questions. How couples would respond if they actually had control over the sex of their children we do not know. The Indianapolis study does

[27] Jeanne E. Clare and Clyde V. Kiser, "Social and Psychological Factors Affecting Fertility. XIV. Preference for Children of Given Sex in Relation to Fertility," *The Milbank Memorial Fund Quarterly*, 29: 440–492, October, 1951.

suggest, however, that to most couples sex control would make no difference. Where it did make a difference, the existence of choice would introduce the possibility of conflict between husband and wife, especially as regards the sex of the first child.

The question of sex preferences can perhaps be considered advantageously from the standpoint of the trend in the United States toward more military power. In the years ahead the United States is expected to become increasingly a garrison state, concerned with national defense and preparation for war. Since population is a factor in military power, we may expect in the future a demand for more population, although in a technological age machines replace men, and resources other than men become increasingly important. But even if population should be emphasized in the future in the United States, there is no indication that the birth of males would be encouraged. Even in dictatorial nations subsidies for babies have been awarded without regard to the sex of the child. While men are needed as warriors, women serve as workers; and the demand for labor is great in a war economy.

Before leaving this topic, it is worth noting that artificial insemination is involved in a number of the scientific discoveries we have had under review. Artificial insemination is involved in the use of preserved semen, and it is involved in the centrifuge method of controlling the sex of the child. There has been a trend for 100 years or more to stress the psychological rather than the procreative aspects of coitus, as birth control has led to smaller families. The new biological developments may be said to accentuate this trend and to lead to a further separation of the physiological and psychological aspects of sex. Artificial insemination also means more emphasis on birth control and on the fertile period, in order to avoid conception when not wanted and to achieve conception when desired.

The sex hormones and sexual behavior. Another area of change in family behavior is the modification of socio-sexual behavior resulting from hormonal therapy. The sex hormones are steroid chemicals, produced by ovaries and testes. The outer part of the adrenal glands also produces steroid hormones much like the hormones of the sex glands. The female sex hormones are called estrogens, and the male sex hormones, androgens. Both are present in varying amounts in normal men and women, and doses of either or both can be used to change the sexual balance of the individual. In normal growth it is the action of these hormones which matures boys and girls into men and women. Testosterone, a powerful androgen early obtained from fresh bull testes, but now synthetically from cholesterol, may — under medical supervision — restore virility to some men and moderate the changes of middle age.[28] Likewise, synthetic sex hormones with estrogenic properties may be used to give relief from the symptoms of menopause.[29] Sex hormones also affect musculature and body tone and may lead somewhat to a return to more zestful living.

In human experiments, 101 women under treatment for endo-crine disorders received androgen administered intramuscularly, subcutaneously, or orally. All but thirteen reported an increase in libido.[30] In another experiment[31] progesterone depressed ex-cessive libido and androgen decidedly increased both libido and general well-being. These observations in no wise imply that learning and experience are not important factors in human sexual behavior but only that constitutional factors are also important determinants, especially the hormones of the glands of internal secretion.

Sexual adjustment is an important factor in marital happiness. Where sexual maladjustment exists, the cause is usually to be sought in some sort of discord between husband and wife, or in a functional sexual disorder in husband and wife. In such cases psychological therapy is called for. But where the basis of the sexual maladjustment is a constitutional condition affecting the vigor or the duration of the sex drive, hormonal therapy may be helpful. As more knowledge is accumulated regarding these glands of internal secretion, more control of the sexual function will be possible. The biochemistry of the reproductive system is a field which is likely to be productive of highly important scientific dis-coveries in the next decade or two. Insofar as adequate sex ad-

28 *Science News Letter*, September 22, 1951, p. 178.
29 H. E. Nieburgs, M.D., *Hormones in Clinical Practice* (London: Cassell & Co., Ltd., 1950).
30 V. J. Salmon and S. H. Geist, "Effect of Androgens upon Libido in Women," *Journal of Clinical Endocrinology*, 3: 235–36, 1943.
31 R. B. Greenblatt, F. Motara, and R. Torpin, "Sexual Libido in the Female," *American Journal of Obstetrics and Gynecology*, 44: 658–63, 1942.

justment in marriage is a factor in companionability between mates, whatever discoveries are made that promote better sex adjustment will also contribute to marital harmony.

Aging. In recent decades, considerable progress has been made in improving the health of young children, mainly because of (a) developments in medicine and public health reducing the incidence of contagious and infectious diseases, and (b) advances in nutrition. One evidence is the lowering of the infant mortality rate; another is the increase in stature of children in the United States in recent generations.

In the years immediately ahead, the interest in the health of young children will continue; but a new interest may overshadow it, namely, a concern for the health and welfare of the aged. One reason is that the law of diminishing returns will set in on the investment of time, money, and effort devoted to children's health, since so much has already been achieved in the way of controlling the diseases of childhood. Another is that the problem of the dependence of the aged will, with an increase in numbers, require more attention. Still another is that the increase in the relative number of the aged in the United States will be reflected in their influence as voters affecting public policy. The results in the improvement of the health and well-being of our elders may, in some ways, be as impressive in the next half-century as the achievements affecting children have been in the years since 1900.

The health of children and the health of elders are, of course, not unrelated, since the gains in the early years of life are reflected in the later years as well. Aging in experimental animals has been greatly postponed by heavy doses of vitamin A in the early years.[32] In the fruit fly, a combination of sodium yeast nucleate, pyridoxin, and calcium pantothenate gave an increase of about 46 per cent in the average life.[33] Vitamins have dominated thinking in nutrition for the past three decades; and if recent discoveries like B_{12}, the anti-anemia vitamin, are an indication, further important discoveries are very likely. But a new nutrition "star" has arisen, the antibiotics, represented by penicillin and aureomycin. When these

[32] H. C. Sherman, *et al.*, *Proceedings, National Academy of Science, U.S.*, 31: 107, 1945; *ibid.*, 35: 90, 1949.
[33] T. S. Gardner, *Journal of Gerontology*, 3: 1, 1948; *ibid.*, 3: 9, 1948.

drugs are fed to non-ruminant animals in the early months of life, growth is greatly stimulated, presumably because the antibiotics kill the germs in the digestive tract and permit the vitamins and other nutrients to work more effectively. Baby pigs fed on penicillin grow to be appreciably bigger and heavier than other pigs from the same litter which are fed a diet that is the same except for the omission of the penicillin.

In the United States in the last century, the gains in the expectation of life have been concentrated at ages under fifty for white males and under sixty for white females. The greatest gains have been in the expectation of life at birth. But for white males in the middle of the twentieth century the expectation of life at age sixty was about the same as in the middle of the nineteenth century.[34] If gains are to be made at the later years, more success will be needed in attacking the degenerative diseases. Some success, as noted above, may be achieved by preventive medicine in the early years of life. Geriatric medicine may also make its contribution. The major cause of death in the United States is the breakdown of the cardiovascular system, and degenerative heart disease can be reduced by lowering the amount of cholesterol in the blood.[35] Drugs have also been developed to reduce and prevent fat deposits in the liver which contribute to hardening of the arteries.[36]

Men and women from sixty-five to eighty-five years of age have been given increased strength and alertness, and a greater interest in life, by suitable diet and hormone treatment.[37] The diet emphasizes proteins; and the male hormone, testosterone, is given to help the aged utilize the proteins. In a similar manner, certain adrenal gland hormones are supplied to help assimilate the sugars and starches, and thyroid gland hormone or iodine is given as needed. Cortisone and female hormones are also used in certain cases, as well as certain hormones of the pituitary gland. When such therapy was used on some 250 old men and women at the St. Louis City Infirmary, it was found that certain organs, such as the genital organs, were revitalized. Elderly women, for in-

[34] Louis I. Dublin, Alfred J. Lotka, and Mortimer Spiegelman, *Length of Life* (New York: The Ronald Press, 1949, Rev. Ed.), p. 51.

[35] L. M. Morrison and W. F. Gonzales, *Proceedings Society Experimental Biological Medicine*, 73: 37, 1950; also *American Heart Journal*, 39: 729, 1950.

[36] *Science News Letter*, September 20, 1952, p. 184.

[37] *Science News Letter*, November 25, 1950, p. 340.

stance, have a return of menstruation. Physical strength and mental alertness are increased; and the oldsters take more interest in life, are more co-operative, and are less dependent upon others.

Based on 1949 vital statistics, white women in the United States had an average life expectancy in 1951 of 71.5 years, white men sixty-five years, eleven months. It is estimated that a woman born in 1970 can expect to live eighty years, a man seventy-four years.[38]

If the length of life is increased, and the health of old people is improved, what will be the effect on family life? It may be helpful to consider the prospect in terms of its (a) economic and (b) psychological aspects. Better health means maintaining physical and psychological potentials and postponing deterioration. At present, chronic illness in old age is a source of considerable drain on the family budget; and in some instances the financial plight becomes desperate. If the health of old people is improved, the medical costs should be reduced. But if old people live longer, this economic gain may be offset by the claims of a longer period of support, where the aged are dependent upon their children for their livelihood. With improved health and vitality, the aged should be more often capable of self-support. The trend is toward greater independence for old people, achieved in part by staying longer on the job. At ages sixty-five to sixty-nine in the United States, more than half the men are still working.[39] Moreover, the shift in responsibility for the economic support of old people has been from their children to public agencies. This makes the burden on families indirect, via taxes; but it also distributes the burden, since those with higher incomes and those without dependents are taxed more heavily.

On the psychological side, better health for the aged should lead to less anxiety and more happiness both for parents and their children. This may be offset in certain instances where the relationship between parents and children is strained and where with longer life for the parents, the children remain for a longer time under the shadow of the despotic parents.

With longer life, more grandchildren will know their grand-

[38] Harold F. Dorn, National Institute of Health, reported in *Science News Letter,* October 27, 1951, p. 261.

[39] Metropolitan Life Insurance Company, *Statistical Bulletin,* February, 1954, p. 1.

parents; and over a longer period of time, will come to know them better. This should result in a sense of greater family continuity, if not solidarity. More grandparents may be available as baby-sitters.

With the size of the family decreasing and the length of life increasing, married couples can expect to spend more years together during the period of the empty nest, after all the children have grown up and married and left home. Based on mortality experience in the United States, 1939–1941, the average couple in the fourth decade of the twentieth century, had at the time of marriage a prospect of married life five years longer than would have been the case two decades earlier.[40] More couples in the future will celebrate their golden wedding anniversaries. With a longer period of life remaining after the children have left home, parents are likely to devote themselves more to community affairs; and there should be more emphasis on adult education and preparation for non-family activities. There will probably be more marital interest in sex apart from procreation and a greater concern about the factors in companionability.

Summary of effects of biological research on the family. Discoveries in biology affecting the family relate to the most intimate aspects of marriage and family living. They deal with the procreational function, which in family life is protected from outside influence so securely that the long arm of the government cannot interfere. Hence when the procreational function is modified by biological research, the effect will be considered revolutionary.

The implication of artificial insemination is that of a departure of the procreational function from the family, though to a limited extent. True, illegitimacy is evidence of that departure in the past. But artificial insemination appears to be of less concern to the state than illegitimacy, for the state sees the family as a guarantee of the rearing of its future citizens. When a wife is artificially impregnated not by her husband but by another man, paternity is delegated, as the educational function is delegated to the school teacher, and with the consent of the wife and husband. This delegation will actually occur only in some of those cases where the

[40] Metropolitan Life Insurance Company, *Statistical Bulletin*, February, 1944, p. 8.

failure of conception is due to the inability of the husband. Though an extensive loss of the procreational function to the family is not to be, the idea that such a loss is possible will be widely-spread knowledge and will have its effect upon the purpose and nature of sexual life.

Another effect will be to re-focus attention on the contribution of heredity and of training on the personality of the child. To those who think that the personality of the child is largely a matter of training, biological paternity is not very important; and the new developments will not be regarded as significant for personality development. On the contrary, for those who place great value on heredity, there will be a recrudescence of interest in eugenics. Indeed the idea of artificial insemination holds great possibilities for eugenics, especially if stores of semen from superior hereditarily-endowed men can be kept indefinitely at below-freezing temperatures. It is, of course, not easy to learn what the hereditary endowment of an individual is. Similarly, husbands whose hereditary equipment is suspect in some regard, and who themselves might not wish to pass on their taints, can nevertheless by artificial insemination of their wives have the psychological experiences of parenthood.

The idea of artificial insemination also further separates the biological aspects of mating from the psychological. The separation is already accentuated by the practice of contraception, although even before the advent of contraceptive practices, the separation of these two purposes of the sex act had long been recognized by many men and some women. That is, the sex act may occur for pleasure rather than for procreation. Not all religions or systems of morals, however, recognize such a separation as proper. This separation gives more approval generally to the pleasurable aspects of marriage than to the dutiful aspects and hence is not without its influence on the personality functions of the family.

The position of the wife is somewhat changed, too, by these new attitudes arising from scientific discovery. For instance, we have observed that women were held responsible for the failure to have offspring or a male child, and that this is an indication of the superior status of the male and of the inferior position of the woman, whose most approved personality trait in the past was obedience. Knowledge of what causes "barrenness" and how the genes produce males and how they produce females automatically raises the status of women. Then, too, the separation of the procreative purpose from the pleasurable purpose of sex changes woman from a mere bearer of children to a potential contributor to the happiness of her husband and herself in other ways as well.

The decrease in the procreational purpose of mating in families will raise in a quite different way the status of women in the family. It will occur through the decrease in the birth rate if it falls as low as or lower than the death rate. As the downward trend in the birth rate approaches the point of a decreasing population, great fear is likely to be shown by those influential economic interests who do not want a market decreasing in numbers and by, let us say, nationalistic-militaristic elements. In which case attempts will be made to encourage child-bearing, which will show itself in an appreciation of motherhood. Various safeguards of family life may be set up by society.

If the birth rate in the United States should decline below the replacement level so that the country faced the prospect of a declining population, what would the popular reaction be? When a similar situation was discovered in Sweden in the 1930's, there was considerable concern; and a population policy was formulated by the government to encourage the having of larger families. Comparable programs, involving bonuses for married couples and subsidies for babies, have been developed in country after country, in both continents, until at present the United States is about the only modern nation without a system of family allowances, although the income tax makes an allowance for dependents. In France, where the birth rate has drastically declined, measures have been sought to prohibit the distribution of contraceptives. So, in the United States, if the birth rate should fall below replacement levels in the future, the politicians may be expected to urge support for a more comprehensive and varied population policy for the nation than we have at the present time. "Be Kind to Families" may become a national slogan, and the President may invite mothers of large families to the White House for special recognition. Efforts may also be made to discourage the use of contraceptives; but in our democracy these efforts, if made, would not be likely to reach the point of outright prohibition, at least not for long, if our earlier experience with Prohibition is a guide.

The control of the procreational function of the family will have its influence on the personal relations of parents and children, also, and hence on the personality of children. This control is expected to lessen the proportion of children who are either unwanted or who are not psychologically welcome, that is, who are rejected emotionally by the mother or father or both. These rejected children, who suffer from lack of attention or the right kind of attention, sometimes become problem children with somewhat deviant personalities.

Procreational control may sometimes mean a different spacing of the births of children from the intervals between births that occur when nature and impulse have their way. Planned spacing when different from natural spacing is likely to enable the mother to give better physical care to her child. These time intervals between births may also affect the personalities of the children and their relations to each other, although how is not definitely known. If controlled procreation results in a larger proportion of children without any brothers or sisters, the problem of rearing the child is somewhat different because of the likelihood that a greater amount of time will be spent with adults or alone. Since interaction between members of a group, especially of little children in the family group, has much to do with forming their personalities, controlled procreation may be of significance for the personality functions of the family.

The accent on the psychological aspects of mating is further emphasized by the possibilities of the use of hormones, particularly of the androgens and of the estrogens. In elderly married couples they mean a prolongation of the sexual life, with various correlated attributes, but without the production of babies. In addition to hormonal therapy, there are discoveries in the chemistry of nutrition which delay somewhat creeping old age with its consequent deterioration. The personal relationships especially in their affectional aspects may be affected by the discoveries regarding the use of hormones.

The influences of these biological discoveries for the near future should be viewed not so much in terms of mass effects and of averages as in terms of individual cases, which may be few in number but which may be quite critical as to happiness and companionship. Thus there are not many men or women, for instance, who are infertile and who might be the beneficiaries of new knowledge in fertility promotion. But where new biological discoveries make it possible for certain couples to have children — couples who would otherwise remain childless — the result in happiness for these couples is often dramatic.

Discoveries in Social Psychology

The reason why social-psychological research is of great significance for the personality functions of the family is easily seen. The personality functions concern affectionate relationships, companionship, and child-rearing. These are all phenomena of the inter-relationships between members of a group. Even happiness, which may come to an individual in solitude, is in marriage dependent upon more than one person. These aspects of the personality functions are then social-psychological. Naturally, therefore, great things are expected from research in this social-psychological area.

The three great divisions of research in this area are those that concern the relationship between husbands and wives, between parents and children, and between children.

Relations between husbands and wives. We consider first the relationship of husbands and wives. Central to this relationship is mutuality in affectional and sexual response. This subject has, until very recent times, not been a topic for scientific research, except by a few bold and pioneering researchers, because of a taboo against investigation into so intimate a subject. There has, of course, always been some folk information on the subject, some of which was approximately true, though this folklore was spread unequally through a community. Some of this lore was, of course, quite inaccurate as, for instance, opinions about women's sexuality and about the consequences to the individual of repression and denial.

Nor has the relationship between sex and sentiments been much investigated. That there is some correlation between sex and love has always been known; but the relationship to love of a highly sentimental or spiritual nature has not been known. The researches have not been definitive regarding the relation of sex to happiness, though happiness and marriage are known to be closely connected. Yet a person may be happy in his work, or his religion may be a source of great happiness to him. Discoveries in psychoanalysis, which have been widely accepted by psychologists and psychiatrists, indicate a rather strong relationship between sex and the various sentiments. Obviously further researches into this relationship will be of great importance for the personality functions of the family.

The theory that certain sentiments have a base in man's biological structure, especially in the physiology of sex, has led to another approach to marital happiness in addition to the approach through attitudes.

This second approach is concerned with the physiology of sex, with the idea that affection and companionability can be enhanced by improved technique in sex relations. This approach deals with dexterity, as is the case in learning to play the violin. Since human sexual behavior is largely learned, it involves technique. Hence there is substantial theoretical basis for expecting some scientific contribution with regard to sex technique which will lead to better adjustment in marriage in the future. There are, however, limits to the success which may be expected to result from such knowledge, since there are factors in the personal relationships of husbands and wives other than the physiological. Furthermore, these non-physiological factors also react upon and influence physiological functioning, either improving or impeding it. This influence of the psychological upon the physiological is the basis of psychosomatic medicine.[41]

These psychological factors that influence the interaction of husbands and wives, though having their basis in the hereditary genes, are the result of learning, which structures our attitudes and habits. This learning comes from others and hence is social-psychological.

The function of the family of providing for sex relations between married couples in the future will not be unaffected by the utilization of opportunities for sex relations outside the family. Several inventions and scientific discoveries relate to such opportunities. One is the expected improvement in reliability and convenience of contraceptives which permit sexual intercourse without conception. Another is the prevention of venereal diseases and their possible eradication. Still another is the growth of cities and of trans-

[41] Flanders Dunbar, *Psychosomatic Diagnosis* (New York: Paul B. Hoebner, Inc., 1943).

portation, which make clandestine relations easier. Finally, there is the possible weakening of religious sanctions against sex relations outside the family, due to the increase of biological knowledge and its effect upon religious rules of conduct. Opposing these are the prospects of more satisfactory sex relations between husbands and wives, earlier marriage, more powerful moral forces, and closer affectional ties. It is difficult to make a forecast, but the technological and scientific influences affecting sex relations will be stronger in the future than they were in the recent past.

As to psychological compatibility of husbands and wives, there has been a vast amount of writing and some scientific research based on statistical measurement, using various rating scales and scores on different personality traits.[42] The psychoanalysts have also made discoveries of many traits affecting marital harmony, not hitherto appreciated, whose origins lie in very early experiences, largely in the family group.[43] These traits are often more readily observable in neurotics and in some psychotics than in normal human beings. The differences are, however, admitted to be differences in degree rather than in kind, so that traits that appear enlarged in neurotics as if under a microscope exist to a lesser degree in the average person.

The factors of a non-physiological kind that have been studied with regard to their influence on marital harmony or discord are very large in number. Some of them emphasize external conditions such as poverty or life with in-laws. Others are inherent in that they are acquired so early and so firmly that they appear part of the person and for practical purposes are ineradicable. Such are altruism and narcissism. In between are habits that are more amenable to alteration, as, for instance, manners and temper. Such an inventory of factors can theoretically be arranged on a continuum from those most susceptible to external alteration such as the residence with relatives to those at the other extreme as, for instance, self-centeredness.

The relationship of very many such factors to marital adjustment has been measured by various researchers. The correlation of no single factor, however, has been found to be very high. These low

---

[42] Instances include the works of Burgess, Cottrell, Wallin, Terman, Locke, and others.

[43] Examples are the works of Freud, Jones, Stechert, Alexander.

coefficients may be due to the fact that very many factors exist in marital adjustment. They may also be due to the fact that no factor appears in extreme form in a normal sample. Thus in a random sample of married persons, extreme immaturity will seldom be found; though, when it does appear in extreme form, its influence on marital discord may be quite great.

But in the future much research on the factors in maladjustment will be done, and the results are expected to be of great value. In these future researches larger and more representative samples will be needed, and the work of one investigator should be checked by others. The mere zero-order correlation coefficients are on the whole not very revealing, because they do not show what are the underlying factors. These can be better determined by partial correlation and by factor analysis. Also it is the combinations of factors that are effective. Hence different groupings should be studied by multiple correlation and by factor analysis. Then, too, it is the pairing of traits in husbands and in wives that produces harmony or disharmony, hence more needs to be known about the pairing of attributes in addition to the possession of these attributes by husband or wife alone.

The problem of companionability of mates depends not only on knowledge of these relationships but also their amenability to alteration. For instance, if a young married couple's happiness is marred by the presence of, say, mothers-in-law living in the family dwelling, the conceptual solution is removal, though practically it may be difficult for many reasons. From the research point of view, the problem is why some husbands and some wives find living with in-laws almost unbearable, while others take the irritations lightly. The answer probably lies in the personality of the husband or of the wife (as well, of course, as of the in-law), and the search will be to ascertain what attributes of the personality produce the strain.

In this manner, the research problems tend to work down into the personality traits that the bride and groom bring to the marriage. Some of the most promising hypotheses of attributes related to marital discord concern the following: immaturity in emotional development, narcissism, self-centeredness, inferiority feelings, rebelliousness, aggressiveness, emotional fixation upon parents, extreme dominance, feelings of guilt and, in general, nervousness.

These terms are popular ones, and there is some overlapping; a few are causes of others; and some are quite generally inclusive. But their listing in this fashion is informative as to lines of research needed. Similarly, there are leads for research in traits often found in harmonious families such as co-operativeness, altruism, empathy, sociability, activity in groups, as well as the opposite of the traits associated with discord. In reviewing these traits, it should be remembered that the influence of any one trait may be overbalanced by the influence of another operating in the opposite direction, as might have been inferred from the low correlation coefficients. It has also been reported that these personality traits affecting harmony and disharmony in personal relationships also affect sexual harmony.

Further reflection on these traits indicates that many are inherent in the personality, that is, they are written deep, probably in early childhood, and are unfortunately not readily changed, from what we know now, although psychoanalysts have reported successes at the cost of much time and labor in individual cases. This observation leads to the interesting but rather grave theory that the potentialities for successful marital adjustment are determined in early childhood. This theory is supported by the findings of many researchers that a happy childhood is correlated with a good later adjustment in marriage.[44] There are, though, many happy children. Nevertheless there are also some whose emotional life is abnormal. Indeed Terman thinks that there is a small percentage of the population that can never attain a happy, successful marriage because of certain personality traits developed in early childhood.[45]

On the basis of the correlations of many factors with success or failure in marriage, attempts have been made to predict the outcome of marriages. Thus a person with a trait of rebelliousness is less likely to adjust than a mate without this trait. It would seem, however, one needs not so much a prediction for success or failure of a marriage, after the marriage has been made or after an engagement has occurred, as one needs a guide for the selection of a mate. These scientific discoveries of personality traits that are conducive to success in marriage or to failure can be used, if this

[44] Burgess, *et. al., op. cit.*
[45] Lewis Terman, *Psychological Factors in Marital Happiness* (New York: McGraw-Hill Book Company, 1938).

knowledge is widely known, in selecting a mate. They can be so used, providing a good list of traits with high correlations is eventually developed; but the question arises as to whether a boy who meets girl and falls in love will ever consult such a chart. Love is blind, they say; and we have shown in Chapter 3 that choice of a marital partner is today more on the basis of romance than for economic considerations. But over most of the world and over most of the past, love has not been the only factor in the choice of a mate. Skills, abilities, property, family status, and religion have all been influential factors. And even today in this age of romance, it is rather in the stories on film or pulp that all practical considerations are thrown to the wind, in favor of love. Among college youth, particularly, there appears to be a growing regard for the importance of traits of personality and character in the choice of a mate.

Suppose that the formation of families of the future should be increasingly done on the basis of scientific knowledge of traits favorable to adjustment. Then there will be discrimination against, say, persons characterized by rebelliousness. For the narcissistic person, too, it may be difficult to find a mate. If the "normal" person discriminates against the "neurotic" in selecting a wife or husband, then the neurotic's chances of marrying another neurotic or of remaining unmarried are increased. And if a neurotic marries a neurotic, the chances of discord and separation are supposedly greater than in the case of the marriage of a normal to a normal. The use therefore of knowledge about marriageable traits will not eliminate unhappy marriages, unless we acquire at some time in the future the knowledge of how to alter the traits discriminated against. When such objectionable traits are inherent as a result of early experiences in childhood, the problem of increasing the number of happy marriages becomes in part a problem of rearing children who will not have these objectionable traits.

The relations of parents to children. The rearing of little children is important not solely because of the marriages they make, for there is much more to life than marriage and family, as, for instance, morality, religion, character, citizenship, business ability, sociability. The rearing of little children is largely, though not wholly, a matter of the relations of parents to children. After a certain age, the influence of brothers or sisters and of playmates from outside the family is significant. It is important to a child not only what family he is born into but what neighborhood and community he lives in.

On the rearing of children by parents there are thousands of books and many more articles. There are research laboratories, professorships, courses, and institutes. The problem is difficult because there are many variables and much emotion. But scientific progress is being made. Some of the fruitful points of attack concern the following items. Prominent is the proper dosage of affection, avoiding too much or too little. One leads to overprotection, a too exclusive fixation of affection on a childhood model, perhaps too much emotional stimulation, and for practical purposes too much sheltering. Too little affection leads to disturbing feelings of insecurity and at times a feeling of rejection by the parents which may develop anti-social aggression.

Extended association with adults and with proportionately little time spent after a certain age with other children has an influence on personality. It seems to have a stimulating effect on mental development, and, if exceptional, makes it more difficult for the child to be identified as a member of a group of children and to play easily with them.

This association with adults is accompanied by some discipline or the lack of it. Much of the discussion of discipline by adults has been seemingly concerned with the comfort and ease of the adults rather than the personality of the child. For the child the effect is different if discipline is moderate and even than if it swings from an extreme of sudden harshness to great laxity. Discipline without understanding may result in rebelliousness; but if it is very frequent and accompanied by affection, it may lead to domination, resulting in submission and lack of initiative.

One way in which a child learns is by imitating an adult, frequently one or both parents. This the child does sometimes by playing the role of the parent more or less unconsciously in building up the concept of self. This process amounts to an identification with the adult. This identification if with a member of the same sex is said to be of aid in promoting the psychological behavior we call masculinity or femininity. If identification is with the opposite sex, appropriate sex typing becomes more difficult to achieve, it is claimed. The affection a child has toward a parent of the opposite sex is thought to be not without stimulation on his love life in later years. Some physical expression of affection between parent and child is also helpful in the development of his capacity for love.

The errors of parents in shaping the child's personality are more likely to occur if the parent does not understand the child or see the world through the child's eyes. These errors are less when there are confidences between parent and child and where they engage in common family activities.

Such are some of the hypotheses being scientifically studied, though they have been listed in the preceding paragraphs in non-scientific language. A great deal of the writing on these and similar topics has consisted of opinions set forth heatedly as in an argument, or persuasively as in propaganda. However, the researchers have supported these hypotheses with much evidence; but the problem has been difficult because of the interrelationships of one hypothesis with another. Perhaps better results would have been obtained if more children had been observed and studied in the home rather than in the laboratory. Certainly the work has been encouraging enough to lead one to think that even more knowledge in the future will be forthcoming on these crucial factors in a child's development.

The relations of brothers and sisters. The effect of brothers and sisters on the personality of a child has been less studied than the influence of parents on a child and than the interaction of husbands and wives. The subject is important, however, for the future because of the decreasing number of children in a family. There are thus fewer middle children and more oldest and youngest. There is less association with brothers and sisters of the oldest child and proportionately more with the parents, who are less experienced and perhaps more anxious with the first born than with later children. There is often a competition and a struggle for dominance between the first and second born if their ages are close together, with varying effects depending on the outcome. The youngest child has more opportunities for play with brothers and sisters if the disparity in age is not too great. There is also more opportunity for being advised and dominated, and also a

better chance for love for his brothers and sisters and less likelihood of love being entirely focused on a mother or a father. In
large families, children get more experience in co-operation, in
not having their own way, and in respecting the rights of others.
These interrelationships are made more complicated by the fact
that there are two sexes. There has been some interest in whether
affection by a parent is spread out a bit thinner in a large family
or concentrated more in a small family. From the foregoing, it is
obvious that the experiences of the child who has no brothers or
sisters are different from those of a child in a large family. The
life of an only child can be made a little more like the life of a
child in a large family if enough playmates can be found to spend
enough time in play with him.

Many of these differences have been reported upon especially
by school psychologists dealing with so-called "problem" children
and also by psychoanalysts who deal with children or who recover
the memories of childhood from adult patients. In any case, it
seems probable that such reports from these sources would mag-
nify the differences occasioned by different sized broods of children. There are many other forces affecting the personality of the
child, especially influences emanating from parents. With the decreased birth rate there is great interest in the personalities of
children according to order of birth and the number of siblings.
So it is confidently expected that much more scientific knowledge
about this influence on personality will be forthcoming in the years
immediately ahead.

The knowledge on interaction in small groups, especially in the
family with or without children, is now, and will continue to be
for a time, highly particularized. It will concern relations between
a single factor and a result in a particular situation at some special
time. This will be in the form of a principle or relationship of limited nature. Later there will be more combinations of factors, or
of a single factor in varying situations. But granted that a considerable body of quite reliable knowledge, tested and demonstrated, accumulates, will it be put to practical use by prospective
mates, by husbands and wives and by parents?

This type of knowledge is more difficult to apply than is the
knowledge of how to raise chickens or pigs. There is much more
emotion involved. Discipline of one's self, and self control, are

needed as truly as knowledge of causes and effects. In other walks of life where will-power is required, aids have been needed from the police, gossip, ostracism, law, religion, and the adversities of climate. Since there is great demand for such knowledge and since husbands and wives want to get along well together and since parents wish to bring their children up to be normal human beings, it is expected that they would try to exercise the necessary self control, for instance so as not to "spoil" a child. Still, such self restraint is difficult considering the power of these emotional drives.

But even if there were a good deal of self discipline possible and the accumulated scientific knowledge were made known far and wide, it would not be put to use very well by the average family unless they were aided by something like a manual giving detailed instruction as to ways and means, proportions and amounts, in varying conditions and situations.

To prepare such manuals for husbands and wives and for parents with limited education and experience, even if the researchers gave us the knowledge, would be a difficult undertaking, much more so than a manual on the care and feeding of infants or one on the techniques of sexual intercourse.

However, we have some confidence that there will be an increasing amount of research by social scientists in the social psychology of family life, and that these efforts will succeed in adding greatly to our reliable knowledge. This expected knowledge is likely to be used widely, because of the great demand for it and because of the highly developed technology of mass dissemination, provided the knowledge can be set forth in the needed detail. With these developments, the results might well be revolutionary in the increase in well adjusted families and a great reduction in the number of maladjusted children.

As we have seen, the functions of the family have been greatly reduced in number, and the family has suffered a great loss in its influence on society apart from its influences on its own members. These productive and protective functions are gone, if not forever, then for the foreseeable future. But there remains the set of personality functions, immeasurably important though fewer in number. There is much promise in science and technology that the family will exercise these functions with greater success. Perfection, as seen through our moralistic glasses, is not to be expected. We know of no society without some adultery or without some premarital sexual intercourse. More success has been had in keeping the family together than in preventing sexual transgressions. But a major objective of the exercise of the personality functions of the family is to produce happy marriages and psychologically healthy children, and future scientific discoveries should make it easier to attain these objectives.

CA62

Index

Adultery, as ground for divorce, 239–42

Adversary proceedings in divorce, 237

Age, changing evidences of, and early marriage, 74

Age at marriage: among preliterate peoples, 65–6; and earlier maturity, 71–4; and place of residence, 81; and sex ratio, 69–71; average, 58; importance of, 58; in colonial times, 64–5; in other countries, 68–9; in United States population, 66–8

Aged: and family life, 306–7; children's responsibility for, 12

Aging, 304–7

Allport, Floyd Henry, 177

Approximate household: composition of, 109–11; decrease in size of, 98–100

Artificial insemination, 297, 302

Atomic energy in the home, 273

Authority: in the home, 167–71; lessening of male, 10; lessening of parental, 11; outside the home, 171–9

Authority of women (See Status of women)

Automobile, 132

Baldwin, Alfred L., and democratic child rearing, 206

Barnett, James Harwood, 243

Bartlett, George A., 241

Beard, Mary, 174

Beers, Howard W., 234

Behaviorism, 199

Benson, Purnell, 233

Biological discoveries and the family, 292–311

Biological family, 100–1; size of, 101–3; trends in size of, 104–8

Biology: and authority of women, 180–1; and family change, 255–6

Birth control (See Contraception)

Birth rate: and contraception, 90–1; and urban residence, 91; decrease in, 104–9

Blackstone, Sir William, 168

Bossard, James H. S., 211

Britten, Florence H., 56

Bromley, Dorothy Dunbar, 56

Brothers and sisters, relations between, 318–9

Brunner, Edmund DeS., 234

Bunge, R. G., 297, 298

Burgess, Ernest W., prediction of marital adjustment, 156, 190, 231, 315

Business cycles: and birth control, 118; and increased income, 83

Cahen, A., 238

Calhoun, Arthur, history of American family, 45, 46, 194

Canham, Erwin D., 173, 283

Cannon, Kenneth L., 245

Carter, W. Paul, 209

Causes of family change: and concomitant variation, 19–21; basic ideas regarding, 18; convergence of, 24–6; dispersion of, 26; how studied, 18–32; how to find important, 26–7; lag in, 29–30; mechanical inventions as, 28–9; motives as, 23–4; pattern of, 30–2; process of, 26; usually complex, 21–2

Chang, M. C., 206, 298

Children: and divorce, 223–4; decrease in number of, 104–8, 113; discipline of, 199–203, in colonial times, 200–1, in modern times, 194; duties of, in colonial times, 194–5, in modern times, 194–5; education of, in colonial times, 193, in recent times, 193; effect of employment of married women on, 13; effect on

323

working wives, 148–9; emphasis on child, 209–11; future relations with parents, 316–8; governmental services for, 197–8; guardianship of, 177; manners of, in colonial times, 194; rearing of, in future family, 283–4; rights of, and growth of state, 197

Children's Charter, 196

Chinoy, Ely, 209

Choice of mate (*See* Choice of wife, Mate selection)

Choice of wife, in Colonial America, 36

Christensen, Harold T., 42

Chromosomes, in control of sex of child, 299–300

Church policy and divorce, 240–2

Cities: and birth control, 116; and birth rate, 91; and economic functions, 129–30; and protective functions, 136; characteristics of, 257; influence on family, 47; rise of, and Industrial Revolution, 258. (*See also* Urbanism, Urbanization)

Clare, Jeanne E., 301

Classes, social: and age at marriage, 80–2; causes of, 82–4

Clothing: making of, in colonial family, 125; in modern United States family, 128

Collusion in divorce, 237

Companionship, marriage for, 8

Concomitant variation versus causes, 19–21

Connecticut, marriage in, 79

Consumption in the home, 274

Contraception, 114–5, 292–5; and birth rate, 90–1; and business cycles, 118; and childlessness, 210; and cities, 116; and cost of rearing children, 119; and early marriage, 89–92; and education, 117; and family change, 269; and improved sex relations, 312; and income, 116, 120; and premarital intercourse, 55–6; and religion, 117; and urban-rural residence, 119; causes of use of, 115–20; chemical means, 293–4; diffusion of, 120–2; increase in, 114–5; physiological means, 293–4; stages in development of, 294–5

Convergence of causes and family change, 24–6

Corporal punishment of children, 200–2

Coser, Lewis A., 237

Cost of rearing children, and birth control, 119

Cottrell, Leonard S., Jr., 156

Crisman, Paul, 52

Davies, Vernon, 153

Davis, Kingsley, 222, 243

Davis, Watson, 297

Democracy, and authority of women, 187–8

DePorte, J. V., 246

Dewhurst, J. Frederic, 128, 131, 133

Dickason, Gladys, 160

Discipline of children (*See* Children, discipline of)

Dispersion of causes, and family change, 26

Divorce: and church policy, 240–2; and court procedure, 240; and early marriage, 92; and Industrial Revolution, 247–8; and loss of family functions, 244–7; and marital happiness, 230–5; and public opinion, 243–4; and remarriage, laws affecting, 239; and residence requirements, 238–9; costs of, 242–3; data on, appraisal of, 228–9; earlier, 219–23; grounds for, 238; increase in, 4, 8, 215–20; and the law, 236–40, and marital unhappiness, 214, worldwide, 217; in Russia, 236–7; legislation in the United States, 237–40; number of children involved, 223–4; obstacles to, 239–40

Domestic roles of wife, dissatisfaction with, 156–8

Domestic skills: in colonial times, 41; reasons for decline in, 45 ff.

Dorn, Harold F., 306

Double standard, changes in, 14

Dowry, 37–8

Dublin, Louis I., 305

Dunbar, Flanders, 312

Duvall, Evelyn, 55, 150

Earle, Alice Morse, 205, on child life in colonial days, 40, 152, 193–201, 205

Early marriage: and changing evidence of age, 74; and changing social contacts of sexes, 88; and contraception, 89–92; and easier divorce, 92; and education, 74–6; and employment of women, 84–6; and increased income, 78–80; and law, 74; and romantic complex, 87–8; and socioeconomic class, 80–2; and war, 77–8; increase in, 59–64; percentages of, 59–60
Economic functions of family (*See* Family functions, economic)
Edin, K. A., 121
Education: and birth control, 117; and early marriage, 74–6; and family functions, 139–40; for children (*See* Children, education of); for women, and status of women, 185–6; in the home, 281–2
Educational advantage of young, and social change, 207–8
Electricity in the home, 270–2
Employment of married women, 12; effect of children on, 13; effect on family, 13; increase in, 12–13 (*See also* Jobs for women, Working wives)
Equalitarianism in marriage, 10
Equality of spouses in the United States, 176–7

Family: and household, 95–8; and rising standard of living, 285; interrelationships of parts, 251–2; outside influences on, 252
Family change: and birth control, 269; and ideologies, 262–3; and scientific discoveries, 260–2; and urbanism, 256–8; and welfare state, 259–60; biological factors in, 255–6; how causes operate in, 253–5
Family changes, list of, 4 ff.
Family feuds, 134
Family functions: changes in, 15; combat, 134, and law, 135; economic, 125–9, and cities, 129–30, and romantic love, 53–4, and technology, 129–30, decline in, 45–8, effect of technology on, 46–7, in Colonial America, 125–6, in twentieth-century United States, 126–9,

reasons for decline in, 129–30; educational, 139–40; governmental, 138; loss of, and divorce, 244–7; protective, 135, and cities, 136; recreational, 130–3, reasons for decrease in, 134; religious, 138–9; transfer of, and status of women, 189–90, and emphasis on children, 205–6
Family types, diversification of, 288–9
Farnham, Marynia F., 176
Fear, in child training, 200
Fertility, promotion of, 295–7
Fisher, Dorothy Canfield, 202
Fiske, John, and "prolongation of infancy," 194
Food preparation: in colonial family, 125; in future family, 270–1; in modern United States family, 126–8
Frampton, Merle, 233
Frank, Lawrence K., 195
Freud, Sigmund, and early years of life, 199
Functions of family (*See* Family functions)

Gardner, T. S., 304
Geist, S. H., 303
Germ cells, preservation of, 297–8
Giedion, Siegfried, 151
Gifted children, remarriage of, 226
Gittler, Joseph B., 119
Glick, Paul C., 147–8, 225
Goldsmith, Raymond, 79, 280, 287
Gonzales, W. F., 305
Goodsell, W., 204
Government: and family functions, 138; and services for children, 197–8
Greenblatt, R. B., 303
Grould, M. R., 73
Grould, N. N., 73
Groves, E. R., 65, 71, 91

Hamilton, G. V., 49
Hammond, Barbara, 47
Hammond, J. L., 47
Hankins, Frank H., 236
Happiness, marital (*See* Marital happiness)
Hart, Hornell, 53, 243
Harvey, E. Newton, and sex determination, 300–1

Henshaw, Paul S., 293
Heron, David, 120
Hill, Reuben, 42, 55, 176
Himes, Norman, 56
Home production and technology, 270–4
Homes: changing structure of, 276–8; increasing attractiveness of, 274–6
Hoover, Herbert, and conference on children, 195
Hopson, Arthur, 248
Horney, Karen, 53
Housecleaning, in modern United States family, 128–9
Household: and family, 95–8; decrease in size of, 15; size of in future, 288–9
Household economy, family of, 123–4
Housework, decrease in, 13, 86–7
Humanitarian movement, 204–5
Husbands and wives, relations between, 311–6
Hutchinson, E. P., 121

Identification, of child with parents, 317
Ideologies and family change, 262–3
Income: and birth control, 116, 120; and early marriage, 78–80; increased, and business cycles, 83; causes of increase, 82–4
Indianapolis study, 210
Industrial Revolution: and divorce, 247–8; and rise of cities, 258; effects on economic function of family, 46–7. (*See also* Technology)
Infancy, prolongation of, 194
Innes, J. W., 120
Inveigling, 36

Jacobson, Alver Hilding, 234
Jacobson, Paul H., 121, 224
Jaffe, A. J., 92, 114, 160
Jenness, Margaret Babcock, 177
Jobs for women, 158–60; and authority of women, 181–4; and urbanization, 162–4. (*See also* Employment of married women, Working wives)
Johnstone, H. W., 174

Karpinos, Bernard D., 116
Katz, Daniel, 177

Key, Ellen, 198
Kinsey, Alfred C., studies of sexual behavior, 50–2, 73, 170
Kirkpatrick, Clifford, 161
Kiser, Clyde V., 116, 117, 118, 119, 121, 301
Klausner, William J., 228
Kluckhohn, Clyde, 49
Koller, Marvin Robert, 169
Komarovsky, Mirra, 45, 177, 182
Kuznets, Simon, 79, 280, 287
Kyrk, Hazel, 86

Laborsaving devices, 150–3; and leisure time, 152
Lag in family change, 29–30
Landis, Paul H., 153, 231
Lang, Richard O., 117
Law: and early marriage, 74; and combat functions, 135; and increase in divorce, 236–40
League of Nations and women's rights, 172–3
Legal status of married women: in Colonial America, 168; in modern United States, 168–9
Leighton, Dorothea, 49
LePlay, Frederic, 233
Lichtenberger, J. P., and studies of divorce, 238, 239
Life expectancy in the United States, 305–7
Linton, Ralph, 124
Locke, Harvey, 156, 190, 228
Lodgers, 112
Lotka, Alfred J., 305
Love (*See* Romantic complex, Romantic love)
Luetkens, Charlotte, 74, 171
Lundberg, Ferdinand, 176
Lunt, Paul, 81

Mackeprang, Muriel, 156
Maisel, Albert Q., 293
Males, lessening of authority of, 10
Marital adjustment: and psychological factors, 313–16; and sex technique, 312
Marital happiness, 8; and divorce, 230–5; factors affecting, 232–5; sex factors in, 51; trend in, 230–5
Marital roles, changes in, 11

Martin, Clyde E., 51
Martin, Edgar W., 151
Martineau, Harriet, on work for women, 159
Maslow, A. H., 187
Massachusetts, marriage in, 63–4
Mate selection: among Navaho Indians, 49; and scientific knowledge, 316; factors in, 37; parental role in, 36–7; role of companionship in, 8; role of love in, 9; romantic complex in, 9; self-determination in, 9
Mead, Margaret, 152, 175, 244; on homemaking, 158
Mechanical invention, as factor in family change, 28–9
Miles, Catherine Cox, 170
Mills, Clarence A., 73
Monahan, Thomas P., 63
Morrison, L. M., 305
Motara, F., 303
Mother's Charter, 170
Mudd, Stuart, 204
Murdock, George P., study of family stability, 227

Navaho Indians, mate selection among, 49
Nazi Germany, woman's role, 161
Neely, Wayne C., 53
New York, divorce in, 229, 237–8, 239–40
Nieburgs, H. E., 303
Nimkoff, M. F., 46, 58, 88, 186
Nuclear family, 100–1; size of, 101–3; trends in size of, 104–8

Oden, Melita H., 226, 234
Ogburn, W. F., 65, 71, 89, 91, 118, 229, 268
Old age and public health, 204
Ova, transplantation of, 298–9

Parents: future relations with children, 316–8; lessening of authority of, 11
Parsons, Talcott, 158
Pearl, Raymond, and study of contraceptives, 90
Personality, effect of technological changes on, 282–3

Physical maturity and early marriage, 71–4
Pincus, G., 298
Pomeroy, Wardwell B., 51
Popenoe, Paul, 187, 231
Powdermaker, Hortense, 41
Power, loss of by family, 16–7
Prefabricated homes, 277
Pregnancy, lessening of fear of, 55–6
Premarital intercourse and contraception, 55–6
Primitive family, 124–5
Pringle, Henry F., 52
Psychology: and accent on child, 198–203; and authority of women, 186–7; and family changes, 311–21; and marital adjustment, 313–6
Public health: and care of children, 203–4; and old age, 204
Public opinion and divorce, 243–4
Puritanism and child training, 198–9

Quasi households, definition of, 95

Raines, Shirley, 228
Rapp, Gustav, 299
Recreation, 130–3; and communication inventions, 131; in the home, 278–80
Reid, Margaret G., 126, 127, 129, 152
Relatives, 111–13
Religion: and birth control, 117; and family functions, 138–9
Remarriage: and marital adjustment, 227–8; and subsequent divorce, 227; increase in, 224–8; in the United States, 227; laws affecting, 239
Reno, 226, 240
Richardson, Garwood C., 299
Role of wife: according to Franklin, 39; in Book of Proverbs, 38–9; in colonial times, 36–41; in modern times, 41–5
Roleplaying of children, 317–8
Romantic complex: and early marriage, 87–8; in mate selection, 9
Romantic love: and decrease of economic functions of family, 53–4; and sex naturalism, 54–5; characteristics of, 48–9; in advertising, 42; in motion pictures, 41–2; in popular songs, 42; student opinion on, 42, 45

Roosevelt, Theodore, and conference on children, 195
Rose, Arnold M., 165
Ruml, Beardsley, 137
Russia, divorce in, 236–7

Salmon, V. J., 303
Sanger, Winogene Pratt, 211
Scheinfeld, Amram, 179
School and emphasis on child, 206
Scientific discoveries and family change, 260–2
Secularization, 138–9
Servants, 111–2
Sex: and sentiment, 311; and shame in little children, 55–6
Sex behavior: changes in, 50–3; of women, changes in, 14
Sex hormones and sexual behavior, 302–4
Sex mores, changes in, 14, 52
Sex naturalism and romantic love, 54–5
Sex of child, control of, 299–302; preference for, 301–2
Sex ratio, and age at marriage, 69–71; and authority of women, 181
Sex taboos, breakdown in, 88–9
Sex technique and marital adjustment, 312
Sex typing of children, 317–8
Sexual behavior and sex hormones, 302–4
Sexual intercourse, premarital, 51–3
Sexual roles, increasing similarity of for men and women, 170
Sheeley, Arlene, 153
Sheen, Fulton J., 214
Sherman, H. C., 304
Sherman, J. K., 298
Siblings, relations between, 318–9
Size of family: decrease in, 14–15; of different types, 103–4; recent changes in, 108–9
Smith, Reginald Heber, 240
Social change and educational advantage of young, 207–8
Social mobility and emphasis on child, 208–9
Spencer, Lyle M., 217
Spiegelman, Mortimer, 305
Stability of family, 227

State, growth of, and children's rights, 197
Status of family members, 287
Status of married women: in Colonial America, 168; in modern United States, 168–9
Status of women: among Anglo-Saxons, 174; among Germanic peoples, 174; among Iroquois, 175; among Romans, 174–5; among Todas, 175; and biological factors, 180–1; and democracy, 187–8; and education for women, 185–6; and jobs for women, 181–4; and psychology, 186–7; and sex ratio, 181; and transfer of family functions, 189–90; in earlier times and other societies, 173; in early England, 173; in Western society, 176 ff.; income lag, 177–9; political leadership lag, 179
Sterility, measures against, 295–7
Stewart, Maxwell S., 178
Stone, Abraham, 204
Stouffer, S. A., 121, 217
Strecker, Edward A., 186

Taeuber, Irene B., 164
Technology: and birth control, 92; and economic functions of family, 46–7, 129–30; and home production, 270–4. (*See also* Industrial Revolution)
Television, 282
Terman, Lewis M.: marital happiness studies, 51; 170; on remarriage of gifted children, 226; study of remarriage, 227–8; marital adjustment studies, 231; 234; marital happiness studies, 315
Thomas, Dorothy, 118
Thomas, W. I., 37
Thompson, Eleanor, 185
Time spent away from home, 13
Trailers, 276–7
Truman, Harry, and conference on children, 196
Turpin, R., 303

United Nations and women's rights, 172–3
Urban population, dispersion of, 284–5

Urbanism, and family change, 256–8. (*See also* Cities)

Urbanization and jobs for women, 162–4

Urban-rural residence and birth control, 119

Venereal disease, lessening of fear of, 56

War: and early marriage, 77–8; and working wives, 160–2

Warner, W. Lloyd, 81

Watson, John, and behaviorism, 199

Weeks, H. Ashley, 234

Weiss, Gertrude S., 127

Welfare state, 137; and family change, 259–60

Whelpton, P. K., 108, 116, 117, 118, 119, 121

White House Conferences on children, 195–7

Whyte, William, 277

Wicks, Donna, 231

Wiesner, B. P., 293

Wife, choice of, in Colonial America, 36

Williams, Robin M., Jr., 184

Williamson, Robert C., 235

Willoughby, Raymond R., 56

Wolfbein, S. L., 160

Women, employment of, and early marriage, 84–6

Women's rights, 11; and League of Nations, 172–3; and United Nations, 172–3; increase in, 172

Wood, Arthur L., 88

Wood, Ethel Mary, 174

Working wives, 12–13; and less work at home, 150–3; and number and age of children, 148–9; and public opinion, 153–6; and smaller families, 147–9; and war, 160–2; desire for income, 146; increase in, 145; reasons for, 147

Wylie, Philip, 186

Yudkin, John, 293

Zimmerman, Carle C., 233

Znaniecki, F., 37

911 2)48